chaucer

Chaucer

THE PROLOGUE AND THREE TALES

Edited with notes & commentary by
Francis King and Bruce Steele

JOHN MURRAY

acknowledgements

For permission to include passages from books published by them, we are indebted to:
Barnes and Noble, Inc. for Curry: *Chaucer and the Mediaeval Sciences;* Basil Blackwell, for Owst: *Literature and Pulpit in Mediaeval England;* Cambridge University Press, for the *Cambridge Economic History of Europe,* Vol. 2, and Power: *Mediaeval English Nunneries;* the Editor, E.L.H. for R.E. Kaske: *Chaucer and Medieval Allegory* in Vol. 30, No. 2, 1963; Oxford University Press for F. N. Robinson (Ed.): *The Works of Geoffrey Chaucer,* 2nd edn.
The woodcuts of the Canterbury pilgrims are reproductions of those commissioned and published by the Chaucer Society. They were issued with the Society's editions of six MSS of *The Canterbury Tales.*

For Sarah and Mary

preface

'Notes are often necessary, but they are necessary evils,' wrote
Dr Johnson in the preface to his edition of the works of Shakes-
peare. Between this apt warning and Chaucer's prayer that his
work 'be understonde' lies the difficult path of editors who present a
late mediaeval masterpiece to modern readers. The five hundred
years which separate Chaucer's English from ours also render the
beliefs and experience of a fourteenth century Englishman remote
from those of mid-twentieth century readers. While little assistance
is needed for him to cross the immediate barrier of Chaucer's language satisfactorily enough, to arrive at a satisfactory and satisfying interpretation or understanding of Chaucer's poetry the
inexperienced reader now, unfortunately, needs considerable
editorial and other assistance. Our aim and our problem in this
book has been to give as much aid as inconspicuously as possible.

Chaucer's text is printed on the right-hand pages, with no gloss
or footnotes to distract the eye. On the pages facing the text and in
smaller type are running notes in which there are glosses of words,
phrases, or even lines, and information of a factual, historical,
literary or linguistic kind which we consider necessary or of particular interest. In some sections where the effect of the work
depends to a significant degree upon the reader's recognition of
what Chaucer is doing with source material, we have inserted
relevant brief quotations from the chief sources (in translation
where necessary), and either given references to readily available
texts like the Bible, or directed the reader to longer extracts in
the Appendixes.

Immediately after the text the reader will find introductory
material and our commentaries on the selections. We give first
a guide to the pronunciation of Chaucerian English, followed by a
discussion of the versification. The meanings of certain 'difficult'
key words which have been asterisked in the running notes are then
examined, and this section ends with two extended notes on
mediaeval Medicine and Astrology in relation to the Canterbury
Tales. In a few instances references are given to Tales outside the
present collection; any complete edition will of course provide the

i

context, but line numbers, where given, refer to our *Selections from Geoffrey Chaucer's The Canterbury Tales* — an edition for university undergraduate use.

The Commentary which follows is a statement of *our* attempt at an interpretation of the meaning and significance of the Prologue and three Tales as works of fourteenth century literary art. It is not uncommon to find Chaucer's work discussed as if he were either a social historian or a pictorial reporter of fourteenth century English life. But Chaucer is above all else a poet, and our aim has been to suggest something of the rich experience we find in his poetry, and to encourage others in their attempts to discover the fullness of Chaucer's meaning.

While we have formally acknowledged only quotations in this book, we are only too aware of our indebtedness to a large number of Chaucerian editors and scholars. Practical assistance has been varied and generous. To the Library of the University of Queensland and the State Public Library of Victoria for the loan of books over many months we record our gratitude. To members of the Department of English at Monash University we express our thanks for their assistance in many ways, direct and indirect, and our admiration of their patience in accommodating our continual discussions and disputations about Chaucer. The difficult task of typing and re-typing various drafts of the book was performed most cheerfully and efficiently by Mrs Betty Moore and Mrs Norma Bolton; their assistance has been invaluable.

Francis King
Bruce Steele
Monash University

contents

And for ther is so gret diversite
In English and in writyng of oure tonge,
So prey I God that non myswrite the
Ne the mysmetre for defaute of tonge;
And red wherso thow be, or elles songe,
That thow be understonde, God I biseche.
Troilus and Criseyde
Bk. v, 1793-8

1 *his*. Although M.E. *his* can mean 'its' as well as 'his', the context suggests an element of personification.
  soote sweet.
2 *droghte* drought, dryness. March is traditionally held to be dry and windy.
  perced pierced.
3 *veyne* vein or sap-bearing vessel.
  swich licour such liquid or moisture; i.e. the sap.
4 *Of which vertu* by the power of which. 'Vertu' has the sense of 'power' or 'vital energy'.
5 *Zephirus* the west wind of Spring.
6 *Inspired* breathed upon with a life-giving breath.
  holt woodland.
7 *croppes* new young shoots; not the modern sense of 'crops'.
  yonge sonne the young sun. The sun was held to begin its course at the vernal equinox, i.e. about March 12th.
8 *Ram* Aries in the Zodiac.
  half cours. During April the sun passed through the latter half of Aries before entering the first half of Taurus (the Bull). As Chaucer states that the half-course in the Ram is complete, the date must be after April 11th. See further Explanatory Notes—Astrology.
9 *foweles* birds.
10 This line either means 'birds are light sleepers', or is a reference to nightingales who sing all night in the Spring; cf. 98 below.
11 'For Nature so spurs them on (priketh hem) in their hearts or inner dispositions (corages)'. But cf. NPT686 and n.
13 *palmeres* palmers; pilgrims or professional pilgrims. The term was originally applied to pilgrims to Palestine who brought back palm branches as tokens. Later the term was applied to pilgrims generally.
  straunge strondes foreign strands or shores.
14 *ferne* far, distant.
  halwes lit. saints; but used of saints' shrines or holy places.
  kouthe known.
16-17 *Caunterbury*. The shrine of St. Thomas a Becket was in Canterbury Cathedral.
  wende make their way.
17 *blisful* blessed.
18 'Who had helped them when they were sick'.
20 'As I was at the Tabard Inn in Southwark'.
22 *ful devout corage* a very devout spirit or disposition.
25 *by aventure* by chance.
  yfalle fallen.
27 *wolden ryde* were intending to ride.
28 *wyde* wide, spacious, roomy. The Tabard was reputed to be very luxuriously appointed for the time.
29 *esed* made comfortable.
  atte beste at the best, in the best manner.

1

HERE BYGYNNETH THE BOOK OF
the tales of caunterbury

WHAN that Aprill with his shoures soote
The droghte of March hath perced to the roote
And bathed every veyne in swich licour
Of which vertu engendred is the flour,
Whan Zephirus eek with his sweete breeth   5
Inspired hath in every holt and heeth
The tendre croppes, and the yonge sonne
Hath in the Ram his half cours yronne,
And smale foweles maken melodye
That slepen al the nyght with open eye,   10
So priketh hem nature in hir corages,
Thanne longen folk to goon on pilgrimages
And palmeres for to seken straunge strondes
To ferne halwes kouthe in sondry londes,
And specially from every shires ende   15
Of Engelond to Caunterbury they wende
The holy blisful martir for to seke
That hem hath holpen whan that they were seeke.
  Bifel that in that sesoun on a day
In Southwerk at the Tabard as I lay   20
Redy to wenden on my pilgrimage
To Caunterbury, with ful devout corage,
At nyght was come into that hostelrye
Wel nyne and twenty in a compaignye
Of sondry folk, by aventure yfalle   25
In felaweshipe, and pilgrimes were they alle
That toward Caunterbury wolden ryde.
The chambres and the stables weren wyde
And wel we weren esed atte beste.

2

30 *shortly* in short.
31 *everichon* every one.
33 'Made arrangements to rise early'.
34 *ther as I yow devyse* to the place I tell you of; i.e. Canterbury.
36 *pace* go.
37 *Me thynketh it* it seems to me it (is).
　acordant to in agreement with.
　resoun reason; a word used in mediaeval rhetoric to cover the
principles of orderly presentation.
38 *condicioun* outward circumstances as well as inward character.
40 *whiche they weren* what were their distinguishing physical
characteristics. 'Which' often translates the Latin *qualis*, 'what kind of'.
　degree rank in society.
41 *array* dress and equipage.

43 *Knyght*. Knights were obliged to serve the king in his wars, but
it was also common for those so inclined to seek service in wars
overseas against the heathen.
45 *chivalrye* the elaborate code of knightly manners, the ideal of
knighthood.
46 'Loyalty, a sense of honour, liberality and courteous behaviour'.
These were the four main virtues of the chivalric code; the words
are loaded with a greater richness of meaning than can be indicated
by translation.
47 *his lordes werre* the king's wars; but also perhaps, the crusades,
the wars of Our Lord.
48 *therto* moreover.
　ferre farther.
51 *Alisaundre* Alexandria, captured by King Peter of Cyprus in 1365.
52 *hadde the bord bigonne* was placed at the head of the table as
a mark of honour.
53 *nacions* representatives of other nations.
53-4 *Pruce* Prussia.
　　Lettow Lithuania.
　　Ruce Russia.
The Teutonic knights of Russia were in a constant state of warfare
with the neighbouring heathen, and this frontier of Christianity became
a common hunting ground for knights unemployed in other chivalric
exercises.
　reysed made an expedition. The word is not connected with
Mod. E. 'raised'.
55 *of his degree* i.e. of the Knight's rank.
56-7 *Gernade* the kingdom of Granada, held by the Moors, from
whom Algeciras was captured in 1344.
　Belmarye Benmarin, a Moorish kingdom corresponding to
modern Morocco.

And shortly, whan the sonne was to reste,   30
So hadde I spoken with hem everichon
That I was of hir felaweshipe anon,
And made forward erly for to ryse
To take oure wey ther as I yow devyse.

   But nathelees whil I have tyme and space   35
Er that I ferther in this tale pace,
Me thynketh it acordant to resoun
To telle yow al the condicioun
Of ech of hem so as it semed me
And whiche they weren and of what degree   40
And eek in what array that they were inne;
And at a knyght than wol I first bigynne.

   A KNYGHT ther was, and that a worthy man
That fro the tyme that he first bigan
To riden out he loved chivalrye,   45
Trouthe and honour, fredom and curteisye.
Ful worthy was he in his lordes werre,
And thereto hadde he riden, no man ferre,
As wel in cristendom as in hethenesse
And evere honoured for his worthynesse.   50
  At Alisaundre he was whan it was wonne;
Ful ofte tyme he hadde the bord bigonne
Aboven alle nacions in Pruce;
In Lettow hadde he reysed and in Ruce,
No Cristen man so ofte of his degree.   55
In Gernade at the seege eek hadde he be
Of Algezir and riden in Belmarye.

58 *Lyeys* Ayas in Armenia, captured from the Turks in 1367.
Satalye ancient Attalia, now Adalia, captured in about 1361.
59 *Grete See* the Mediterranean.
60 *armee* armada, rather than army; an armed expedition.
62 *Tramyssene* Tremessen, now Tlemcen, then in Moorish North Africa.
63 *lystes* lists; in this case, in direct combat with a heathen.
ay always.
65 *Palatye* Palathia, probably the modern Balat in Turkey. The Lord of Palatye was a heathen, but bound in treaty to the chivalric King Peter of Cyprus.
67 *a sovereyn prys* a supreme renown.
68-9 *wys* prudent, rather than wise.
port bearing, manner. The two lines mean that, though he was an excellent man of war, he was courteously unaggressive in behaviour, as the chivalric code enjoined.
70 *vileynye** coarseness of speech; speech appropriate to a 'vilein' or churl.
71 *maner wight* kind of man.
72 *verray* true.
parfit perfect or complete.
*gentil** cf. gentleman.
74 *hors* horses (plural).
gay referring to his clothing.
75 *fustian* a thick cotton cloth.
gypoun a tunic worn under the chain mail.
76 *bismotered* stained, spotted.
habergeoun hauberk, coat of mail.
77 *viage* voyage or expedition.
78 *his pilgrimage.* The word 'his' implies that it was the usual pilgrimage offered to a saint in return for safety or honour in battle.

79 *Squyer* attendant and arm bearer for a knight. He would usually have been of aristocratic birth; his duties would include carving at table.
80 *lusty* a word used by many writers to describe such 'bachelers', and conveying such qualities as high-spirits and exuberance as well as amorousness.
bacheler a man training for knighthood; cf. Bachelor of Arts.
81 *crulle* curled.
leyd in presse pressed in a curling iron of some sort.

At Lyeys was he and at Satalye
Whan they were wonne and in the Grete See
At many a noble armee hadde he be.   60
At mortal batailles hadde he been fiftene,
And foghten for oure feith at Tramyssene
In lystes thryes and ay slayn his foo.
This ilke worthy knyght hadde been also
Som tyme with the lord of Palatye   . 65
Agayn another hethen in Turkye.
    And evere moore he hadde a sovereyn prys,
And though that he were worthy he was wys
And of his port as meeke as is a mayde.
He nevere yet no vileynye ne sayde   70
In al his lyf unto no maner wight:
He was a verray parfit gentil knyght.
    But for to tellen yow of his array,
Hise hors were goode but he was nat gay:
Of fustian he wered a gypoun   75
Al bismotered with his habergeoun
For he was late ycome from his viage
And wente for to doon his pilgrimage.

    With hym ther was his sone, a young Squyer,
A lovere and a lusty bacheler   80
With lokkes crulle as they were leyd in presse;

83 *evene lengthe* middle height.
84 *delyvere* agile.
85 *chivachye* cavalry raid or expedition; or, feat of horsemanship.
86 In contrast with the Knight, the Squire has not yet ventured farther afield than France.
87 *as of so litel space* i.e. considering the shortness of his service.
88 *his lady grace* his lady's favour.
89 *Embrouded* embroidered. The excessive decoration of clothing was forbidden to esquires having an annual income of less than £200. Elaborate dressing often came under the moral condemnation of preachers, but courtly literature positively praised and encouraged it.
   meede meadow.
91 *floytynge* playing the flute.
94 *koude* knew how to.
95 *endite* write the words for the songs he composed.
96 *Juste* joust.
   purtreye draw.
   write an uncommon ability at the time.
97 *hoote* fervently.
   nyghtertale night-time.
99 *lowely* humble, modest.
   servysable willing to serve.
101 *Yeman* a servant ranking next above a groom.
   he i.e. the Knight.
   namo no more.
102 *hym liste* it pleased him.
104 *pecok arwes* arrows with peacock feathers for gaiety of appearance.
   kene sharp.
105 *bar* bore.
   thriftily carefully, properly.
106 *dresse* prepare, arrange.
   takel. The word was most often used specifically of arrows, though it could also mean 'shooting gear' in general.
   yemanly in a yeomanlike fashion.
107 'His arrows did not droop in flight as a result of weak feathers or of feathers cut too close to the shaft!'
109 *not heed* closely cropped skull.
110 *wodecraft* more concerned with game-keeping and the chase than with forestry in the modern sense.
   usage customs, practice.
111 *bracer* armguard used in archery.
112 *bokeler* buckler, small shield.
114 *Harneysed* mounted or embellished, probably with silver or some other precious metal.
115 *Cristofre* a figure of St. Christopher, the patron saint of foresters and travellers. Such a figure was believed to ward off danger and ill-luck of all kinds.
   sheene bright.
116 *bawdryk* a belt slung over one shoulder and under the opposite arm.
117 *forster* forester, more concerned with preserving game than trees.
   as I gesse an inspired guess on Chaucer's part!

7

Of twenty yeer of age he was I gesse.
　Of his stature he was of evene lengthe
And wonderly delyvere and of greet strengthe.
And he hadde been som tyme in chivachye　　　　85
In Flaundres, in Artoys and Picardye,
And born hym wel, as of so litel space,
In hope to stonden in his lady grace.
　Embrouded was he as it were a meede
Al ful of fresshe floures white and reede,　　　　90
Syngynge he was or floytynge al the day:
He was as fressh as is the monthe of May.
Short was his gowne with sleves longe and wyde.
Wel koude he sitte on hors and faire ryde,
He koude songes make and wel endite,　　　　95
Juste and eek daunce and wel purtreye and write.
So hoote he lovede that by nyghtertale
He slepte namoore than dooth a nyghtyngale.
　Curteys he was, lowely and servysable,
And carf biforn his fader at the table.　　　　100

　A Yeman hadde he and servantz namo
At that tyme for hym liste ryde so,
And he was clad in cote and hood of grene.
A sheef of pecok arwes bright and kene
Under his belt he bar ful thriftily —　　　　105
Wel koude he dresse his takel yemanly,
His arwes drouped noght with fetheres lowe —
And in his hand he bar a myghty bowe.
A not heed hadde he with a broun visage.
Of wodecraft wel koude he al the usage.　　　　110
Upon his arm he bar a gay bracer
And by his syde a swerd and a bokeler
And on that oother syde a gay daggere
Harneysed wel and sharp as point of spere;
A Cristofre on his brest of silver sheene,　　　　115
An horn he bar, the bawdryk was of grene:
A forster was he soothly as I gesse.

8

118 *Prioresse.* A prioress was in charge of a small religious house, as an abbess was in charge of a major house. However, prioresses would have enjoyed 'the same prestige as the lords of the manors and some extra deference on account of their religion', (Power); often their duties included the entertainment of wayfarers and the education of the daughters of the nobility.

119 *symple and coy* modest and shy. 'Coy' has none of the modern sense of coquetry.

120 *Seint Loy* the seventh century St. Eligius (Fr. S. Eloi), a peculiarly suitable saint to form the basis of the Prioress's 'gretteste' oath. He had been a goldsmith's apprentice in his youth, was famed for his craftsmanship, and later, as Bishop of Noyon, devoted himself to the beautification of the church. His cult, as celebrated in Chaucer's time, concentrated on "his peculiar office of lending beauty to the symbols of holiness" (Lowes). He had been a man of court, famed for his personal beauty and courtesy; and on one occasion he is supposed to have refused to make an oath.

121 *Madame* the usual courtesy title of a nun.
Eglentyne an incongruous though not impossible name for a 14th century nun; lit. 'briar-rose'.

123 *Entuned* intoned.
semely fittingly.

124 *fetisly* prettily, neatly.

125 *After the scole of* as it was spoken at.
Stratford atte Bowe Stratford, Essex.

127 *mete* food, meals. See Appendix A for background to this passage.

130 *keepe* take care, manage.

132 *curteisye** courtliness of manners.
lest desire, delight.

134 *ferthyng* lit. a fourth part, a farthing; fig. a tiny piece.
sene visible.

136 *raughte* past tense of 'reche(n)', to reach, to stretch.

137 *sikerly* certainly, surely.
desport affability, gaiety.

138 *plesaunt* pleasant, easy of manner.
amyable kind, courteous.
port behaviour.

139-40 'She took care to adopt or maintain standards of courtly behaviour'. The word 'countrefete' bears in itself no suggestion of fraudulence or mere cheap copying.

140 *estatlich of manere* stately of bearing befitting a person of rank.

141 *digne of reverence* worthy of respect. For a significant contrast cf. 527 below.

Ther was also a nonne, a PRIORESSE,
That of hir smylyng was ful symple and coy;
Hir gretteste ooth was but by Seint Loy,   120
And she was cleped Madame Eglentyne.
    Ful wel she soong the service dyvyne
Entuned in hir nose ful semely,
And Frenssh she spak ful faire and fetisly
After the scole of Stratford atte Bowe   125
For Frenssh of Parys was to hire unknowe.
    At mete wel ytaught was she with alle:
She leet no morsel from hir lippes falle
Ne wette hir fyngres in hir sauce deepe;
Wel koude she carie a morsel and wel keepe   130
That no drope ne fille upon hire brest.
In curteisye was set ful muchel hir lest:
Hir over lippe wyped she so clene
That in hir coppe ther was no ferthyng sene
Of grece whan she dronken hadde hir draughte;   135
Ful semely after hir mete she raughte,
And sikerly she was of greet desport
And ful plesaunt and amyable of port,
And peyned hire to countrefete cheere
Of court and to been estatlich of manere   140
And to been holden digne of reverence.

142 *conscience* moral conscience; but also sensibility, tender feeling.
143 *charitable* showing Christian charity; but also, tender-hearted.
    pitous pious or devout; but also, full of pity.
146 *houndes* dogs.
147 *wastel breed* fine white bread, which was something of a luxury.
149 *yerde* stick or rod.
    smerte sharply.
151 *wympel* wimple, covering for the neck.
    pynched pleated.
152 *tretys* long, well-shaped.
    greye less the actual colour than the brilliance and light of the
eyes.
156 *hardily* certainly.
    undergrowe small in stature.
157 *fetys* well-made, neat, elegant.
    was war perceived, was aware.
159 *peyre of bedes* a set of beads, a rosary.
    gauded. The large beads or gaudies of her rosary were green.
160 *sheene* bright.
162 *Amor vincit omnia* Love conquers all. This popular Latin tag
could equally well apply to sacred or profane love.

164 *chapeleyne* a nun acting as secretary and attendant.
    preestes thre a textual problem since the presence of *three* priests
with the other pilgrims conflicts with Chaucer's figure of 'nyne and
twenty'. It seems unlikely that the Prioress would have had as many
as three priests attending her; only one is referred to later — the
Nonnes Preeste. The most likely explanation is that Chaucer intended
to give descriptions of the Chapeleyne and the Nonnes Preeste, since
each subsequently tells a tale, but left a blank half-line which some
scribe filled in with these words.

But for to speken of hir conscience,
She was so charitable and so pitous
She wolde wepe if that she sawe a mous
Caught in a trappe if it were deed or bledde.   145
Of smale houndes hadde she that she fedde
With rosted flessh or milk and wastel breed,
But soore wepte she if oon of hem were deed
Or if men smoot it with a yerde smerte,
And al was conscience and tendre herte.   150
   Ful semely hir wympel pynched was,
Hir nose tretys, hir eyen greye as glas,
Hir mouth ful smal and therto softe and reed,
But sikerly she hadde a fair forheed —
It was almoost a spanne brood I trowe,   155
For hardily she was nat undergrowe.
Ful fetys was hir cloke as I was war.
Of smal coral aboute hir arm she bar
A peyre of bedes gauded al with grene
And theron heng a brooch of gold ful sheene   160
On which ther was first writen a crowned A
And after *Amor vincit omnia.*

Another NONNE with hire hadde she
That was hir chapeleyne, and preestes thre.

165 *maistrie* lit. mastery; command, pre-eminence. To be fit for the 'maistrie' in any field implies the greatest degree of skill, experience or power. The phrase 'fair for the maistrie' is idiomatic, meaning 'fine in the highest degree'. The line means 'there was a monk and an exceedingly fine (one)'.

166 *outridere* a monk appointed by the abbot to manage the estates belonging to the abbey. His duties were those of a business man in continual contact with the outside world. Consequently the temptations to worldliness were greater for him than for other monks.

venerie hunting.

167 *able* worthy or fit (to be an abbot).

For 'manly man' see 397n. below.

168 *deyntee* fine and valuable.

172 *Ther as* where.

kepere head or custodian.

celle a small priory or dependant house, or perhaps an estate with a chapel, belonging to the abbey.

173 St. Maurus was a disciple of St. Benedict and was regarded as the founder of the French Benedictines.

St. Benedict was the founder of the Benedictine order, whose rule enjoined strict claustration and manual labour as essential elements in the monastic life.

174 *som del* somewhat.

streit narrow, strict. Cf. St. Matthew vii, 14: 'How narrow is the gate and how straight is the way that leadeth to life; and few there are that find it.'

175 *pace* pass by.

176 *heeld* held, followed; cf. 'held his course'.

space space, in the sense of room or opportunity, in contrast with the strict rule of St. Benedict. (Some scholars have even suggested 'course or custom' and 'meanwhile'; but see OED.)

177 *text* any common saying, or frequently quoted writing.

pulled plucked; a 'pulled hen', like 'an oystre', was a common contemptuous epithet.

178 The idea that hunting was sinful was a commonplace of the fourteenth century, although derived ultimately from a pronouncement of St. Jerome (d. 420) — 'Esau was a hunter, because he was a sinner; and in Holy Scripture we do not find any holy man who is a hunter. We do find holy men as fishermen'.

179 *recchelees* careless; here, 'neglectful of his rule', a common application of the word.

180 *til* to. The comparison of a gadding monk to a fish out of water was frequent, being found in writings as early as the fourth century, and in works by Chaucer's contemporaries Gower, Langland and Wycliff.

181-2 These two lines are an ironic reversal of two lines from *Le testament de Jehan de Meung* (Jean de Meun, author of the second part of *Le Roman de la Rose*): 'Whoever wants to find them should seek them in their cloister; for they do not hold the world as worth an oyster'.

184 *What* why.

wood mad.

13

A Monk ther was, a fair for the maistrie,   165
An outridere that lovede venerie,
A manly man, to been an abbot able.
Ful many a deyntee hors hadde he in stable
And whan he rood men myghte his brydel heere
Gynglen in a whistlynge wynd as cleere   170
And eek as loude as dooth the chapel belle
Ther as this lord was kepere of the celle.
     The reule of Seint Maure or of Seint Beneit
By cause that it was old and som del streit,
This ilke monk leet olde thynges pace   175
And heeld after the newe world the space.
He yaf nat of that text a pulled hen,
That seith that hunters been nat holy men
Ne that a monk whan he is recchelees
Is likned til a fissh that is waterlees,   180
This is to seyn, a monk out of his cloystre;
But thilke text heeld he nat worth an oystre,
And I seyde his opinioun was good:
What sholde he studie and make hym selven wood

14

186 *swynken* to toil.
187 *Austyn* St. Augustine of Hippo (b. 354), from whose writings was compiled the Augustinian monastic rule. In anti-monastic polemics of Chaucer's time, the rule requiring manual labour was used to justify attacks against the luxury and ease which many monks preferred.

bit commands (pres. tense).

189 *prikasour*. The word is usually taken to mean 'hard-rider', 'quick-rider', related to 'pricking' meaning 'spurring'; cf. Spenser's 'A gentle Knight was pricking on the plaine'. But since the word is only found in this line of Chaucer and is here placed in close relation with 'pricking' meaning 'hunting' (cf. 191n. below) something of this sense must enter into the meaning. Perhaps 'mounted huntsman' translates it most neatly.

191 *prikyng* the tracking of a hare by its pricks or footprints.
192 *lust* pleasure, intent, desire.
193 *saugh* saw.

ypurfiled trimmed or edged.

hond hand, wrist.

194 *grys* valuable gray fur of squirrels. The use of 'grys' was specifically forbidden to monks, who were allowed to use sheepskin, and that only when protection from the cold was necessary.

of a lond in the land.

196 *wroght* wrought or fashioned.

curious skilfully made.

197 *love knotte* a traditional intertwined knot with loops.
200 *in good poynt* cf. Fr. *embonpoint*, occasionally used in English today, meaning 'plumpness' or 'of a well-nourished appearance'.
201 *stepe* large, prominent, perhaps bright.
202 'Which (his eyes) shone like a furnace or fire under a cauldron'.
203 *in greet estat* in good condition.
205 *forpyned* tormented, emaciated by suffering.
206 *roost* roast.
207 *palfrey* a riding horse, perhaps also used for hunting.

208 *Frere* a member of one of the four mendicant orders, who supported themselves by begging. They were pledged to a life of service to men in contrast with the secluded and contemplative life of the monks. Chaucer's criticism of the Friar is typical of that levelled against the mendicant orders of his time.

wantowne lively, high-spirited; but also 'wanton'.

209 *lymytour* the Friar was licenced to beg within a certain 'limitacioun' or limited area.

solempne. The word draws on such meanings as pompous, ceremonious and festive and does not exclude merriment as does the modern word 'solemn'.

210 *the ordres foure* the four orders of friars: Franciscans, Dominicans, Carmelites and Augustinians.

kan knows.

Upon a book in cloystre alwey to poure,   185
Or swynken with his handes and laboure
As Austyn bit? How shal the world be served?
Lat Austyn have his swynk to hym reserved!
Ther fore he was a prikasour aright:
Grehoundes he hadde as swift as fowel in flight;   190
Of prikyng and of huntyng for the hare
Was al his lust, for no cost wolde he spare.
  I saugh his sleves ypurfiled at the hond
With grys and that the fyneste of a lond,
And for to festne his hood under his chyn   195
He hadde of gold wroght a ful curious pyn:
A love knotte in the gretter ende ther was.
His heed was balled that shoon as any glas
And eek his face as he hadde been enoynt;
He was a lord ful fat and in good poynt;   200
Hise eyen stepe and rollynge in his heed
That stemed as a fourneys of a leed,
His bootes souple, his hors in greet estat,
Now certeynly he was a fair prelat:
He was nat pale as a forpyned goost,   205
A fat swan loved he best of any roost,
His palfrey was as broun as is a berye.

  A Frere ther was, a wantowne and a merye,
A lymytour, a ful solempne man:
In alle the ordres foure is noon that kan   210

16

211 *daliaunce* flirting and idle gossip.

fair langage flowery and beguiling talk.

212-3 *maad* made. The suggestion is that he found husbands, and therefore probably dowries, for women whom he had himself seduced.

214 *post* pillar, support.

216 *frankeleyns.* See 333 ff. below. This explains why the Friar enjoyed the company of franklins.

in his contree in his territory. Cf. 209n. above.

220 *licenciat.* He had a licence from his order with papal authority to hear confessions and grant absolutions beyond the jurisdiction of the local priests, who had to refer serious cases, e.g. murder, to the bishop.

224 *a good pitaunce* a substantial offering of food or, more likely, money.

226 *yshryve* shriven.

227 *he yaf* he (the penitent) gave.

he dorst make avaunt he (the Friar) dared make a boast.

230 *hym soore smerte* it pains him sorely; i.e. he is sorely pained.

232 *Men moote yeve* one should give.

233 *typet* hood, used as a pocket.

ay always.

farsed stuffed.

235 *note* lit. tune, i.e. a melodious voice.

236 *a rote* a stringed instrument, a kind of fiddle.

237 'He completely carried off the prize for songs (romances and ballads)'.

238 The white neck and lisping (266 below) were regarded as signs of licentiousness or sensuality.

239 *Therto* moreover.

241 *tappestere* barmaid.

242 *Bet* better.

lazar leper, or perhaps just any diseased person.

beggestere a beggar; the feminine form, used perhaps for the rime.

244 'Was unfitting for a man of his profession'; or perhaps 'of his ability'.

245 *sike* sick.

246 'It is not respectable or becoming, it will not advance (one's profits)'.

247 *poraille* poor rabble.

248 *al* only, just.

vitaille victuals, foodstuffs. The victual merchants were influential, as well as being plentifully supplied with offerings in kind.

249 *over al* everywhere.

ther as wherever.

250 Ironic reference to 99 above.

251 Note the ironic over-emphasis of the triple negative.

17

So muche of daliaunce and fair langage;
He hadde maad ful many a mariage
Of yonge wommen at his owene cost.
   Unto his ordre he was a noble post.
Ful wel biloved and famylier was he   215
With frankeleyns over al in his contree
And with worthy wommen of the toun,
For he hadde power of confessioun,
As seyde him self, moore than a curat,
For of his ordre he was a licenciat.   220
Ful swetely herde he confessioun
And plesaunt was his absolucioun:
He was an esy man to yeve penaunce
Ther as he wiste to have a good pitaunce,
For unto a poure ordre for to yive   225
Is signe that a man is wel yshryve;
For if he yaf, he dorst make avaunt,
He wiste that a man was repentaunt:
For many a man so hard is of his herte
He may nat wepe althogh hym soore smerte;   230
Ther fore in stede of wepynge and preyeres
Men moote yeve silver to the poure freres.
   His typet was ay farsed ful of knyves
And pynnes for to yeven faire wyves.
   And certeynly he hadde a murye note: 235
Wel koude he synge and pleyen on a rote;
Of yeddynges he bar outrely the prys.
His nekke whit was as the flour-delys,
Therto he strong was as a champioun.
   He knew the tavernes wel in every toun   240
And every hostiler and tappestere
Bet than a lazar or a beggestere,
For onto swich a worthy man as he
Acorded nat as by his facultee
To have with sike lazars aqueyntaunce,   245
It is nat honeste, it may nat avaunce
For to deelen with no swich poraille,
But al with riche and selleres of vitaille.
And over al ther as profit sholde arise
Curteys he was and lowely of servyse;   250
Ther nas no man no wher so vertuous.

18

253-4 These two lines are thought to be genuine, although perhaps deliberately cancelled by Chaucer in a later draft.

ferme rent.

graunt the right to beg in his district or haunt.

255 *widwe* widow.

sho shoe.

256 *In principio* the opening words of St. John's Gospel, 'In the beginning (was the word)'. The phrase had come to be regarded by the ignorant as a potent charm, and was much used by the friars in their begging. Cf. NPT397.

257 *ferthyng* farthing; perhaps meaning 'any small gift'.

258 'His fraudulent income was greater than his honest income'.

259 *rage* to play about, very often in a wanton manner.

whelpe. Puppies were often associated with wantonness of behaviour.

260 *lovedayes* days appointed for the amicable rather than legal settling of disputes, often with a churchman as umpire. The institution was easily corrupted to the financial benefit of the umpire.

262 *cope* cape or cloak.

263 *maister* in the sense of a learned Master, a title which implies learning and dignity; cf. Master of Divinity.

264 *double worstede* a broad and substantial worsted fabric.

semycope short ecclesiastical cape.

265 *out of the presse* out of the mould in which the bell was made.

266 *lipsed* lisped; a characteristic often associated with lasciviousness.

for his wantownesse from a desire; as a conscious mannerism.

269 *aryght* certainly, really.

271 *Huberd*. A connection has been suggested with the kite (a bird of prey) called Hubert, in the French *Roman de Renart*.

273 *mottelee* cloth woven with a design in various colours, perhaps referring to the distinctive dress of the company to which this merchant belonged.

hye on hors on a saddle constructed to increase the rider's height.

274 *Flaundryssh bevere hat* an expensive hat of beaver fur, as made in Flanders.

275 *clasped* fastened with clasps.

276 *resons* opinions.

solempnely impressively, with a sense of importance.

277 *Sownynge* proclaiming.

encrees increase.

wynnyng profit.

278 *kept for any thyng* guarded at any cost (against the prevalent pirates and privateers — like the Shipman, perhaps. Cf. 390ff. below).

279 *Middelburgh* a wool town in Holland. It was the staple town (through which most English exports were sent) between 1384 and 1388, when the hostility of the French was threatening the usual staple town, Calais.

Orewelle Orwell, a now submerged port on the River Orwell, near Ipswich, and presumably the port through which the Merchant operated.

280 *sheeldes* French coins. Foreign exchange and the profits therefrom were a royal prerogative and therefore illegal for the Merchant.

281 *his wit bisette* employed his wits and cunning.

19

He was the beste beggere in his hous,
[And yaf a certeyn ferme for the graunt:
Noon of his bretheren cam ther in his haunt;]
For thogh a widwe hadde noght a sho,   255
So plesaunt was his *In principio,*
Yet wolde he have a ferthyng er he wente:
His purchas was wel bettre than his rente.
And rage he koude as it were right a whelpe.
   In lovedayes ther koude he muchel helpe: 260
For ther he was nat lyk a cloystrer
With a thredbare cope as is a poure scoler,
But he was lyk a maister or a pope:
Of double worstede was his semycope
That rounded as a belle out of the presse.   265
   Som what he lipsed for his wantownesse
To make his Englissh sweete upon his tonge,
And in his harpyng whan that he hadde songe
Hise eyen twinkled in his heed aryght
As doon the sterres in the frosty nyght.   270
This worthy lymytour was cleped Huberd.

   A MARCHANT was ther with a forked berd,
In mottelee, and hye on hors he sat;
Upon his heed a Flaundryssh bevere hat,
His bootes clasped faire and fetisly.   275
   Hise resons he spak ful solempnely
Sownynge alwey th'encrees of his wynnyng.
He wolde the see were kept for any thyng
Bitwixe Middelburgh and Orewelle.
Wel koude he in eschaunge sheeldes selle.   280
   This worthy man ful wel his wit bisette:

20

283 *estatly* dignified.
  of his governaunce in the conduct of his business; and perhaps 'in his behaviour'.
284 *chevysaunce* referring to the borrowing and lending of money, perhaps a form of usury. As with the word 'bargayn', it was often used with implications of dishonesty.
285 *For soothe* truly, indeed.
286 *how men hym calle* what men call him, what name he goes by.

287 *Clerk* an ecclesiastical student, though the word came to mean any man of learning.
288 *ygo* gone, taken to. The line means that the Clerk had been studying logic for a considerable time, implying that he was an advanced student. Logic, the science of rational argument, was a major part of the University course.
291 *holwe* hollow.
  and therto sobrely and also grave.
292 *overeste courtepy* the outer short coat or cloak.
293 *geten* got.
  benefice an ecclesiastical appointment, such as a chaplaincy or a curacy.
294 *office* by contrast with benefice, a secular employment of some kind, in government or legal business, for instance. It was a common charge against clerks that they turned to worldly advancement instead of pursuing their religious duties.
295 *hym was levere* 'it was preferable to him' i.e. he had rather.
296-7 Aristotle's works were textbooks for the study of Rhetoric and Logic, and of Natural, Moral and Metaphysical Philosophy. At a conservative estimate, twenty such volumes would have cost about £ stg. 4,000 in modern money.
298 *fithele* fiddle.
  sautrye psaltery, a kind of small harp held on the lap.
299-300 *al be that* although.
  philosophre. As well as meaning a philosopher in the modern sense, the word also had a more specialised meaning, referring to alchemists who performed chemical experiments in the hope of producing gold from base metal. The couplet is a satirical pun directed at both kinds of philosopher.
  cofre coffer, chest for holding money.
301 *hente* get.
303 *bisily* earnestly.
  gan did.
304 *hem* them.
  scoleye study.
305 *cure* care.
306 *o* one.
  neede necessary.
307 *in forme and reverence* with suitable formality and respect.
308 *quyk* not modern 'quick', but 'lively and perceptive'.
  *by sentence** lofty or weighty significance.
309 *Sownynge in* full of, inclining to.

Ther wiste no wight that he was in dette,
So estatly was he of his governaunce,
With his bargaynes and with his chevysaunce.
    For soothe he was a worthy man with alle,   285
But sooth to seyn I noot how men hym calle.

    A CLERK ther was of Oxenford also
That unto logyk hadde longe ygo.
    As leene was his hors as is a rake
And he nas nat right fat I undertake   290
But looked holwe and therto sobrely.
Ful thredbare was his overeste courtepy
For he hadde geten hym yet no benefice
Ne was so worldly for to have office,
For hym was levere have at his beddes heed   295
Twenty bookes clad in blak or reed
Of Aristotle and his philosophye
Than robes riche or fithele or gay sautrye.
    But al be that he was a philosophre
Yet hadde he but litel gold in cofre,   300
But al that he myghte of his frendes hente
On bookes and on lernynge he it spente,
And bisily gan for the soules preye
Of hem that yaf hym wherwith to scoleye.
    Of studye took he moost cure and moost heede;   305
Noght o word spak he moore than was neede
And that was seyd in forme and reverence
And short and quyk and ful of hy sentence:
Sownynge in moral vertu was his speche
And gladly wolde he lerne and gladly teche.   310

311 *war and wys* cautious and prudent.
312 *the Parvys* probably the porch or nave of St. Paul's, where lawyers were assigned pillars to meet clients for consultation. There is some doubt, however, about this interpretation.
313 *ful riche of excellence* of great ability. Is there a pun on the word 'riche'?
314 *of greet reverence* i.e. he had a bearing demanding respect.
316 *assise* county courts.
317 *patente* a letter patent; the letter authorizing his appointment to the assizes, issued by the king or by a judge.
pleyn commissioun full commission giving him jurisdiction over all kinds of cases.
318 *For his science* as a result of his learning.
for his heigh renoun as a result of his great reputation.
319 *robes* full sets of clothing, a common form of payment.
many oon many a one.
320 *purchasour* a buyer (of land) presumably for himself rather than for his clients. This common form of social self-promotion was often attacked by reformers.
321 *fee symple* absolute possession, without entail.
in effect in the end result.
322 *infect* invalidated. The implication of these lines is that he is an expert in converting entailed or defective titles into freehold for his own benefit.
325 *In termes* with formal accuracy.
caas and doomes alle all cases and judgements.
326 *Kyng William* William the Conqueror (1066-1087).
were falle had befallen, were.
327 *endite* compose.
make a thyng draw up a legal document.
328 *pynchen* find fault. Manly has suggested that this is a punning reference to an actual Sergeant at Law, Thomas Pynchbeck, who signed a writ to arrest Chaucer for a small debt in 1388, and who fits neatly the other characteristics of Chaucer's portrait.
329 *koude he pleyn by rote* he knew in full by heart.
330 *rood* rode.
hoomly in a homely manner, unpretentiously, informally.
medlee a cloth of mixed colours, perhaps reminiscent of those of his formal robes.
331 *ceint* girdle.
barres smale ornamental metal strips, running transversely across the width of the girdle.

A Sergeaunt of the lawe, war and wys,
That often hadde been at the Parvys,
Ther was also, ful riche of excellence.
Discreet he was and of greet reverence:
He seemed swich, hise wordes weren so wise.   315
    Justice he was ful often in assise
By patente and by pleyn commissioun.
For his science and for his heigh renoun,
Of fees and robes hadde he many oon.
So greet a purchasour was nowher noon: 320
Al was fee symple to hym in effect,
His purchasyng myghte nat been infect.
    Nowher so bisy a man as he ther nas
And yet he semed bisier than he was.
    In termes hadde he caas and doomes alle   325
That from the tyme of Kyng William were falle.
Therto he koude endite and make a thyng
Ther koude no wight pynchen at his writyng,
And every statut koude he pleyn by rote.
    He rood but hoomly in a medlee cote   330
Girt with a ceint of silk with barres smale;
Of his array telle I no lenger tale.

333 *Frankeleyn.* Franklins were wealthy country landowners, probably considered members of the gentry, but ranking immediately below knights in company with Sergeants of Law and squires. They were perhaps equivalent to the country squires of a later period.

334 *dayesye* daisy; etymologically 'day's eye'.

335 A sanguine complexion, accompanied by a red face, was considered the most cheerful and handsome, and implied a good digestion and liberality. See further Explanatory Notes—Medicine.

336 *by the morwe* in the morning.

sop in wyn wine containing pieces of bread or cake.

337 *delyt* pleasure.

wone custom or habit.

338 *Epicurus* a Greek philosopher (b. 342 B.C.) who held that pleasure is the chief good and aim of life. By pleasure he meant freedom from pain and fear, and certainly not the luxury and sensuality (pleyn delit) which some of his followers practised and taught, and which mediaeval preachers commonly attributed to him.

340 *verray* true.

341 *housholdere* the owner of a house, not a tenant.

342 *Seint Julian* the patron saint of hospitality. He was supposed to have built a hostel for travellers, and to have fed, entertained and helped strangers.

contree country or region.

343 *breed* bread.

after oon uniformly good.

344 *envyned* stocked with wines.

349 *After* according to.

350 *mete and . . . soper* dinner and supper. For medical reasons, it was customary to change one's diet with the seasons.

351 *muwe* coop.

352 *luce* pike.

stuwe fish pond.

353 *Wo was* woe betide.

but if unless.

354 *Poynaunt* piquant.

his gere his eating utensils.

355 *table dormaunt* a large fixed table in contrast to the normal 'board' which was a removable trestle-table.

halle the large main room of the house.

357 *sessiouns* sessions, meetings of Justices of the Peace, (at which he presided).

358 *knyght of the shire* representative of his county in parliament.

A FRANKELEYN was in his compaignye.
Whit was his berd as is the dayesye;
Of his complexioun he was sangwyn.   335
Wel loved he by the morwe a sop in wyn;
To lyven in delyt was evere his wone
For he was Epicurus owene sone
That heeld opinioun that pleyn delit
Was verray felicitee parfit.   340
    An housholdere and that a greet was he;
Seint Julian he was in his contree.
His breed, his ale was alweys after oon,
A bettre envyned man was no wher noon;
Withoute bake mete was nevere his hous,   345
Of fissh and flessh and that so plentevous
It snewed in his hous of mete and drynke
Of alle deyntees that men koude thynke.
After the sondry sesons of the yeer
So chaunged he his mete and his soper.   350
Ful many a fat partrich hadde he in muwe
And many a breem and many a luce in stuwe.
Wo was his cook but if his sauce were
Poynaunt and sharp, and redy al his gere.
His table dormaunt in his halle alway   355
Stood redy covered al the longe day.
    At sessiouns ther was he lord and sire;
Ful ofte tyme he was knyght of the shire.

359 *anlaas* a short, two-edged dagger or knife.
    gipser purse or pouch.
361 *shirreve* sheriff, the King's administrative officer or reeve in the shire or county.
    countour probably a reference to his function as county auditor.
362 *vavasour* a country gentleman or squire.

363 *Haberdasshere* a seller either of hats or of small wares such as needles and buttons.
364 *Webbe* weaver.
    Tapycer a maker of tapestry and carpets.
365 *o lyveree* one livery.
366 *solempne* august, solemn.
367 *geere* apparel or trappings.
    apyked trimmed, adorned.
368 *chaped* tipped. A chape was a metal tip or cap on the point of a scabard.
370 *everydel* every one, every piece (of equipment).
371 *burgeys* burgess, a magistrate or member of the governing body of a town.
372 *yeldehalle* guildhall.
    on a deys on a dias (where the mayor and alderman sat).
373 *Everich* each one.
    can knows, is in possession of.
374 *shaply* suitable, fit, or perhaps 'likely'.
    alderman a magistrate, in the early sense of a civil officer, next in dignity to a mayor; the chief officer of a ward.
375 *catel* chattels, property, goods.
    rente income.
    A certain degree of wealth was a necessary qualification for the position of alderman.
376 'And also their wives would certainly agree'.
377 *to blame* blameable, deserving of censure.
379 *vigilies* vigils; either the celebrations before guild festivals, or the saint's day vigils, at both of which aldermen's wives would have precedence.
380 *ybore* born or carried.

381 *for the nones* for the occasion.
382 *marybones* marrowbones.
383 *poudre marchaunt* a seasoning for which a variety of recipes exist.
    tart tart or sharp.
    galyngale a spice, made from the root of sweet cyperus.
384 London ale was celebrated and expensive.
385 *seethe* boil.
386 *mortreux* a thick soup.
387 *as it thoughte me* as it seemed to me.
388 *shyne* shin.
    mormal 'malum mortuum', a species of scabies or dry scabbed ulcer.
389 *blankmanger* not blancmange, but a dish of creamed capon with rice, almonds, sugar and salt.

27

An anlaas and a gipser al of silk
Heeng at his girdel, whit as morne milk. 360
A shirreve hadde he been and a countour.
Was nowhere swich a worthy vavasour.

AN HABERDASSHERE and a CARPENTER,
A WEBBE, a DYERE and a TAPYCER
And they were clothed alle in o lyveree 365
Of a solempne and a greet fraternitee.
Ful fressh and newe hir geere apyked was,
Hir knyves were chaped noght with bras
But al with silver, wroght ful clene and wel,
Hire girdles and hir pouches everydel. 370
Wel semed ech of hem a fair burgeys
To sitten in a yeldehalle on a deys;
Everich for the wisdom that he can
Was shaply for to been an alderman,
For catel hadde they ynogh and rente 375
And eek hir wyves wolde it wel assente,
And ellis certeyn were they to blame:
It is ful fair to been ycleped 'Madame'
And goon to vigilies al bifore
And have a mantel roialliche ybore. 380

A COOK they hadde with hem for the nones
To boille the chiknes with the marybones
And poudre marchaunt tart and galyngale.
Wel koude he knowe a draughte of Londoun ale.
He koude rooste and seethe and broille and frye, 385
Maken mortreux and wel bake a pye,
But greet harm was it as it thoughte me
That on his shyne a mormal hadde he;
For blankmanger, that made he with the beste.

390 *wonyng* dwelling.
   fer by weste away in the west country.
391 'For all I know he was from Dartmouth (Devon)'. Dartmouth was notoriously a haven for privateers.
392 *rouncy*. The term appears to have been used variously to denote a poor hack, a nag, or a heavy sturdy horse; the illustration shows a rather stolid animal. Any of these would hardly be the choice of an experienced rider.   *as he kouthe* as best he could.
393 *faldyng* a coarse, long-lasting woollen fabric.
394 *a laas* a cord.
395 i.e. worn as a baldric.
397 *a good felawe* a good companion, in the sense defined by Chaucer's following lines. Mediaeval preachers, who never tired of preaching against moral abuses, sometimes deplored abuse of language too: 'he that is a . . . grete bragger, a grete swerer or a grete fyghter, soche men ben callyd "manly men" . . . He that is a ryatour and a grete hawnter of tavernys or of ale howsys, and a grete waster of his goodes, than is he callyd "a good felaw"' (Owst).
398 *drawe* drawn from the casks.
399 *Fro Burdeuxward* on the way from Bordeaux. Bordeaux was an English possession and renowned for its red wines.
   chapman the wine merchant who accompanied his cargo.
   sleep slept.
400 *nyce conscience*. There seems no necessity at this point for adopting the meaning of 'conscience' as tender feelings, as several editors have done. The word 'nyce', meaning both foolish and scrupulous, really sums up the shipman's attitude to conscience.
   took he no keep he took no heed.
402 i.e. he threw his prisoners overboard.
403 *of his craft* in the matter of his trade or special skill.
404 *stremes* currents.
   daungers hym bisydes the perils near at hand.
405 *herberwe* harbour in the abstract sense of shelter; cf. 'to seek harbour from'. To 'rekene' 'his herberwe' would involve a knowledge of where particular harbours were to be found and of their condition and accessibility.   *moone* the phases of the moon.
   lodemenage navigation, pilotage; cf. lodestone.
406 *noon swich* none such.   *Hulle* Hull.
   Cartage probably Cartagena in the south east of Spain, rather than Carthage in Africa.
407 *wys to undertake* prudent in judging what business to undertake.
409 *as they were* in order.
410 *Gootlond* Gotland, an island off the coast of Sweden, an important trading post. It is sometimes suggested that Jutland might be intended.
   Fynystere probably Cape Finistere, the western tip of Spain.
411 *cryke* inlet.   *Britaigne* Brittany.
412 *barge* a sea-going merchant vessel of less than 200 tons.
   Maudelayne Magdalen.

A SHIPMAN was ther wonyng fer by weste: 390
For aught I woot he was of Dertemouthe.
He rood upon a rouncy as he kouthe
In a gowne of faldyng to the knee;
A daggere hangynge on a laas hadde he
Aboute his nekke under his arm adoun.   395
The hoote somer hadde maad his hewe al broun.
   And certeinly he was a good felawe:
Ful many a draughte of wyn hadde he drawe
Fro Burdeuxward whil that the chapman sleep;
Of nyce conscience took he no keep;   400
If that he faught and hadde the hyer hond
By water he sente hem hoom to every lond.
   But of his craft, to rekene wel his tydes,
His stremes and his daungers hym bisydes,
His herberwe and his moone, his lodemenage,   405
Ther nas noon swich from Hulle to Cartage.
Hardy he was and wys to undertake;
With many a tempest hadde his berd been shake.
He knew alle the havenes as they were
Fro Gootlond to the cape of Fynystere,   410
And every cryke in Britaigne and in Spayne.
His barge ycleped was the *Maudelayne*.

415 *To speke of* in the matter of, concerning.
416 *grounded in astronomye* well trained in astrology. See Explanatory Notes—Medicine, for the whole of this passage.
417-8 'He took care of his patient thoroughly in the matter of hourly prescription and treatment, as dictated by his natural magic, his astrology and charms.' 'Natural magic' was not connected with witchcraft, the attempt to procure the services of spirits, or with legerdemain; it was the attempt to influence the course of natural events by drawing on such occult natural principles as the influence of the stars, and the curative powers of 'pure' metals. The construction of images is a good example of such natural magic.
419 'Images', usually seals or medallions inscribed with signs of the Zodiac and appropriate incantations, were used copiously in medicine. Their power depended on their being constructed and inscribed under exactly the right confluence of planetary influences relevant to the particular malady of the patient. The ascendant — when a planet or zodiacal sign is rising above the horizon — was the most potent moment of such influence. This Doctor of Physic was adept at determining the ascendants that would produce the greatest curative effect, and at inscribing their symbols on his images in the right or 'fortunate' position to dominate the 'unfortunate' influences.
422 See Explanatory Notes.
423 *engendred* originated.
   humour see Explanatory Notes.
424 *a verray, parfit practisour* a true, perfect (or complete) practitioner.
425 *of his harm the roote* the source of its ill-effect.
426 *yaf . . . his boote* gave . . . his remedy.
428 *letuaries* electuaries, medicines in syrup.
429 *to wynne* to profit financially.
430 'Their friendship didn't begin yesterday!'
431-6 The authorities here paraded are the authors of the most notable mediaeval medical textbooks, varying from Aesculapius, the legendary founder of medicine, through Hippocrates, of the 5th century B.C., who expounded the theory of the four humours, to such contemporaries as John Gaddesden, a doctor famous for his 'love of gold'.
437 *mesurable* moderate.
439 *of greet* greatly.
440 Atheism and irreligion were common charges laid to the medical profession.

With us ther was a DOCTOUR OF PHISIK:
In al this world ne was ther noon hym lik
To speke of phisik and of surgerye,   415
For he was grounded in astronomye:
He kepte his pacient a ful greet del
In houres bv his magyk naturel;
Wel koude he fortunen the ascendent
Of his ymages for his pacient.   420
He knew the cause of every maladye,
Were it of hoot or coold or moyste or drye
And where engendred and of what humour:
He was a verray, parfit practisour.
   The cause yknowe and of his harm the roote,   425
Anon he yaf the sike man his boote.
Ful redy hadde he hise apothecaries
To sende hym drogges and his letuaries,
For ech of hem made oother for to wynne;
Hir frendshipe nas nat newe to bigynne.   430
   Wel knew he the olde Esculapius
And Deyscorides and eek Rufus,
Olde Ypocras, Haly and Galyen,
Serapion, Razis and Avycen,
Averrois, Damascien and Constantyn,   435
Bernard and Gatesden and Gilbertyn.
   Of his diete mesurable was he
For it was of no superfluitee
But of greet norissyng and digestible.
His studye was but litel on the Bible.   440

441 *sangwyn* blood red, scarlet (cloth).

pers blue (cloth); 'a rich deep shade dyed in woad; cloths of this colour sometimes nearly reached the price of scarlet' (Carus-Wilson).

442 *taffata . . . sendal* kinds of fine and expensive silk.

443 *esy of dispence* cautious in spending.

444 *wan in pestilence* gained in time of plague.

445-6 *cordial* tonic for the heart. Mediaeval medicine held that gold strengthened the heart. There is an obvious double meaning in this final couplet.

447 *A good Wyf* a compound title, later to become 'a goodwife', possibly meaning a mistress of a household.

of biside Bathe. St. Michael's juxta Bathon, a suburb of Bath, was largely devoted to the industry of weaving.

448 *scathe* lit. harm; here 'a pity'.

449 *swich an haunt* such a knowledge of the trade.

450 *passed* surpassed.

Ypres and Ghent, with Bruges, had been the foremost weaving towns of Europe, with England the leading supplier of wool. By the third quarter of the 14th century, however, what with political and social disturbances in Flanders, the active immigration policy of Edward III welcoming Flemish weavers to England, and the rise of the water-powered weaving mills, England had surpassed Flanders in the quantity and probably the quality of her cloth exports. The Wife may, therefore, be taken as representative of the English industry in surpassing the Flemish weavers and the line may also reflect the rivalry between the native weavers and the Flemish immigrants — cf. NPT 628 & n. There is no good evidence for any ironic reflection on the Wife's skill — some of the best cloth came from the West Country. Chaucer, with his close knowledge of the import and export situation, would have been aware of the strength and energy of the weaving industry.

452 *to the offrynge.* At this point in the mass, known as the offertory, the congregation went up to the altar-rail in order of precedence to make their offerings.

454 *out of alle charitee* angry, a common phrase. However, to be literally out of charity with one's neighbour was a serious sin.

455 *coverchiefs* kerchiefs, coverings for the head massed on a structure of wire. *ground* texture.

456 *dorste* durst, would dare; 'might go so far as to'.

458 *hosen* stockings.

459 *Ful streite yteyd* tightly fastened.

moyste supple, not dried out; characteristic of fine-quality leather.

461 *worthy* basically 'respectable' but used with considerable irony.

462 *at chirche dore.* Marriages were performed outside the church door or in the vestibule, after which the couple proceeded into the church for the nuptial mass.

463 *Withouten oother compaignye* apart from other 'company'.

464 *as nouthe* now. There is no need to amplify the statement here as the Wife herself fully reveals her youthful adventures in her Prologue.

In sangwyn and in pers he clad was al
Lyned with taffata and with sendal,
And yet he was but esy of dispence:
He kepte that he wan in pestilence,
For gold in phisik is a cordial;   445
Ther fore he loved gold in special.

A good WYF was ther of biside BATHE
But she was som del deef and that was scathe.
  Of clooth makyng she hadde swich an haunt
She passed hem of Ypres and of Gaunt.   450
In al the parisshe wyf ne was ther noon
That to the offrynge bifore hire sholde goon,
And if ther dide, certeyn so wrooth was she
That she was out of alle charitee.
  Hir coverchiefs ful fyne were of ground,   455
I dorste swere they weyeden ten pound
That on a Sonday weren upon hir heed;
Hir hosen weren of fyn scarlet reed
Ful streite yteyd, and shoes ful moyste and newe.
Boold was hir face and fair and reed of hewe.   460
She was a worthy womman al hir lyve:
Housbondes at chirche dore she hadde fyve
Withouten oother compaignye in youthe,
But therof nedeth nat to speke as nouthe.

34

465 'Jerusalem' was probably pronounced 'Iersalem', as it was often spelt.

466 *straunge strem* foreign river.

467-8 Apart from Jerusalem and Rome, holy cities *par excellence* for pilgrims, the Wife had visited the shrines of the Blessed Virgin at Boulogne, of St. James Compostela in Galicia, Spain, and the tomb of the Magi at Cologne in Germany.

469 'She knew much about travelling'. A more questionable wandering may also be implied, either that of the purely pleasure-seeking pilgrim, or even of the moral wandering from the straight and narrow path.

470 *Gat tothed* gap-toothed, with teeth set wide apart. Curry has found that mediaeval physiognomists regarded this feature as a sign of 'boldness, falseness, gluttony and lasciviousness'.

471 *amblere* a saddle horse.

472 *Ywympled wel* see 151n. above.

473 *bokeler . . . targe* kinds of shield.

474 *A foot mantel* an outer, protective skirt.   *large* broad.

475 *spores* spurs.

476 *In felawshipe* in company.   *carpe* chatter.

477 *remedies of love* lit. cures for love, in the sense of 'how to manage a love affair without getting your fingers burnt'. The phrase refers to Ovid's *Remedia Amoris* which, giving just this sort of advice, points to the gross and often cynical sensuality of the Wife's management of the 'olde daunce'.

   par chaunce as it happened; perhaps 'by experience'.

478 'She knew all the ins and outs of that game'.

   'Art' refers to Ovid's *Ars Amatoria*, a 'young person's guide to profane love'.

480 *a poure Persoun of a toun* a poor parson or parish priest. 'Toun' meant village, hamlet or even parish.

482 *a lerned man.* Ignorance, even of the Bible, was a common criticism of parish priests, a criticism all too frequently justified.

484 *parisshens* parishioners.

487 'And he was proved such many times'.

488 *to cursen* to excommunicate. Excommunication was the usual punishment for non-payment of the tithes which supported the incumbent of a parish. Many of the more radical critics in the Church decried this practice.

489 *out of doute* indeed, certainly.

491 i.e. from the Easter offering given to the priest, and from the regular income derived from his benefice, including the tithes.

492 'He knew how to subsist and be content on very little'.

And thries hadde she been at Jerusalem;   465
She hadde passed many a straunge strem:
At Rome she hadde been and at Boloyne,
In Galice at Seint Jame and at Coloyne;
She koude muche of wandrynge by the weye:
Gat tothed was she soothly for to seye.   470
    Upon an amblere esily she sat
Ywympled wel and on hir heed an hat
As brood as is a bokeler or a targe,
A foot mantel aboute hir hipes large
And on hir feet a peyre of spores sharpe.   475
    In felawshipe wel koude she laughe and carpe;
Of remedies of love she knew par chaunce,
For she koude of that art the olde daunce.

    A good man was ther of religioun
And was a poure PERSOUN of a toun   480
But riche he was of holy thoght and werk.
He was also a lerned man, a clerk
That Cristes gospel trewely wolde preche:
His parisshens devoutly wolde he teche.
Benygne he was and wonder diligent   485
And in adversitee ful pacient
And swich he was preved ofte sithes.
    Ful looth were hym to cursen for his tithes,
But rather wolde he yeven out of doute
Unto his poure parisshens aboute   490
Of his offryng and eek of his substaunce;
He koude in litel thyng have suffisaunce.

493 *Wyd* extensive.

494 *he ne lefte nat* he was never deterred (from visiting).

495 *meschief* trouble, mishap.

496 *ferreste* farthest.

muche and lite the great and the small, i.e. of high and low rank.

498 *his sheep* his parishioners.

499 '. . . he first put into practice what he subsequently taught'.

500 *tho* those.

501 *figure* metaphor, figure of speech.

502 Gold, the purest of metals, was often used as a metaphor for the perfections of the ideal priesthood, in contrast with the common metals of ordinary men.

503 *foul* defiled, unclean.

504 *lewed* ignorant. Cf. PaT 75n.

505 *if a preest take keep* if a priest takes heed (he will realize).

509-16 The reference in these lines is to the common practice of parish priests who left their parishes either vacant or in charge of a curate, meagrely paid (line 509), while they sought employment in richly endowed chantries, or as chaplains to a guild or fraternity. The chantry was an altar or chapel, endowed 'for the maintenance of priests to sing masses, usually for the soul of the founder' (OED); it usually paid as much as the parish benefice and without any of the hard work of teaching and visitation.

510 *leet* left.

511 At the time, Saint Paul's cathedral had thirty-five chantries, served by fifty-four priests.

513 *to been witholde* to be retained.

515 *myscarye* come to harm.

5.6 *a mercenarye.* The reference is to the hireling of St. John x, 12: 'He that is a hireling and not the shepherd, whose own the sheep are not, seeth the wolf coming, and leaveth the sheep and fleeth'.

518 *despitous* contemptuous.

519 *daungerous** haughty or arrogant.

digne superior.

520 *discreet* prudenᵗ, showing good sense; perhaps 'civil'.

525 *snybben* rebuke.

for the nonys on the occasion.

526 *I trowe* I believe, think.

527 *He waited after* he expected or looked for.

528 'He did not assume an over-scrupulous conscience'; lit. a highly-seasoned conscience.

529 *loore* lore, teaching.

532 *ylad* led or carried.

dong dung.

fother cartload

Wyd was his parisshe and houses fer asonder,
But he ne lefte nat for reyn ne thonder,
In siknesse nor in meschief to visite   495
The ferreste in his parisshe, muche and lite,
Upon his feet, and in his hand a staf.
This noble ensample to his sheep he yaf
That first he wroghte and afterward he taughte;
Out of the gospel he tho wordes caughte,   500
And this figure he added eek therto
That if gold ruste, what shal iren do?
For if a preest be foul on whom we truste,
No wonder is a lewed man to ruste;
And shame it is, if a preest take keep,   505
A shiten shepherde and a clene sheep;
Wel oghte a preest ensample for to yive
By his clennesse how that his sheep sholde lyve.
    He sette nat his benefice to hyre
And leet his sheep encombred in the myre   510
And ran to Londoun unto Seint Poules
To seken hym a chauntrye for soules
Or with a bretherhede to been witholde,
But dwelte at hoom and kepte wel his folde
So that the wolf ne made it nat myscarye: 515
He was a shepherde and noght a mercenarye.
    And thogh he holy were and vertuous,
He was to synful men nat despitous
Ne of his speche daungerous ne digne,
But in his techyng discreet and benigne;   520
To drawen folk to hevene by fairnesse,
By good ensample, this was his bisynesse;
But it were any persone obstinat,
What so he were, of heigh or lowe estat,
Hym wolde he snybben sharply for the nonys.   525
    A bettre preest I trowe that nowher noon ys:
He waited after no pompe and reverence
Ne maked him a spiced conscience,
But Cristes loore and his apostles twelve
He taughte but first he folwed it hym selve.   530

    With hym ther was a PLOWMAN, was his brother,
That hadde ylad of dong ful many a fother;

533 *A trewe swynkere* an honest workman, labourer.
534 *pees* peace.
535 *hoole* whole.
536 *thogh him gamed or smerte* whether it was pleasant or unpleasant
to him.
538 *therto* also.
dyke make ditches.
delve dig.
539 *wight* person.
540 *Withouten hire* without payment.
541 *ful faire* fairly, honestly.
542 'Both of his own labour (on the priest's land) and of his goods'.
543 *a tabard* a smock.
a mere a mare, ridden only by the poor.

547 *a stout carl* a tough fellow or churl.
for the nones here probably meaning 'indeed' rather than 'for
the occasion'.
548 *brawn* muscles.
549 'That was well proved, for wherever he went'.
550 *ram* the usual prize at a wrestling match.
551 *short sholdred* probably of high, bunched shoulders; cf. the
illustration. There is no other known use of this phrase.
brood broad.
a thikke knarre a thick knotty fellow, knave, bloke.
552 *that he nolde heve of harre* that he would not heave off its hinges.
553 *at a rennyng* at a run. Modern instances of this feat are known.
554 *berd* beard.
556 *the cop right* the very top.
557 *A werte* a wart.
herys hairs.
558 *erys* ears.
559 *nosethirles* nostrils.

A trewe swynkere and a good was he
Lyvynge in pees and parfit charitee.
God loved he best with al his hoole herte 535
At alle tymes thogh him gamed or smerte,
And thanne his neighebore right as hym selve:
He wolde thresshe and therto dyke and delve
For Cristes sake, for every poure wight,
Withouten hire, if it lay in his myght; 540
His tithes payde he ful faire and wel
Both of his propre swynk and his catel.
In a tabard he rood upon a mere.
    Ther was also a REVE and a MILLERE,
A SOMNOUR and a PARDONER also, 545
A MAUNCIPLE and my self, ther were namo.

    The MILLERE was a stout carl for the nones,
Ful byg he was of brawn and eek of bones;
That proved wel, for over al ther he cam
At wrastlynge he wolde have alwey the ram. 550
He was short sholdred, brood, a thikke knarre:
Ther was no dore that he nolde heve of harre
Or breke it at a rennyng with his heed.
His berd as any sowe or fox was reed
And therto brood as thogh it were a spade; 555
Upon the cop right of his nose he hade
A werte, and theron stood a tuft of herys
Reed as the bristles of a sowes erys;
His nosethirles blake were and wyde.
A swerd and bokeler bar he by his syde. 560

561 The image is the common mediaeval one of the gaping and flaming mouth of hell, 'with its fuyre and brimston', its 'venemous wormes and naddris', its 'oribull rorynge', 'a sound like the grunting of many hogs, so horrible that it seems that heaven and earth crash together at the sound' (Owst).

562 *a janglere* a loud-mouth; cf. Parson's Tale 406: 'janglynge is when a man speketh to much biforn folk, and clappeth as a mille, and taketh no kepe what he seith.'

a goliardeys a ribald and indecent story-teller.

563 *harlotries* ribaldries.

564 *stelen* steal.

tollen thries take his toll (payment in kind) three times over.

565 Chaucer appears to be saying that he was an excellent judge of corn since corn was tested by trying it with the thumb. But he is ironically referring to the proverb 'An honest miller has a thumb of gold', which, if taken literally, means 'there are no honest millers'.

569 *gentil** mild. The meaning 'well-bred' is presumably present in an ironic sense.

Maunciple a buyer of provisions, in this case for one of the Inns of Court.

570 *achatours* purchasers.

571 *wise* prudent, careful.

vitaille victuals, provisions.

572 *by taille* by tally, on account.

573 *Algate* always.

wayted so in his achaat waited or watched for the right moment in his buying.

574 *ay biforn and in good staat* always ahead and in a sound financial position.

576 *lewed* unlearned. Cf. PaT75n.

pace surpass.

578 *maistres* either masters in the sense of superiors or 'Masters' in the sense of Masters of Law.

579 *curious* skilful, careful.

581 *stywardes* chief managers of estates or manors.

583 *by his propre good* on or within his own income.

584 *In honour dettelees* honourably without debts. A great deal more moral fervour was attached to the idea of a lord's living within his own income and without debts than exists in the present age of time payments and big business ethics.

but if he were wood unless he were mad.

585 *scarsly* economically.

as hym list desire as he might wish.

586 *al a shire* a whole county.

587 *In any caas* in any contingency.

588 *sette hir aller cappe* 'tipped the cap of all of them', meaning 'made fools of them all'. Skeat comments, 'To come behind a man and alter the look of his head-gear was no doubt a common trick'.

His mouth as greet was as a greet fourneys,
He was a janglere and a goliardeys,
And that was moost of synne and harlotries.
Wel koude he stelen corn and tollen thries
And yet he hadde a thombe of gold, pardee.   565
A whit cote and a blew hood wered he,
A baggepipe wel koude he blowe and sowne
And therwithal he broghte us out of towne.

A gentil MAUNCIPLE was ther of a temple,
Of which achatours myghte take exemple   570
For to be wise in byynge of vitaille:
For wheither that he payde or took by taille
Algate he wayted so in his achaat
That he was ay biforn and in good staat.
Now is nat that of God a ful fair grace   575
That swich a lewed mannes wit shal pace
The wisdom of an heep of lerned men?
Of maistres hadde he mo than thries ten
That weren of lawe expert and curious,
Of whiche ther were a dozeyne in that hous   580
Worthy to been stywardes of rente and lond
Of any lord that is in Engelond
To make hym lyve by his propre good
In honour dettelees, but if he were wood,
Or lyve as scarsly as hym list desire;   585
And able for to helpen al a shire
In any caas that myghte falle or happe;
And yet this maunciple sette hir aller cappe.

42

589 *Reve* technically a subordinate manager of a manorial estate chosen from among the more prosperous serfs. A reeve could rise in authority above a bailiff, his nominal superior, and even take over some of the responsibilities of a steward.

sclendre slender.

colerik see Explanatory Notes—Medicine. The predominance of the humour choler produced irascibility, keen wits and a good memory, lustfulness and leanness of body.

591 *erys* ears. His hair was cut off evenly round his head above his ears.

592 *dokked* cut very short.

biforn in front, across the forehead. The Reeve's close-cropped head was an indication of his servile status.

594 Narrow calfless legs, further attributes of the choleric man, were a sign of lustful intemperance.

595 *kepe* manage.

gerner granary.

bynne a corn-bin.

596 *on him wynne* catch him out in his accounts, or stock.

597-8 *wiste* knew. He could estimate what his grain and seed would amount to in any season by the proportion of wet and dry weather.

599 *neet* cattle.

600 *stoor* livestock.

602 *covenant* contract or terms of appointment.

yaf the rekenynge presented the accounts.

604 'No man could successfully accuse him of being in arrears.'

605 *hierde* herdsman.

hyne hind or servant, farm-labourer.

606 'Of whose cunning and fraud he was not aware'.

607 *the deeth* the plague.

608 *wonyng* dwelling.

610 *purchace* buy or acquire.

611 *astored pryvely* stocked privately or in secret.

612 *subtilly* shrewdly.

613-4 'By giving and lending to his lord the lord's own goods, and receiving thanks for it and a reward of a coat and hood into the bargain.' Such rewards were common.

615 *mister* trade, craft.

616 *wrighte* craftsman, artisan.

The REVE was a sclendre colerik man.
His berd was shave as neigh as ever he kan,   590
His heer was by his erys ful round yshorn,
His top was dokked lyk a preest biforn,
Ful longe were his legges and ful lene
Ylyk a staf, ther was no calf ysene.
   Wel koude he kepe a gerner and a bynne,   595
Ther was noon auditour koude on him wynne;
Wel wiste he by the droghte and by the reyn
The yeldynge of his seed and of his greyn.
His lordes sheep, his neet, his dayerye,
His swyn, his hors, his stoor and his pultrye   600
Was hoolly in this reves governynge,
And by his covenant yaf the rekenynge
Syn that his lord was twenty yeer of age;
Ther koude no man brynge hym in arrerage.
Ther nas baillif ne hierde nor oother hyne   605
That he ne knew his sleighte and his covyne;
They were adrad of hym as of the deeth.
   His wonyng was ful faire upon an heeth;
With grene trees shadwed was his place.
He koude bettre than his lord purchace;   610
Ful riche he was astored pryvely;
His lord wel koude he plesen subtilly
To yeve and lene hym of his owene good
And have a thank and yet a cote and hood.
   In youthe he hadde lerned a good mister: 615
He was a wel good wrighte, a carpenter.

617　*stot*　plain farm-horse, probably a stallion.
618　*pomely*　dappled.　　*highte*　was called.
　　Scot　for centuries a common name given to farm horses in the
county of Norfolk.
619　*surcote*　outer coat.
　　pers　a rich blue, cf. 441n. above.
621　*Northfolk*　Norfolk.
622　*Biside*　near.
　　Baldeswelle　Bawdswell, in northern Norfolk.
623　His surcote was tucked up into his girdle for ease of movement.
624　*hyndreste of oure route*　last of our company.

625　*Somnour*　an officer of the Archdeacon's court, which dealt with
matrimonial cases and moral offences. His duty was to summon
offenders to appear in court, and like many summoners of his time,
he was open to bribery and other forms of corruption.
626　*fyr reed cherubynnes face.*　The cherubin, one of the angelic
orders standing about the throne of God in heaven, were traditionally
depicted with red faces.
627　*saucefleem*　suffering from red pimples and inflamed skin.
　　eyen narwe　slit eyes caused by the swelling and inflammation
of the face.
628　*sparwe.*　Sparrows were held to be lecherous birds.
629　*scalled*　scaly or scabrous.
　　piled berd　a beard from which much of the hair had fallen.
630　*visage*　countenance, face.　　*aferd*　afraid.
631　*quyk silver*　mercury ointment.
　　lytarge　litharge or white lead.
　　brymstoon　sulphur ointment.
632　*Boras*　borax.
　　ceruce　ceruse, another name for white lead.
　　oile of tartre　cream of tartar.
634　*helpen of*　rid (him) of.
　　whelkes　pus-filled pimples, perhaps boils.
635　*knobbes*　pimples.
638　*wood*　mad.
643　*it*　i.e. Latin. He would hear the Latin phrases and terms
daily in the Archdeacon's court.
645　*Kan clepen 'Watte'*　knows how to say Wat (Walter). Jays
(magpie-like birds) were taught to say this, it seems, as modern parrots
say 'Poll' or 'Cocky'.

This reve sat upon a ful good stot
That was al pomely grey and highte Scot;
A long surcote of pers upon he hade
And by his syde he bar a rusty blade.   620
Of Northfolk was this reve of which I telle,
Biside a toun men clepen Baldeswelle.
Tukked he was as is a frere aboute
And evere he rood the hyndreste of oure route.

A SOMNOUR was ther with us in that place   625
That hadde a fyr reed cherubynnes face,
For saucefleem he was with eyen narwe;
As hoot he was and lecherous as a sparwe,
With scalled browes blake and piled berd;
Of his visage children were aferd: 630
Ther nas quyk silver, lytarge ne brymstoon,
Boras, ceruce ne oile of tartre noon
Ne oynement that wolde clense and byte
That hym myghte helpen of his whelkes white
Nor of the knobbes sittynge on his chekes.   635
    Wel loved he garleek, oynons and eek lekes
And for to drynken strong wyn reed as blood;
Thanne wolde he speke and crie as he were wood,
And whan that he wel dronken hadde the wyn
Thanne wolde he speke no word but Latyn.   640
    A fewe termes hadde he, two or three
That he had lerned out of som decree:
No wonder is, he herde it al the day,
And eek ye knowen wel how that a jay
Kan clepen 'Watte' as wel as kan the pope.   645

646 'But if anyone set about testing him on other matters'.
647 *philosophye* an ironic hyperbole for knowledge.
648 *Ay* always.
  Questio quid iuris (the) question (is): which (section) of the law (applies here). One of the Summoner's Latin 'termes' from court.
649 *gentil* harlot* good natured rogue.
650 *bettre felawe* a better mate or companion; cf. 397n. above.
651 *suffre* allow.
652 *to have his concubyn* to keep, or live immorally with, a woman.
653 *atte fulle* to the full, completely.
654 *Ful prively* in secret, on the quiet.
  a fynch eek koude he pulle he knew how to pull a finch (or pluck a bird) too. The phrase is often explained as 'to cheat a person'; in this context it undoubtedly means that he had immoral relations with women — just like the other 'good felawe'.
655 *foond owher* found anywhere.
656-7 'He used to tell him not to have any fear of the archdeacon's curse (excommunication) in such a case'.
658 *But if* unless.
659 He would be punished in the purse; i.e. his 'punishment' would involve a decent bribe.
661 'But I know very well that he was really lying in fact'.
662 *cursyng* excommunication.
  him drede be afraid.
663 *slee* kill (the soul).
  right as just as.
  assoillyng absolution.
664 *war hym* beware.
  Significavit the first Latin word of the writ which ordered that the unrepentant sinner be imprisoned by the civil authorities.
665 *In daunger** in his power.
  at his owene gise at his own will.
666 *gerles* young people of either sex.
667 *conseil* confidences, secrets.
  al hir reed their adviser in all things.
668 *gerland* garland, wreath of flowers.
669 *ale stake* a pole set horizontally out from above the door of an ale-house, with a garland or bush attached to the end.
670 *bokeler* buckler, shield.
  cake a round flat loaf of bread.

671 *gentil** worthy, excellent, perhaps courteous.
  Pardoner. The pardoners were ecclesiastical officers, usually but not always in Orders, appointed to distribute papal indulgences. See further, Commentaries and Appendix B.
672 *Rouncivale.* The Order of St. Mary Roncevalles (in the Pyrenees) established a subsidiary House at Charing Cross, in London, in the thirteenth century. By Chaucer's time, this House had become notorious for scandals connected mainly with the traffic in 'pardons' — it had even been seized by the crown for this reason, between 1379 and 1382.
  comper comrade, close friend. The friendship of summoners and pardoners was notorious, since they could be professionally useful to each other.

But whoso koude in oother thyng hym grope,
Thanne hadde he spent al his philosophye:
Ay *Questio quid iuris* wolde he crie.
He was a gentil harlot and a kynde,
A bettre felawe sholde men noght fynde: 650
He wolde suffre for a quart of wyn
A good felawe to have his concubyn
A twelf month and excuse hym atte fulle;
Ful prively a fynch eek koude he pulle.
And if he foond owher a good felawe   655
He wolde techen him to have noon awe
In swich caas of the ercedeknes curs,
But if a mannes soule were in his purs,
For in his purs he sholde ypunysshed be:
Purs is the ercedeknes helle, seyde he;   660
But wel I woot he lyed right in dede:
Of cursyng oghte ech gilty man him drede
For curs wol slee right as assoillyng savith,
And also war hym of a *significavit*.
In daunger hadde he at his owene gise   665
The yonge gerles of the diocise,
And knew hir conseil and was al hir reed.
A gerland hadde he set upon his heed
As greet as it were for an ale stake;
A bokeler hadde he maad hym of a cake.   670

With hym ther rood a gentil PARDONER
Of Rouncivale, his freend and his comper

673 *the court of Rome* the Vatican, the source of the indulgences.

675 *stif* strong, powerful.

burdoun ground melody or bass part. The word also means a pilgrim's staff, or a cudgel; this line, with the next, by a number of coarse double meanings, suggests a homosexual relationship between the two singers.

676 *trompe*. In mediaeval manuscript illustrations the short trumpet, like the bagpipe, was often a symbol of masculine sexuality and one of the instruments representing the sensual, earthly music.

soun sound.

677 *heer* hair.

wex wax.

678 *strike of flex* hank of flax.

679 *ounces* bits, shreds, bunches.

681 *by colpons oon and oon* by separate or scattered strands.

683 *trussed up in his walet* packed away in his carry-all.

684 *al of the newe jet* in the very latest fashion.

685 'With unkempt hair, he rode bare-headed, except for his cap' (which could only cover the top of the head and not control the long hair he spread over his shoulders).

686 'He had prominent and shining eyes like a hare.' The hare was commonly a symbol of lust and of cowardice; glaring eyes signified shamelessness and were thought to be a characteristic of the eunuch.

687 *A vernycle*. A vernicle was a small copy of the handkerchief with which St. Veronica wiped the face of Christ and which received the imprint of His face. It was a token of the wearer's pilgrimage to Rome.

689 *Bretful* brimful.

690 *smal* light, reedy (a sign of effeminacy).

The goat was a symbol of lust.

693 'I think (in the positive sense of I am sure) he was a gelding or a mare', i.e. a eunuch or a 'woman'.

694 *craft* the word could mean either 'trade' or 'cunning'.

fro Berwyk into Ware from Berwick-on-Tweed on the Scottish border to Ware, north of London, in Hertfordshire. The phrase presumably means from the North to the South of England, though the choice of the town Ware is unexplained except as a useful rime.

696 *male* bag.

pilwe beer pillow case.

698 *gobet* small portion, scrap.

seyl sail.

698-700 *wente* went or walked.

hente caught, caught hold of, took.

These lines refer either to St. Peter's attempt to walk on the sea and his having to be rescued by Christ, or to his having been a fisherman until called by Christ to be a fisher of men.

701 *a croys of latoun* a cross of latten, a cheap metal compounded of copper and zinc. The cross was set with 'precious stones', presumably as worthless as the pig's bones and the Pardoner's other holy relics.

702 *in a glas* in a monstrance or glass container.

704 'A poor parson living in the country'.

705-6 *Upon a day* in one day. The Pardoner later claims to 'earn' 100 marks per annum (£66/13/4); a parson might receive £5 per annum.

That streight was comen fro the court of Rome.
Ful loude he soong *Com hider love to me.*
This somnour bar to hym a stif burdoun,   675
Was nevere trompe of half so greet a soun.
  This pardoner hadde heer as yelow as wex,
But smothe it heeng as dooth a strike of flex;
By ounces henge his lokkes that he hadde
And therwith he his shuldres overspradde,   680
But thynne it lay by colpons oon and oon;
But hood, for jolitee wered he noon
For it was trussed up in his walet;
Hym thoughte he rood al of the newe jet:
Dischevelee save his cappe he rood al bare.   685
Swiche glarynge eyen hadde he as an hare.

  A vernycle hadde he sowed upon his cappe,
His walet biforn hym in his lappe
Bretful of pardoun comen from Rome al hoot.
  A voys he hadde as smal as hath a goot;   690
No berd hadde he ne nevere sholde have,
As smothe it was as it were late yshave:
I trowe he were a geldyng or a mare.
  But of his craft, fro Berwyk into Ware
Ne was ther swich another pardoner,   695
For in his male he hadde a pilwe beer
Which that he seyde was Oure Lady veyl;
He· seyde he hadde a gobet of the seyl
That Seint Peter hadde whan that he wente
Upon the see til Jesu Crist hym hente;   700
He hadde a croys of latoun ful of stones
And in a glas he hadde pigges bones;
But with thise relikes, whan that he fond
A poure persoun dwellynge upon lond,
Upon a day he gat hym moore moneye   705
Than that the persoun gat in monthes tweye;

707 *feyned flaterye and japes* false flattery (of the parson) and tricks.
708 'He duped, made fools of, the parson and the people.'
711 *lessoun* the lesson, or 'lectio', a reading from scripture or other sacred writing.
    storie the 'historia', a series of lessons, covering a book of the Bible or a life of a saint.
712 *alderbest* best of all.
    offertorie the anthem during which the members of the congregation made their offerings; cf. 452n. above.
713 *wiste* knew.
714 *wel affile his tonge* smooth or sharpen his tongue.
715 *as he ful wel koude.* In his subsequent tale, the Pardoner demonstrates the real brilliance of his preaching for gain.
716 *murierly* the more merrily.
    loude loudly (an adverb).

717 *soothly in a clause* truly and briefly.
718 *Th'estaat* the social rank.
    th'array the dress or condition.
721 *faste by the Belle* close to the Bell, presumably another tavern.
723 'How we occupied ourselves on that (same) night'.
724 *were . . . alyght* had alighted or dismounted.
725 *viage* journey.
728 *n'arette it nat my vileynye** don't put it down to my ill breeding or coarseness.
730 *hir cheere* their behaviour.
731 *proprely* exactly; but also in the sense of 'proper to' the speaker, i.e. 'as they expressed themselves'.
735 *if it be in his charge* if it is committed to him.
736 *Al speke he* although he speaks.
    rudeliche vulgarly; cf. 'the rude multitude'.
    large freely, broadly.
737 *moot* must, is forced to.
    untrewe falsely.
738 *feyne* invent. Chaucer speaks these two lines ironically as though distortion or invention were inconceivable for an honest reporter, though of course they describe exactly what he *is* doing.
739 *spare* omit.
740 i.e. he must repeat the coarse words as well as the other, respectable, ones.
741 *brode* broadly.
743 *whoso kan hym rede.* Chaucer himself would not have found this statement in Plato, but at second hand in Boethius or *Le Roman de la Rose.*
746 *degree* social order.

And thus with feyned flaterye and japes
He made the persoun and the peple his apes.
    But trewely to tellen atte laste
He was in chirche a noble ecclesiaste: 710
Wel koude he rede a lessoun or a storie
But alderbest he song an offertorie,
For wel he wiste whan that song was songe
He moste preche and wel affile his tonge
To wynne silver, as he ful wel koude; 715
Ther fore he song the murierly and loude.

    Now have I toold you soothly in a clause
Th'estaat, th'array, the nombre and eek the cause
Why that assembled was this compaignye
In Southwerk at this gentil hostelrye 720
That highte the Tabard, faste by the Belle;
But now is tyme to yow for to telle
How that we baren us that ilke nyght
Whan we were in that hostelrye alyght;
And after wol I telle of our viage 725
And al the remenaunt of oure pilgrymage.
    But first I pray yow of youre curteisye
That ye n'arette it nat my vileynye
Thogh that I pleynly speke in this mateere
To telle yow hir wordes and hir cheere, 730
Ne thogh I speke hir wordes proprely,
For this ye knowen al so wel as I,
Whoso shal telle a tale after a man,
He moot reherce as neigh as evere he kan
Everich a word, if it be in his charge, 735
Al speke he nevere so rudeliche and large,
Or ellis he moot telle his tale untrewe
Or feyne thyng or fynde wordes newe;
He may nat spare althogh he were his brother,
He may as wel seye o word as another. 740
Crist spak hym self ful brode in holy writ
And wel ye woot no vileynye is it;
Eek Plato seith, whoso kan hym rede,
The wordes mote be cosyn to the dede.
    Also I prey yow to foryeve it me 745
Al have I nat set folk in hir degree

749 'Our host gave each of us a hearty welcome'.
751 *vitaille* victuals, food.
at the beste in the best manner.
752 *wel to drynke us leste* we were very glad to drink.

753 *semely* fitting.
754 *marchal in an halle* a master of ceremonies or guest-master in the house of a lord.
755 *stepe* large, prominent, perhaps bright; cf. 201 above.
756 *burgeys* a solid citizen.
Chepe Cheapside, one of the principal streets and mercantile areas of London.
757 *Boold of his speche* commanding and vigorous in his manner of speaking.
wys capable.
wel ytaught well-instructed or well-informed.
759 *right* certainly.
760 *pleyen* to joke, to be sociable.
761 *myrthe* pleasure, entertainment.
762 *maad oure rekenynges* paid our bills (in advance, be it noted!)
763 *lordynges* equivalent to 'ladies and gentlemen'.
767 *At ones in this herberwe* at one time in this inn.
768 'I would gladly entertain you if I knew how'.
769 *I am right now bythoght* I have just now thought.
770 *To doon yow ese* to give you pleasure.
772 *quyte yow youre meede* give you your reward.
774 'You intend to tell tales and to amuse yourselves'.
777 *disport* amusement.
778 *erst* first.
780 *stonden at my juggement* abide by my decision.
781 *to werken* to do.
783 'Now by my dead father's soul'.
784 *But* unless.
786 *conseil* decision.
seche seek.

Heere in this tale as that they sholde stonde:
My wit is short ye may wel understonde.
    Greet cheere made oure hoost us everichon
And to the souper sette he us anon.   750
He served us with vitaille at the beste:
Strong was the wyn and wel to drynke us leste.

    A semely man oure HOOST was with alle
For to been a marchal in an halle:
A large man he was with eyen stepe,   755
A fairer burgeys is ther noon in Chepe,
Boold of his speche and wys and wel ytaught
And of manhode hym lakked right naught.
    Eek therto he was right a murye man,
And after souper pleyen he bigan   760
And spak of myrthe amonges othere thynges
Whan that we hadde maad oure rekenynges,
And seyde thus: "Now lordynges, trewely
Ye been to me right welcome hertely,
For by my trouthe if that I shal nat lye,   765
I saugh nat this yeer so murye a compaignye
At ones in this herberwe as is now.
Fayn wolde I doon yow myrthe, wiste I how;
And of a myrthe I am right now bythoght
To doon yow ese, and it shal coste noght.   770
    Ye goon to Caunterbury, God yow speede;
The blisful martir quyte yow youre meede!
And wel I woot as ye goon by the weye
Ye shapen yow to talen and to pleye;
For trewely confort ne myrthe is noon   775
To ride by the weye domb as a stoon,
And ther fore wol I maken yow disport
As I seyde erst, and doon yow som confort;
And if yow liketh alle by oon assent
For to stonden at my juggement   780
And for to werken as I shal yow seye,
Tomorwe whan ye ryden by the weye,
Now by my fader soule that is deed,
But ye be myrie I wol yeve yow myn heed.
Hoold up youre hondes withouten moore speche."   785
    Oure conseil was nat longe for to seche,

787 'It seemed to us not worth making a grave matter of it'.
788 *graunted hym* agreed with him.
     avys deliberation.
789 'And asked him to make his proposal as it pleased him'.
791 *in desdeyn* in disdain, as if it gave offence.
793 *to shorte with oure weye* with which to shorten our way.
797 *whilom* once upon a time.
798 *which* whichever.
     bereth hym performs.
800 *sentence** moral truth or teaching.
     solas amusement, entertainment.
801 *oure aller cost* the expense of all of us.
805 *goodly* kindly, or perhaps gladly.
806 'Entirely at my own expense . . .'
807 *withseye* dispute.
809 *vouche sauf* vouchsafe, grant or agree.
810 *anon* at once.
     mo more.
811 *shape me* prepare myself.
812 *swore*. The subject 'we' is implied.
815 *governour* leader, referee.
816 *reportour*. He was to report on their merits.
817 *certeyn* i.e. specified, agreed.
818 'And we will be guided by his planning'.
819 *In heigh and lough* in all respects.
820 *been acorded* submitted ourselves.
821 *fet* fetched.
822 *echon* each one.
824 *A-morwe* next morning.
825 *oure aller cok* the cock (who roused) us all.
827 *a litel moore than pas* a little more than foot-pace.

Us thoughte it was noght worth to make it wys,
And graunted hym withouten moore avys
And bad him seye his voirdit as hym leste.
   "Lordynges," quod he, "now herkneth for the beste,   790
But taketh it not, I preye yow, in desdeyn;
This is the poynt, to speken short and pleyn,
That ech of yow to shorte with oure weye
In this viage shal telle tales tweye
To Caunterburyward, I mene it so,   795
And homward he shal tellen othere two,
Of aventures that whilom han bifalle;
And which of yow that bereth hym best of alle,
That is to seyn, that telleth in this cas
Tales of best sentence and moost solas,   800
Shal have a souper at oure aller cost
Here in this place, sittynge by this post,
Whan that we come agayn fro Caunterbury.
And for to make yow the moore mury
I wol my self goodly with yow ryde   805
Right at my owene cost, and be youre gyde;
And whoso wol my juggement withseye
Shal paye al that we spenden by the weye.
And if ye vouche sauf that it be so
Tel me anon withouten wordes mo   810
And I wol erly shape me ther fore."
   This thyng was graunted and oure othes swore
With ful glad herte, and preyden hym also
That he wolde vouche sauf for to do so
And that he wolde been oure governour   815
And of oure tales juge and reportour
And sette a souper at a certeyn prys
And we wol reuled been at his devys
In heigh and lough; and thus by oon assent
We been acorded to his juggement.   820
And therupon the wyn was fet anon,
We dronken and to reste wente echon
Withouten any lenger taryynge.
   A-morwe whan that day bigan to sprynge,
Up roos oure hoost and was oure aller cok   825
And gadred us togidre in a flok
And forth we riden a litel moore than pas

56

828 St. Thomas-a-Watering was a brook at the second mile-post, where horses were watered.
829 *areste* rein in.
831 'You know your agreement, and (you) recall it to yourselves'. This reflexive use of 'recorde' is rare.
832 'If evensong and matins agree', a proverbial expression meaning, 'If you still affirm this morning what you agreed to last night'.
834 A colloquial expression meaning roughly 'As surely as I ever hope to drink wine or ale . . .'
837 *draweth cut* draw lots (using straws).
ferrer twynne go any further on our way; lit. depart further.
840 *myn acord* the agreement I suggested.
841 *Cometh* pronounce 'comth'.
842 *shamefastnesse* modesty.
843 *Ne studieth noght* don't deliberate over it.
ley hond to i.e. take one (in your hand).
846 *aventure or sort or cas* luck, lot, or chance.
847 *sothe* truth.
849 *resoun* right, fitting, proper.
850 Both words mean agreement.
853 *As he that* as one who.
856 *a Goddes name!* in God's name.
859 *right 1 myrie cheere* a most cheerful demeanour.

Unto the wateryng of Seint Thomas;
And there oure hoost bigan his hors areste
And seyde, "Lordynges, herkneth if yow leste!   830
Ye woot youre foreward and it yow recorde.
If evensong and morwesong acorde,
Lat se now who shal telle the firste tale.
As evere mote I drynke wyn or ale,
Whoso be rebel to my juggement   835
Shal paye for al that by the wey is spent.
Now draweth cut er that we ferrer twynne:
He which that hath the shorteste shal bigynne.
Sire knyght", quod he, "my mayster and my lord,
Now draweth cut, for that is myn acord.   840
Cometh neer", quod he, "my lady prioresse,
And ye sire clerk, lat be youre shamefastnesse
Ne studieth noght; ley hond to, every man."
    Anon to drawen every wight bigan,
And shortly for to tellen as it was,   845
Were it by aventure or sort or cas
The sothe is this, the cut fel to the knyght,
Of which ful blithe and glad was every wyght;
And telle he moste his tale, as was resoun
By foreward and by composicioun   850
As ye han herd; what nedeth wordes mo?
    And whan this goode man saugh that it was so,
As he that wys was and obedient
To kepe his foreward by his free assent,
He seyde, "Syn I shal bigynne the game,   855
What, welcome be the cut, a Goddes name!
Now lat us ryde and herkneth what I seye."
And with that word we ryden forth oure weye,
And he bigan with right a myrie cheere
His tale anon, and seyde as ye may heere.   860

    There follows the Romance of the young knights Palamon
and Arcite, a courtly history of their amorous tribulations and
absurdities in the common pursuit of 'Emelye the brighte'.

1 *beel amy* fair friend, from Fr. *bel ami*.
2 *myrthe* entertainment or entertaining tale.
  japes jokes.
3 *Seint Ronyon.* In view of the frequent sexual innuendoes shadowing the Pardoner, there may be an obscure pun on "runnion" — a colloquial term for the male organ. This may partly explain the reaction of the 'gentils'.
4-5 By stopping at the 'ale stake' for a 'cake' (cf. GP669-70) and a 'draughte of corny ale' i.e. at a common tavern, the Pardoner allies himself with the world of ribaldry and immorality — like the 'yonge folk' of his tale.
6 *gentils* the gentle-folk of the pilgrimage
8 *leere* learn.
9 *wit* practical wisdom.
10 *graunte* agree.
   ywis certainly.
   moot must.

the wordes of the hoost to the pardoner

"Thow beel amy, thow pardoner," he sayde,
"Tel us som myrthe or japes right anon."
  "It shal be doon," quod he, "by Seint Ronyon!
But first," quod he, "heere at this ale stake
I wol bothe drynke and eten of a cake."   5
  But right anon thise gentils gonne to crye,
"Nay, lat hym telle us of no ribawdye!
Tel us som moral thyng that we may leere
Som wit, and thanne wol we gladly heere."
  "I graunte, ywis," quod he, "but I moot thynke   10
Upon som honest thyng while that I drynke."

12 *Lordynges* Sirs.
13 *I peyne me* I take pains.
   hauteyn lofty and loud.
14 *round* smoothly without pausing.
   'And make my voice ring out as continuously and resonantly as a
   bell'.
15 *kan* know.
16 *theme* text, topic.
17 1 Timothy vi, 10: 'The root of all evil is cupidity . Although
   cupiditas is translated as 'the love of money' or avarice, and the
   Pardoner claims that avarice is his chief motivation, nevertheless the
   love of money is only the most striking instance in human action of
   cupiditas, the love of the things of this world.
19 *bulles* authorities with seals or *bullae* attached, which he produced
   to establish his authority as a pardoner.
   alle and some every one.
20 *Oure lige lordes seel* the seal either of his bishop or of the King.
   patente a bull licencing him to operate in a particular diocese.
21 *to warente* to protect. That the Pardoner should need official
   protection is an indication of the resentment felt towards pardoners
   both false and genuine by the regular clergy; cf. GP703-6. See further,
   Appendix B.
25 *Bulles.* So extensive a collection of bulls is used only to impress
   his heaters.
28 'To colour and flavour my preaching with'. Saffron is a spice.
30 *cristal stones* crystal or glass flasks or cases in which his relics
   were displayed; cf. GP702.
31 *cloutes* clothes.
32 *as wenen they echon* as each (member of the congregation)
   believes.
34 In the light of lines 44-8 it would seem that the Pardoner has in
   mind the story of Jacob in Genesis xxx, 37ff., though most of the
   details are of his own invention.
38 'That has eaten any snake or which has been bitten (ystonge)
   by any snake'.
44 *oweth* owns.
45 *wike* week.
48 *stoor* stock.

"Lordynges," quod he, "in chirches whan I preche
I peyne me to han an hauteyn speche
And rynge it out as round as gooth a belle,
For I kan al by rote that I telle: 15
My theme is alwey oon, and evere was
Radix malorum est Cupiditas.
　　First I pronounce whennes that I come
And thanne my bulles shewe I, alle and some.
Oure lige lordes seel on my patente,   20
That shewe I first, my body to warente,
That no man be so boold, ne preest ne clerk,
Me to destourbe of Cristes holy werk;
And after that thanne telle I forth my tales.
Bulles of popes and of cardynales,   25
Of patriarkes and bisshopes I shewe
And in Latyn I speke a wordes fewe
To saffron with my predicacioun
And for to stire hem to devocioun.
　　Thanne shewe I forth my longe cristal stones   30
Ycrammed ful of cloutes and of bones:
Relikes been they, as wenen they echon.
Thanne have I in latoun a shulder bon
Which that was of an holy Jewes sheep.
'Goode men,' I seye, 'tak of my wordes keep: 35
If that this boon be wasshe in any welle,
If cow or calf or sheep or oxe swelle
That any worm hath ete or worm ystonge,
Taak water of that welle and wassh his tonge
And it is hool anon; and forther moor   40
Of pokkes and of scabbe and every soor
Shal every sheep be hool that of this welle
Drynketh a draughte. Taak kepe eek what I telle:
If that the goode man that the bestes oweth
Wol every wike, er that the cok hym croweth,   45
Fastynge, drynken of this welle a draughte
As thilke holy Jew oure eldres taughte,
Hise bestes and his stoor shal multiplie.
　　And, sires, also it heeleth jalousie:
For thogh a man be falle in jalous rage,   50

51 'Let his soup or stew be made with this water'.
52 *mystriste* distrust.
54 *Al* even though.
Another instance of the ill-feeling between Pardoners and Parsons.
55 *miteyn* mitten or glove.
59 *So that* provided that.
grotes groats: worth about 4d.
63 *yshryven be* confess and be absolved.
65 *cokewold* cuckold, the husband of an adulterous wife.
66 *power* permission.
68 *out of* without.
blame cause of blame, guilt.
70 *assoille* absolve from the penance due to sin. But the Pardoner never makes a clear distinction between forgiveness of sin and absolution from penance; cf. GP671n.
72 *gaude* trick. This trick he has described nicely in the preceding twelve lines. Relying on the doctrine that people in mortal sin are not in the state of grace necessary to benefit from the sacraments, and are indeed forbidden by the church even to receive them, the Pardoner says that those of his congregation in such a state are excluded from offering money and venerating his relics, and from the benefit of his absolution. Of course few would admit in public to having cuckolded their husbands, or to being in mortal sin, and would therefore feel obliged to come forward and make their offering to the Pardoner in order to avoid scandalous speculations and gossip.
73 *An hundred mark.* A mark was 13/4d., so that the Pardoner's 'earnings' would be £66/13/4d. per annum. This would be the equivalent of perhaps £4,000 stg.
74 *clerk* cleric.
75 *lewed.* Originally, the word meant 'lay' in contrast to 'clerical'; but since the clergy had a monopoly of learning, the word came to mean 'unlearned', 'ignorant', and finally 'base, low, vulgar'. All of these senses are relevant here.
76 *so as* in the manner of.
79 *bekke* nod the head.
80 *dowve* dove.
berne barn.
81 *goon so yerne* move so briskly and eagerly.
84-5 *free To yeven* liberal or eager in giving.
85 *namely* especially.
86 'For my purpose is nothing but gain'.
88 *rekke* care.
89 *goon a-blakeberyed* go a-blackberrying, go wandering at will.

Lat maken with this water his potage
And nevere shal he moore his wyf mystriste
Thogh he the soothe of hir defaute wiste,
Al hadde she taken preestes two or thre.
  Heere is a miteyn eek that ye may se: 55
He that his hand wol putte in this mitayn
He shal have multiplyyng of his grayn
Whan he hath sowen, be it whete or otes,
So that he offre pens or ellis grotes.
  Goode men and wommen, o thyng warne I yow: 60
If any wight be in this chirche now
That hath doon synne horrible that he
Dar nat for shame of it yshryven be,
Or any womman, be she yong or old,
That hath ymaked hir housbond cokewold,   65
Swich folk shal have no power ne no grace
To offren to my relikes in this place.
And whoso fyndeth hym out of swich blame,
They wol come up and offre in Goddes name
And I assoille hym by the auctoritee   70
Which that by bulle ygraunted was to me.'
  By this gaude have I wonne yeer by yeer
An hundred mark sith I was pardoner.
I stonde lyk a clerk in my pulpet
And whan the lewed peple is doun yset   75
I preche so as ye han herd bifore
And telle an hundred false japes more;
Thanne peyne I me to strecche forth the nekke
And est and west upon the peple I bekke
As dooth a dowve sittyng on a berne;   80
Myne handes and my tonge goon so yerne
That it is joye to se my bisynesse.
Of avarice and of swich cursednesse
Is al my prechyng, for to make hem free
To yeven hir pens and namely unto me.   85
For myn entente is nat but for to wynne
And no thyng for correccioun of synne.
I rekke nevere, whan that they been beryed,
Thogh that hire soules goon a-blakeberyed!
For certes many a predicacioun   90
Comth ofte tyme of yvel entencioun:

92 *plesance* the giving of pleasure.
95 *debate* argue or contend.
96 *hym* one of his listeners.
   smerte smartly, sharply.
97-8 *asterte To been* escape being.
99 *trespased to* offended against.
103 *quyte* pay back.
104 *hewe* hue, colour, i.e. pretence.
106 'But briefly I will explain my purpose'.
107 'I preach for nothing but what I can get out of it'.
113 *twynne* depart.
114 *soore* bitterly.
117 'Concerning this matter it (i.e. what I have said) ought to suffice'.
118 *ensamples* exempla; traditional stories for the illustration of sermons.
121 *reporte* repeat.
   holde retain, commit to memory.
123 *for I teche* for what I teach, i.e. about avarice.
125 *I thoghte it never* it never occurred to me.
126 *landes* districts rather than countries.
129 *ydelly* in vain. The Pardoner will not follow the example of holy men, labouring or making baskets, because he will make so much money by begging that he won't have to do so — a striking inversion of Christian teaching! Manual labour was part of the monastic regimen. Both Chaucer and his contemporary Langland for some reason held that St. Paul the apostle was a basket-maker; he was in fact a tent-maker, and did at times support himself by 'labouring with his hands' at this trade.
130 *countrefete* imitate, follow the example of.
131 *wolle* wool.
132 'Although it were given by the poorest servant lad'.

Som for plesance of folk and flaterye,
To been avanced by ypocrisye,
And som for veyne glorie and som for hate;
For whan I dar noon oother weyes debate   95
Thanne wol I stynge hym with my tonge smerte
In prechyng so that he shal nat asterte
To been defamed falsly if that he
Hath trespased to my bretheren or to me;
For thogh I telle noght his propre name,   100
Men shal wel knowe that it is the same
By signes and by othere circumstances:
Thus quyte I folk that doon us displesances,
Thus spitte I out my venym under hewe
Of holynesse, to seme holy and trewe.   105
  But shortly myn entente I wol devyse:
I preche of no thyng but for coveityse.
Ther fore my theme is yet and evere was
Radix malorum est Cupiditas.
Thus kan I preche agayn that same vice   110
Which that I use, and that is avarice.
But though my self be gilty in that synne
Yet kan I maken oother folk to twynne
From avarice, and soore to repente.
But that is nat my principal entente;   115
I preche no thyng but for coveitise.
Of this matere it oghte ynow suffise.
  Thanne telle I hem ensamples many oon
Of olde stories longe tyme agoon,
For lewed peple loven tales olde;   120
Swiche thynges kan they wel reporte and holde.
What, trowe ye that whiles I may preche,
And wynne gold and silver for I teche,
That I wol lyve in poverte wilfully?
Nay, nay, I thoghte it never, trewely!   125
For I wol preche and begge in sondry landes,
I wol nat do no labour with myne handes
Ne make baskettes and lyve therby,
By cause I wol nat beggen ydelly.
I wol noon of the apostles countrefete,   130
I wol have moneye, wolle, cheese and whete
Al were it yeven of the poverest page

134 *sterve for famyne* die of hunger.
138 *likyng* desire.
139 'Now that I have . . .'
141 *by resoun* with every reason.
145 This line is a conventional opening, deriving from the time when minstrels had to gain the attention of an audience. It had become something of a cliché and Chaucer actually parodies it in his Tale of Sir Thopas: 'Now holde youre mouth, par charitee/Bothe knyght and lady free'.

146 *In Flandres whilom.* 'Once upon a time in Flanders' may just be a conventional opening for the story, any country being as suitable. However, Manly has given reasons for supposing that Flanders was notorious in England for such goings on.
147 *that haunteden folye* that made a habit of folly (or dissipation).
148 'Such as unrestrained dissipation, games of chance, brothels and taverns'. Hasard was also a particular dice game.
149 *gyternes* stringed musical instruments, rather like lutes or guitars.
150 *dees* dice.
151 *over hir myght* beyond their capacity.
153 *that develes temple* a typical preacher's phrase for taverns and brothels.
  wise fashion.
154 *superfluytee abhomynable.* Superfluity or excess carried a load of moral condemnation not always present in modern usage. The word 'abhomynable' was mistakenly thought to be derived from the Latin *ab homine*, thus meaning inhuman, unnatural.
157 *to-tere.* tear to pieces.
158 *Hem thoughte* it seemed to them.
160 *comen* come.
  tombesteres female dancers.
161 *Fetys and smale* neat and slender.
  frutesteres female fruitsellers.
162 *baudes* harlots, perhaps procurers.
  wafereres cake sellers (sellers of wafers, etc.) who apparently had a reputation as intermediaries in sexual affairs.
163 This group of 'entertainers' seems to have had some of the reputation still clinging to 'show-girls'.
165 *annexed unto* inextricably connected with.
167 *luxure.* At this time the word meant 'lechery', although the text he is quoting (St. Paul: Ephesians v, 18) uses the word *luxuria* in the sense of 'vicious excess'.
168 *Loth* Lot. See Genesis xix, 30-38.
  unkyndely unnaturally; cf. kind in the word 'mankind'.
169 *unwityngly* unknowingly.
170 *he nyste what he wroghte* he didn't know what he was doing.

Or of the povereste widwe in a village
Al sholde hir children sterve for famyne;
Nay, I wol drynke licour of the vyne   135
And have a joly wenche in every toun.
    But herkneth lordynges, in conclusioun,
Youre likyng is that I shal telle a tale:
Now have I dronke a draughte of corny ale,
By God I hope I shal yow telle a thyng   140
That shal by resoun been at youre likyng;
For thogh my self be a ful vicious man,
A moral tale yet I yow telle kan
Which I am wont to preche for to wynne.
Now holde youre pees! My tale I wol bigynne."   145

Heere bigynneth the Pardoners Tale

    In Flandres whilom was a compaignye
Of yonge folk that haunteden folye,
As riot, hasard, stewes and tavernes
Where as with harpes, lutes and gyternes
They daunce and pleyen at dees bothe day and nyght   150
And ete also and drynke over hir myght,
Thurgh which they doon the devel sacrifise
Withinne that develes temple in cursed wise
By superfluytee abhomynable.
Hir othes been so grete and so dampnable   155
That it is grisly for to heere hem swere:
Oure blissed lordes body they to-tere,
Hem thoughte that Jewes rente hym noght ynough,
And ech of hem at otheres synne lough.
And right anon thanne comen tombesteres   160
Fetys and smale, and yonge frutesteres,
Syngeres with harpes, baudes, wafereres,
Whiche been the verray develes officeres
To kyndle and blowe the fyr of lecherye
That is annexed unto glotonye.   165
The holy writ take I to my witnesse
That luxure is in wyn and dronkenesse.
    Lo, how that dronken Loth, unkyndely,
Lay by his doghtres two unwityngly:
So dronke he was he nyste what he wroghte.   170

171 *whoso wel the stories soghte* (as would be found by) whoever should search the stories carefully. Drunkenness is not in fact to be found in any biblical version of the story of Herod and John the Baptist.

173 *he yaf his heste* he gave his command.

175 *Senec* Seneca: Epistola lxxxiii: '. . . Drunkenness is nothing but a condition of insanity purposely assumed. Prolong the drunkard's condition to several days; will you have any doubt about his madness? Even as it is, the madness is no less; it merely lasts a shorter time'.
word saying.

178 *dronkelewe* drunken, habitually drunk.

179 *woodnesse yfallen in a shrewe* madness, when it occurs in a worthless person (of either sex).

182 The first cause of man's fallen state was the eating of the apple, as the Pardoner goes on to say.

185-6 . . . *how deere* . . . *Aboght was* . . . i.e. what a price was paid for . . .

188 Much of the following passage draws heavily on St. Jerome: *Adversus Jovinianum*.

190 *it is no drede* without doubt.

191 *as I rede* i.e. in St. Jerome, where it is implied that Adam's eating of the apple was in part an act of gluttony.

193 *defended* forbidden.

195 *pleyne (on)* complain (about).

196 *wiste a man* if a man knew.

197 *Folwen of* follow as a result of.

198 *mesurable* moderate; cf. 'a measured statement'.

200 *the shorte throte*. Chaucer is here translating a phrase from Pope Innocent III's *De Contemptu Mundi* referring to the brevity of the pleasure of eating: '*Tam brevis est gulae uoluptas, ut spatio loci uix sit quatuor digitorum*' 'The sensual pleasure of gluttony is as short as the length of the place (i.e. the gullet) is scarcely four fingers'.

202 *swynke* labour.

203 *deyntee* rare and delicate.
mete food.

204 *kanstow* canst thou.

205-6 St. Paul: 1 Corinthians vi, 13.
wombe belly.

208 *To seye this word* to repeat this saying.

209 *the white and rede* white and red wine.

210 *pryvee* privy.

211 *thilke* that same.

Herodes, whoso wel the stories soghte,
Whan he of wyn was replet at his feste,
Right at his owene table he yaf his heste
To sleen the Baptist John ful giltelees.
  Senec seith a good word doutelees;   175
He seith he kan no difference fynde
Bitwix a man that is out of his mynde
And a man which that is dronkelewe
But that woodnesse yfallen in a shrewe
Persevereth lenger than dooth dronkenesse.   180
O glotonye ful of cursednesse!
O cause first of oure confusioun!
O original of oure dampnacioun
Til Crist hadde boght us with his blood agayn!
Lo, how deere, shortly for to sayn,   185
Aboght was thilke cursed vileynye!
Corrupt was al this world for glotonye.
  Adam oure fader and his wyf also
Fro Paradys to labour and to wo
Were dryven for that vice, it is no drede.   190
For whil that Adam fasted, as I rede,
He was in Paradys; and whan that he
Eet of the fruyt defended on the tree,
Anon he was out cast to wo and peyne.
O glotonye, on thee wel oghte us pleyne!   195
O wiste a man how manye maladies
Folwen of excesse and of glotonyes,
He wolde been the moore mesurable
Of his diete, sittyng at his table.
Allas! the shorte throte, the tendre mouth,   200
Maketh that est and west and north and south,
In erthe, in eyr, in water, men to swynke
To gete a glotoun deyntee mete and drynke!
Of this matere, O Paul, wel kanstow trete:
'Mete unto wombe and wombe eek unto mete,   205
Shal God destroyen bothe,' as Paulus seith.
Allas! a foul thyng is it, by my feith,
To seye this word, and fouler is the dede,
Whan man so drynketh of the white and rede
That of his throte he maketh his pryvee   210
Thurgh thilke cursed superfluitee.

212 *The apostel* St. Paul. See Philippians iii, 18ff.

215 *croys* cross.

216 *Of whiche* of whom.

217 *cod* bag; used metaphorically here for stomach.

218 *Fulfilled* filled full.

219 *soun* sound.

220 *to fynde* to provide for.

221 *stampe* pound (as in a mortar). This description of cooks labouring to pamper a delicate appetite comes from an attack on elaborate cooking by Pope Innocent III.

222 This line is a witty play on current philosophical terminology. The idea is that such cooks so torture and confuse the real nature (substance) of what they are cooking that only a mess of unidentifiable tastes and colours (accidents) remains.

223 *likerous* gluttonous, rather than its associated meaning of lecherous.

　　talent desire, appetite.

225 *mary* marrow.

226 *softe and soote* softly and sweetly.

228 *by delit* for delight.

230 *haunteth* indulges in, makes a habit of; cf. 147 above.

　　delices delights; cf. 'delicious'.

231 *deed* dead; spiritually dead, in mortal sin.

232-3 Proverbs xx, 1, in the Vulgate version; quoted by St. Jerome.

　　stryvyng fighting; cf. strife.

237 *Sampsoun.* The name is chosen for the sound, but the Pardoner knows how to make capital out of the reference to the biblical Samson, who was called a 'Nazarite to God', and forbidden 'liquor of grapes'.

238 *God woot* God knows.

239 *stiked swyn* stuck pig.

240 *thyn honeste cure* care for thine honour, i.e. self respect.

244 *conseil* confided secrets.

246 *namely* especially.

　　Lepe a town not far from Cadiz in Spain. It has been suggested that the wines of Lepe were either very strong or were laced with powerful spirits.

247 *to selle* on sale.

　　Fysshstrete now Fish Hill Street.

　　Chepe Cheapside, a market street.

246-54 These lines allude to the practice of adulterating good French wines of La Rochelle and Bordeaux with cheap and potent Spanish ones. The suggestion that it is their proximity while growing that produces the mixture is neatly ironic.

250 *fumositee.* It was thought that the fumes of alcohol rose into the brain to cause drunkenness.

252 *weneth* believes.

The apostel wepyng seith ful pitously,
'Ther walken manye of whiche yow toold have I —
I seye it now wepyng, with pitous voys —
They been enemys of Cristes croys,   215
Of whiche the ende is deth, wombe is hir god!'
O wombe! O bely! O stynkyng cod
Fulfilled of dong and of corrupcioun!
At either ende of thee foul is the soun.
How greet labour and cost is thee to fynde!   220
Thise cokes, how they stampe and streyne and grynde
And turnen substaunce into accident
To fulfillen al thy likerous talent!
Out of the harde bones knokke they
The mary, for they caste noght awey   225
That may go thurgh the golet softe and soote;
Of spicerie of leef and bark and roote
Shal been his sauce ymaked by delit
To make hym yet a newer appetit.
But certes, he that haunteth swiche delices   230
Is deed whil that he lyveth in tho vices.
   A lecherous thyng is wyn, and dronkenesse
Is ful of stryvyng and of wrecchednesse.
O dronke man, disfigured is thy face,
Sour is thy breeth, foul artow to embrace,   235
And thurgh thy dronke nose semeth the soun
As thogh thow seydest ay 'Sampsoun, Sampsoun!'
And yet, God woot, Sampsoun drank nevere no wyn.
Thow fallest as it were a stiked swyn,
Thy tonge is lost, and al thyn honeste cure;   240
For dronkenesse is verray sepulture
Of mannes wit and his descrecioun.
In whom that drynke hath dominacioun
He kan no conseil kepe, it is no drede.
Now kepe yow fro the white and fro the rede   245
And namely fro the white wyn of Lepe
That is to selle in Fysshstrete or in Chepe.
This wyn of Spaigne crepeth subtilly
In othere wynes growynge faste by,
Of which ther ryseth swich fumositee   250
That whan a man hath dronken draughtes thre,
And weneth that he be at hoom in Chepe,

256 *o* one.
257 *sovereyn actes* chief deeds.
dar I seye I dare say.
259 *verray* true.
261 *leere* learn.
262 Attila the Hun died in A.D. 453, reputedly after riotous celebrations on his wedding night.
266 *avyseth yow* consider.
267-8 *Lamuel.* Proverbs xxxi, 4-5: 'Give not to kings, O Lamuel, give not wine to kings; because there is no secret where drunkenness reigneth: And lest they drink and forget judgements, and pervert the cause of the children of the poor'.
270 *Of* concerning.
han justise are responsible for justice.
273 *yow defenden hasardrye* present to you the case against gambling.
274 *moder of lesynges* mother of lies.
275 *forswerynges* perjuries.
276-7 *wast . . . Of catel* waste of property.
278 *repreeve* reproach.
280 *estat* social rank.
281 *holden* held to be.
desolat destitute (of honour), disgraced; but also in a state of spiritual desolation.
286 *Stilbon.* The incident is from John of Salisbury's *Policraticus,* where the ambassador is called Chilon.
288 *make hire alliaunce* make an alliance with them.
289 *hym happed* it happened to him.
293 *stal hym hoom* went quietly home.

He is in Spaigne right at the toune of Lepe,
Nat at the Rochel ne at Burdeux toun;
And thanne wol he seye 'Sampsoun, Sampsoun!'   255
    But herkneth lordynges, o word, I yow preye!
That alle the sovereyn actes, dar I seye,
Of victories in the Olde Testament,
Thurgh verray God that is omnipotent,
Were doon in abstinence and in prayere,   260
Looketh the Bible, and ther ye may it leere.
    Looke, Attila, the grete conquerour
Deyde in his sleep with shame and dishonour
Bledyng ay at his nose in dronkenesse.
A capitayn sholde lyve in sobrenesse.   265
And over al this, avyseth yow right wel
What was comaunded unto Lamuel;
Nat Samuel but Lamuel seye I;
Redeth the Bible and fynde it expresly
Of wyn-yevyng to hem that han justise.   270
Namoore of this, for it may wel suffise.
    And now that I have spoken of glotonye,
Now wol I yow defenden hasardrye.
Hasard is verray moder of lesynges
And of deceite and cursed forswerynges,   275
Blaspheme of Crist, manslaughtre and wast also
Of catel and of tyme; and forther mo
It is repreeve and contrarie of honour
For to ben holde a commune hasardour;
And ever the hyer he is of estat,   280
The moore is he holden desolat.
If that a prynce useth hasardrye
In alle governaunce and policye,
He is, as by commune opinioun,
Yholde the lasse in reputacioun.   285
    Stilbon, that was a wys embassadour,
Was sent to Corynthe in ful gret honour
Fro Lacedomye to make hire alliaunce.
And whan he cam, hym happed, par chaunce,
That alle the gretteste that were of that lond,   290
Pleiynge atte hasard he hem fond.
For which, as soone as it myghte be,
He stal hym hoom agayn to his contree

294 *lese* lose.
298 *me were levere dye* I would rather die.
302 'As a result of my decision or of discussion undertaken by me'.
305 *the book.* John of Salisbury's *Policraticus* also has the story of the King of Parthia sending dice to a certain King Demetrius in scorn.
310 *oother manere pley* other kinds of diversion.
317 cf. Matthew v, 34: 'But I say unto you: swear not at all'.
318 *Jeremye* Jeremiah iv, 2.
319 *sooth* true.
320 *doom* judgement.
      rightwisnesse righteousness.
321 *ydel* vain, empty, thoughtless.
323 *hestes* commandments given to Moses and inscribed on two tablets of stone (Exodus xxxi, 18).
326-8 *rather . . . Than* earlier than, sooner than. The Pardoner's implication is that the order of the commandments from I to X represents the decreasing degrees of God's disapproval, i.e. he equates 'earlier in order' and 'more'.
331 *forther over* further more.
      al plat flatly.
332 *parten* depart. See Ecclesiasticus xxiii, 12: 'A man that sweareth much shall be filled with iniquity: and a scourge shall not depart from his house'.
334 *By his nayles.* The oath usually would have referred to the nails that pierced Christ's hands, though here it may possibly refer to Christ's fingernails, an example of the tearing apart of Christ's body referred to in line 157 above.

And seyde, "Ther wol I nat lese my name,
N' I wol nat take on me so greet defame   295
Yow for to allie unto none hasardours.
Sendeth othere wise embassadours
For, by my trouthe, me were levere dye
Than I yow sholde to hasardours allye.
For ye that been so glorious in honours   300
Shal nat allye yow with hasardours
As by my wyl ne as by my tretee."
This wise philosophre, thus seyde he.
   Looke eek that to the kyng Demetrius,
The kyng of Parthes, as the book seith us,   305
Sente him a paire of dees of gold in scorn,
For he hadde used hasard ther biforn;
For which he heeld his glorie or his renoun
At no value or reputacioun.
Lordes may fynden oother manere pley   310
Honeste ynow to dryve the day awey.
   Now wol I speke of othes false and grete
A word or two, as olde bokes trete.
Greet sweryng is a thyng abhomynable,
And fals sweryng is yet moore reprevable.   315
The heighe God forbad sweryng at al,
Witnesse on Mathew; but in special
Of sweryng seith the holy Jeremye,
"Thow shalt swere sooth thyne othes and nat lye,
And swere in doom and eek in rightwisnesse";   320
But ydel sweryng is a cursednesse.
Bihoold and se that in the firste table
Of heighe Goddes hestes honurable
How that the seconde heste of hym is this:
"Take nat my name in ydel or amys."   325
Lo, rather he forbedeth swich sweryng
Than homycide or many a cursed thyng;
I seye that, as by ordre, thus it standeth;
This knowen that hise hestes understandeth,
How that the seconde heste of God is that.   330
And forther over I wol thee telle al plat
That vengeance shal nat parten from his hous
That of hise othes is to outrageous.
"By Goddes precious herte," and "By his nayles,"

76

335 *Hayles.* Hayles Abbey in Gloucestershire possessed a phial supposedly containing some of Christ's blood.

336 The line uses terminology from the game of hasard, 'cynk' and 'treye' being the O.Fr. words for five and three.

339 *bicched bones* cursed dice. There has been some discussion as to whether the adjective is merely a term of abuse, as is the modern word 'bitch', or a technical word, meaning knuckle-bone, from which dice were often made. Perhaps both are implied, as in a parallel phrase 'dog-bones', used by Vincent of Beauvais in referring to dice.

342 *Lete* leave, quit.

344 *riotoures* that is, men engaged in riotous living. Cf. 148n. above.

345 'Long before prime was rung (announced) by any bell'. Prime, the third of the canonical hours, was rung at 6 a.m.

347 It was the habit to ring a 'lich-bell' in front of the body being carried to its grave.

348 The relative is frequently omitted, as here.

349 *gan callen* called.

    knave servant, boy.

350 *Go bet* lit. 'go better', meaning 'go quickly'. The phrase was one used to encourage hunting dogs.

    axe redily ask immediately or promptly.

351 *forby* by.

353 *it nedeth never a del* it is quite unnecessary.

355 *pardee* a word derived from the O.Fr. *par de* (by God), but by this time merely an intensive meaning perhaps 'indeed'.

    old felawe old friend, i.e. a friend of long standing.

357 *Fordronke* completely drunk.

358 *privee* secret.

    men clepeth who is called. The word 'man' or 'men' was commonly used as we say 'one', in 'one calls him Death'.

362 *this pestilence* during this plague. There had been four serious outbreaks of plague in Chaucer's lifetime.

365 *be war of* beware.

366 *Beth* be.

367 *my dame* my mother.

368 *taverner* tavern-keeper.

370 *Henne over a myle* over a mile hence.

371 *hyne and page* farm labourer and servant.

373 *To been avysed* to be wary, forewarned.

374 i.e. before Death slays a man.

And "By the blood of Crist that is in Hayles,   335
Sevene is my chaunce, and thyn is cynk and treye!"
"By Goddes armes, if thow falsly pleye,
This dagger shal thurghout thyn herte go!"
This fruyt cometh of the bicched bones two,
Forsweryng, ire, falsnesse, homycide.   340
Now, for the love of Crist that for us dyde,
Lete youre othes bothe grete and smale.
But sires, now wol I telle forth my tale.
    Thise riotoures thre of which I telle,
Longe erst er prime rong of any belle,   345
Were set hem in a taverne to drynke
And as they sat they herde a belle clynke
Biforn a cors was caried to his grave.
That oon of hem gan callen to his knave:
"Go bet," quod he, "and axe redily   350
What cors is this that passeth heer forby,
And looke that thow reporte his name wel."
    "Sire," quod this boy, "it nedeth never a del;
It was me told er ye came heer two houres.
He was, pardee, an old felawe of youres,   355
And sodeynly he was yslayn to-nyght
Fordronke as he sat on his bench upright.
Ther cam a privee theef men clepeth Deeth
That in this contree al the peple sleeth,
And with his spere he smoot his herte atwo   360
And wente his wey withouten wordes mo.
He hath a thousand slayn this pestilence.
And maister, er ye come in his presence,
Me thynketh that it were necessarie
For to be war of swich an adversarie.   365
Beth redy for to meete hym evere moore;
Thus taughte me my dame; I sey namoore."
    "By Seinte Marie!" seyde this taverner,
"The child seith sooth, for he hath slayn this yer
Henne over a myle, withinne a greet village,   370
Bothe man and womman, child and hyne and page;
I trowe his habitacioun be there.
To been avysed greet wisdom it were
Er that he dide a man a dishonour."
    "Ye, Goddes armes!" quod this riotour,   375

377 *wey* way, path.
  strete paved road (as in Watling Street).
378 *digne* worthy.
379 *al ones* completely at one.
380 *til* to.
381 To swear brotherhood in this way, with oaths and raised hands, was a common mediaeval, and indeed, ancient practice.
385 *hir trouthes plight* the phrase 'plight thee my troth' is still used in some marriage services. It means 'to pledge one's word'.
387 *ybore* born, i.e. natural.
388 *rage* passion or frenzy, rather than anger.
392 *to-rente* rent in pieces.
393 *hente* catch.
395 *Right as* just as.
396 For a discussion of the old man and his significance, see commentary.
397 *hem grette* greeted them.
398 *God yow se* lit. 'God see you', meaning 'God watch over you'; but the literal meaning, implying 'God keep an eye on you', is ironically suitable here.
400 *agayn* in return.
  carl, with sory grace 'churl, ill fortune to you', a common imprecation.
401 *forwrapped* heavily or completely wrapped up.
403 *gan looke* looked.
404 *For* because.
405 *Inde* India, often used at this time to mean the remotest limits of the world.
410-6 These lines are imitated from an elegy on the miseries of old age, by Maximian, a 6th century Latin poet.
411 *caytyf* Derived from the Lat. *captivum,* 'captive', the word had come to mean 'miserable wretch'.
414 *Leeve* dear.

"Is it swich peril with hym for to meete?
I shal hym seke by wey and eek by strete!
I make avow to Goddes digne bones!
Herkneth, felawes, we thre been al ones;
Lat ech of us holde up his hand til oother   380
And ech of us bicome otheres brother,
And we wol sleen this false traytour Deeth.
He shal be slayn, he that so manye sleeth,
By Goddes dignytee, er it be nyght!"
 Togidres han thise thre hir trouthes plight   385
To lyve and dyen ech of hem for oother
As thogh he were his owene ybore brother;
And up they stirte al dronken in this rage
And forth they goon towardes that village
Of which the taverner hadde spoke biforn;   390
And many a grisly ooth thanne han they sworn,
And Cristes blessed body they to-rente;
Deeth shal be deed, if that they may hym hente!
 Whan they han goon nat fully half a mile,
Right as they wolde han treden over a stile,   395
An old man and a poure with hem mette.
This olde man ful mekely hem grette
And seyde thus, "Now, lordes, God yow se!"
 The proudeste of thise riotoures thre
Answerde agayn, "What, carl, with sory grace!   400
Why artow al forwrapped save thy face?
Why lyvestow so longe in so greet age?"
 This olde man gan looke in his visage
And seyde thus: "For I ne kan nat fynde
A man, thogh that I walked into Inde,   405
Neither in citee ne in no village,
That wolde chaunge his youthe for myn age;
And ther fore moot I han myn age stille
As longe tyme as it is Goddes wille.
 Ne Deeth, allas! ne wol nat han my lyf.   410
Thus walke I lyk a restelees caytyf
And on the ground which is my modres gate
I knokke with my staf bothe erly and late
And seye, 'Leeve moder, leet me in!
Lo how I vanysshe, flessh and blood and skyn!   415
Allas! when shal my bones been at reste?

417 *cheste* wardrobe; meaning the clothes themselves.
419 *an heyre clowt* a cloth of hair used as a winding-sheet.
420 *grace* favour.
421 *welked* withered.
422 *to yow* in you.
423 *vileynye** rudeness.
424 *But* unless.
425 Leviticus xix, 32: 'Rise up before the hoary head, and honour the person of the aged man: and fear the Lord thy God'.
426 *Agayns* before, in the presence of.
427 *yeve yow reed* give you advice.
430 'In old age, if you live that long'.
431 *where ye go or ryde* whether you go (on foot) or ride (on horseback).
432 *thider as* where.
435 *lightly* easily.
   by Seint John the closest and most devoted of Christ's apostles.
438 'Here is my true word; since you are his spy . . .'
439 *abye* pay for.
441 *assent* assent, party.
443 *leef* keen, desirous.
445 *by my fey* by my faith.
446 '. . . there he will wait (for you)'.
447 i.e. 'he is not in the least likely to hide on account of your boast (to kill him)'.
448 *ook* oak.
453 'Fine round florins minted of gold'.
455 *thanne* then.
457 *been* were.
   faire beautiful.

Moder, with yow wolde I chaunge my cheste
That in my chambre longe tyme hath be,
Ye, for an heyre clowt to wrappe me!'
But yet to me she wol nat do that grace,   420
For which ful pale and welked is my face.
  But sires, to yow it is no curteisye
To speken to an old man vileynye
But he trespase in word or ellis in dede.
In holy writ ye may your self wel rede: 425
'Agayns an old man, hoor upon his heed,
Ye sholde arise;' wherfore I y�ve yow reed:
Ne dooth unto an old man noon harm now,
Namoore than that ye wolde men dide to yow
In age, if that ye so longe abyde.   430
And God be with yow where ye go or ryde!
I moot go thider as I have to go."
  "Nay, olde cherl, by God, thow shalt nat so,"
Seyde this oother hasardour anon;
"Thow partest nat so lightly, by Seint John!   435
Thow spak right now of thilke traytour Deeth
That in this contree alle oure freendes sleeth.
Have here my trouthe, as thow art his espye,
Telle wher he is or thow shalt it abye,
By God and by the holy sacrament!   440
For soothly thow art oon of his assent
To sleen us yonge folk, thow false theef!"
  "Now, sires," quod he, "if that yow be so leef
To fynde Deeth, turn up this croked wey,
For in the grove I lafte hym, by my fey,   445
Under a tree, and there he wol abyde;
Nat for youre boost he wol him no thyng hyde.
Se ye that ook? Right ther ye shal hym fynde.
God save yow, that boghte agayn mankynde,
And yow amende!" Thus seyde this olde man;   450
And everich of thise riotoures ran
Til they came to that tree, and ther they founde
Of floryns fyne of gold ycoyned rounde
Wel ny an eighte busshels as hem thoughte.
No lenger thanne after Deeth they soughte,   455
But ech of hem so glad was of the sighte,
For that the floryns been so faire and brighte,

82

458 *they sette hem* they sat.
460 *taak kepe* take notice of.
461 *bourde* jest.
464 'Let's spend it as easily as it came to us'.
465 *wende* would have thought.
466 *so fair a grace* so great a blessing, i.e. such good luck.
469 Any treasure found was properly the property of the Crown.
473 *doon us honge* have us hanged; lit. cause us to hang.
475 *wisely* circumspectly.
        slyly cunningly.
476 *rede* advise.
        cut lots, by drawing straws cut to different lengths.
477 *drawe* drawn.
        the cut i.e. the shortest straw.
478 *herte blithe* light heart.
479 *ful swithe* very quickly.
480 *ful prively* secretly. The line may suggest a blasphemous parody
of the Sacrament.
481 *kepen* guard.
        subtilly cunningly.
484 *us thynketh* it seems to us.
485 *That oon* the one; cf. the t'un and the t'other; cf. 490 below.
        fest fist or hand.
489 *also* as.
492 *Thy profit* something which is to your profit.
495 *departed* divided.
496 *shape it* bring it about.
498 *torn* turn.

That doun they sette hem by this precious hoord.
The worste of hem, he spak the firste word.
    "Bretheren," quod he, "taak kepe what I seye;   460
My wit is greet, thogh that I bourde and pleye.
This tresor hath Fortune unto us yeven,
In myrthe and jolitee oure lyf to lyven,
And lightly as it cometh so wol we spende.
By Goddes precious dignytee! who wende   465
To-day that we sholde han so fair a grace?
But myghte this gold be caried fro this place
Hoom to myn hous, or ellis unto youres —
For wel ye woot that al this gold is oures —
Thanne were we in heigh felicitee.   470
But trewely, by daye it may nat be;
Men wolde seyn that we were theves stronge
And for oure owene tresor doon us honge.
This tresor moste ycaried be by nyghte
As wisely and as slyly as it myghte.   475
Wher fore I rede that cut among us alle
Be drawe, and lat se wher the cut wol falle;
And he that hath the cut, with herte blithe
Shal renne to the toune, and that ful swithe,
And brynge us breed and wyn ful prively;   480
And two of us shal kepen subtilly
This tresor wel, and if he wol nat tarye,
Whan it is nyght, we wol this tresor carye
By oon assent wher as us thynketh best."
That oon of hem the cut broghte in his fest   485
And bad hem drawe and looke where it wol falle;
And it fil on the yongeste of hem alle,
And forth toward the town he wente anon.
And also soone as that he was agon,
That oon of hem spak thus unto that oother: 490
"Thow knowest wel thow art my sworn brother;
Thy profit wol I telle thee anon.
Thow woost wel that oure felawe is agon
And heere is gold and that ful greet plentee
That shal departed been among us thre;   495
But nathelees, if I kan shape it so
That it departed were among us two,
Hadde I nat doon a freendes torn to thee?"

499 *noot* know not.
500 *tweye* two.
502 *conseil* a secret.
    shrewe scoundrel.
505 *graunte* promise.
    out of doute without any doubt.
506 *biwreye* betray.
509 *is set* has sat down.
511 *ryve* stab.
512 *in game* in sport, for fun.
516 *lustes* desires.
517 *right at oure owene wille* just as and when we want to.
518 *acorded been* are in agreement.
519 *sleen* kill, slay.
525-6 *trone Of God* the throne of God, i.e. the heavens.
528 *beye* buy.
530 *For why* because.
    swich lyvynge such a way of life.
531 'That he had permission to bring him (the reveller) to a state of sorrow'; cf. Job i, 12: 'Then the Lord said to Satan: Behold, all that he hath is in thy hand'.
532 *outrely* entirely.
    entente intention.
537 *quelle* kill, rather than the vaguer modern 'put down'.
538 *eek* also.
    polcat polecat, a sort of weasel.
    hawe lit. hedge, but here an enclosure or 'fowl-run'.
539 *yslawe* killed.

That oother answerde, "I noot how that may be.
He woot that the gold is with us tweye;   500
What shal we doon? What shal we to hym seye?"
   "Shal it be conseil?" seyde the firste shrewe,
"And I shal tellen in a wordes fewe
What we shal doon, and brynge it wel aboute."
   "I graunte," quod that oother, "out of doute,   505
That, by my trouthe, I wol thee nat biwreye."
   "Now," quod the firste, "thow woost wel we be tweye
And two of us shul strenger be than oon.
Looke whan that he is set that right anoon
Arys as though thow woldest with hym pleye   510
And I shal ryve hym thurgh the sydes tweye
Whil that thow strogelest with hym as in game,
And with thy daggere looke thow do the same;
And thanne shal al this gold departed be,
My deere freend, bitwixe me and thee.   515
Thanne may we bothe oure lustes al fulfille
And pleye at dees right at oure owene wille."
And thus acorded been thise shrewes tweye
To sleen the thridde as ye han herd me seye.
   This yongeste, which that wente to the toun,   520
Ful ofte in herte he rolleth up and doun
The beautee of thise floryns newe and brighte.
"O Lord!" quod he, "if so were that I myghte
Have al this tresor to my self allone,
Ther is no man that lyveth under the trone   525
Of God that sholde lyve so myrie as I!"
And atte laste the feend, oure enemy,
Putte in his thoght that he sholde poyson beye,
With which he myghte sleen his felawes tweye;
For why the feend foond hym in swich lyvynge   530
That he hadde leve hym to sorwe brynge.
For this was outrely his ful entente,
To sleen hem bothe and nevere to repente.
And forth he goth, no lenger wolde he tarye,
Into the toun unto a pothecarye,   535
And preyed hym that he hym wolde selle
Som poyson that he myghte his rattes quelle;
And eek ther was a polcat in his hawe,
That, as he seyde, his capons hadde yslawe,

540 *wreke hym* take vengeance.
541 *destroyed hym* were ruining him, or perhaps, disturbed or worried him.
543 *also God my soule save* as God may save my soul.
545 *confiture* mixture, preparation.
546 'Nothing but the amount of a grain of wheat'.
547 *anoon forlete* at once give up, end.
548 *sterve* die.
549 'Than you would take to go scarcely a mile at walking pace'.
551 *yhent* taken.
552 *sith* afterwards, then.
554 *borwed of hym* borrowed from him; cf. modern 'borrow *off* someone'.
557 'For he planned to work all night'.
561 *repaireth* returns.
562 *sermone of* make a sermon of, go on about.
563 *right as* just as, exactly as.
   cast plotted.
568 *it happed hym par cas* he happened by chance.
569 *ther* where.
571 *storven* died.
572 *certes* certainly.
   Avycen Avicenna, an Arabic physician.
573 *canon*. Avicenna's great work was the *Canon Medicinae. Canon* means 'rule' or 'prescription'.
   fen chapter.
574 'More amazing symptoms of poisoning'.
575 *er hir endyng* before their end, i.e. death.
579 *traytours* traitorous.
580 *luxure* lechery.

And fayn he wolde wreke hym, if he myghte,   540
On vermyn that destroyed hym by nyghte.
   The pothecarie answerde, "And thow shalt have
A thyng that, also God my soule save,
In al this world ther is no creature
That ete or dronke hath of this confiture   545
Nat but the montaunce of a corn of whete,
That he ne shal his lyf anoon forlete;
Ye, sterve he shal, and that in lasse while
Than thow wolt goon a paas nat but a mile,
The poysoun is so strong and violent."   550
   This cursed man hath in his hond yhent
This poyson in a box, and sith he ran
Into the nexte strete unto a man
And borwed of hym large botels thre
And in the two his poyson poured he,   555
The thridde he kepte clene for his drynke.
For al the nyght he shoop hym for to swynke
In cariyng of the gold out of that place.
And whan this riotour with sory grace
Hadde filled with wyn hise grete botels thre,   560
To hise felawes agayn repaireth he.
  ꞮWhat nedeth it to sermone of it moore?
For right as they hadde cast his deeth bifore
Right so they han hym slayn and that anon.
And whan that this was doon, thus spak that oon: 565
"Now lat us sitte and drynke and make us merye
And afterward we wol his body berye."
And with that word it happed hym par cas
To take the botel ther the poyson was
And drank and yaf his felawe drynke also,   570
For which anon they storven bothe two.
   But certes I suppose that Avycen
Wroot nevere in no canon ne in no fen
Mo wonder signes of empoysonyng
Than hadde thise wrecches two er hir endyng.   575
Thus ended been thise homicides two,
And eek the false empoysonere also.
   O cursed synne of alle cursednesse!
O traytours homicide, O wikkednesse!
O glotonye, luxure, and hasardrye!   580

581 *vileynye** evil speech.
582 *usage* habit.
583 *how may it bityde* how can it happen.
584 'That to thy creator who made thee'.
586 *unkynde* unnatural; i.e. exhibiting behaviour unfitting for a creature towards his creator.
588 *ware yow* guard yourselves, beware.
589 *warice* cure.
590 *So that* provided that.
  nobles golden coins.
  sterlynges silver pence.
591 Coin was in short supply in the Middle Ages, so that offerings in kind were quite usual.
593 *wolle* wool.
594 *my rolle.* In the Summoner's Tale there is another such charlatan entering the names of people he absolved on a roll as though certifying their entry into heaven.
596 *assoille* absolve.
598 The Pardoner here turns from his imaginary congregation to address the pilgrims.
599 *leche* physician.
603 *male* bag.
604 *faire* fine.
608 *adoun* down.
610 *wende* go along.
612 *So that* provided that.
  alwey newe and newe anew each time.
614 *honour* privilege.
  everich everyone.
  heer here.
615 *mowe* may.
  suffisant capable and efficient.
617 *aventures* chances, accidents.
  bityde happen, befall.
618 *Par aventure* perhaps.
620 *which* what.
  seuretee security.
621 'That I have happened to be in your company'.

Thow blasphemour of Crist with vileynye
And othes grete, of usage and of pryde!
Allas! mankynde, how may it bityde
That to thy creatour, which that thee wroghte
And with his precious herte blood thee boghte,   585
Thow art so fals and so unkynde, allas?
   Now goode men, God foryeve yow youre trespas,
And ware yow fro the synne of avarice!
Myn holy pardoun may yow alle warice,
So that ye offre nobles or sterlynges,   590
Or ellis silver broches, spones, rynges.
Boweth youre heed under this holy bulle!
Cometh up, ye wyves, offreth of youre wolle!
Youre name I entre here in my rolle anon;
Into the blisse of hevene shul ye gon.   595
I yow assoille, by myn heigh power,
Yow that wol offre, as clene and eek as cler
As ye were born. —And lo sires, thus I preche.
And Jesu Crist that is oure soules leche
So graunte yow his pardoun to receyve,   600
For that is best, I wol yow nat deceyve.
   But, sires, o word forgat I in my tale:
I have relikes and pardoun in my male,
As faire as any man in Engelond,
Whiche were me yeven by the popes hond.   605
If any of yow wol of devocioun
Offren and han myn absolucioun,
Com forth anon and kneleth here adoun
And mekely receyveth my pardoun;
Or ellis taketh pardoun as ye wende,   610
Al newe and fressh at every miles ende,
So that ye offren, alwey newe and newe,
Nobles or pens whiche that been good and trewe.
It is an honour to everich that is heer
That ye mowe have a suffisant pardoner   615
T'assoille yow, in contree as ye ryde,
For aventures whiche that may bityde.
Par aventure ther may falle oon or two
Doun of his hors and breke his nekke atwo.
Looke which a seuretee is it to yow alle   620
That I am in youre felaweshipe yfalle,

622 *bothe moore and lasse* both high and low in rank.
624 *I rede* I suggest.
625 *envoluped* enveloped, involved.
630 *so theech* from archaic 'so thee ich', 'as I may thrive'.
631 *breech* a covering for thighs and hips; possibly a breech-cloth, underpants.
633 *with* by.
     fundement anus.
     depeint stained, soiled.
634 *Seint Eleyne.* St. Helena, the mother of the emperor Constantine, was supposed to have been the finder of the true cross of Christ.
635 *coylons* cullions, testicles.
636 *In stede* instead.
     seintuarie reliquary, box containing relics.
637 *Lat cutte hem of* have them cut off.
641 *pleye* sport, joke.
643 *bigan* began (to intervene and say).
645 *right ynough* quite enough; 'it has gone far enough'.
646 *cheere* countenance, demeanour.
651 *ryden* rode.

That may assoille you, bothe moore and lasse,
Whan that the soule shal fro the body passe.
I rede that oure hoost shal bigynne,
For he is moost envoluped in synne.   625
Com forth, sire hoost, and offre first anon.
And thow shalt kisse the relikes everychon,
Ye, for a grote! Unbokele anon thy purs."
    "Nay, nay!" quod he, "thanne have I Cristes curs!
Lat be," quod he, "it shal nat be, so theech!   630
Thow woldest make me kisse thyn olde breech,
And swere it were a relyk of a seint
Thogh it were with thy fundement depeint!
But by the croys which that Seint Eleyne fond,
I wolde I hadde thy coylons in myn hond   635
In stede of relikes or of seintuarie.
Lat cutte hem of, I wol thee helpe hem carie,
They shul be shryned in an hogges toord!"
    This pardoner answerde nat a word;
So wrooth he was, no word ne wolde he seye.   640
    "Now," quod oure hoost, "I wol no lenger pleye
With thee, ne with noon oother angry man."
But right anon the worthy knyght bigan,
Whan that he saugh that al the peple lough,
"Namoore of this, for it is right ynough!   645
Sire pardoner be glad and murye of cheere;
And ye, sire hoost, that been to me so deere,
I prey yow that ye kisse the pardoner.
And pardoner I pray thee drawe thee neer
And, as we diden, lat us laughe and pleye."   650
Anon they kiste, and ryden forth hir weye.

Heere is ended the Pardoners Tale.

1 *corpus dominus* properly *corpus domini*, the Lord's body.
2 *moote* may.
  by the coost along the coast.
4 *a thousand last quade yeer* a thousand (cart-)loads (of) bad years.
  last. Related to 'load', originally meaning a burden, then a very large measure of, for instance, grain, the word came to mean just any large load.
  quade bad.
  Both 'last' and 'yeer' have no plural inflection in Chaucer's English; the preposition 'of' is idiomatically omitted; cf. Mod. E. 'two dozen eggs' and 'two pints *of* milk'; hence the obscurity of the phrase to modern eyes.
  The line refers to the scheming monk in the tale which the Shipman has just told.
5 *jape* practical joke.
6 i.e. made a fool of the man; cf. GP707-8.
7 'And in his wife's hood too, by St. Augustine'. There is an ironic appropriateness in the Host's swearing by one who was held to be a founding father of monasticism, St. Augustine of Hippo.
8 *in* not necessarily an inn, but a house of lodging.

10 *route* company.
14 *So that I wiste* provided that I knew.
15 *demen* decide.
  The contrast in tone in these lines, reflecting a change in the Host's demeanour, may well remind us of the Prioress's 'peyning hir to ben held digne of reverence'. The Host's almost obsequious courtesy in addressing her is a measure of the Prioress's success in her efforts. (Or is the Host being ironic?)

The Shipman has told another tale of bawdy trickery — a monk borrows a hundred francs from a merchant as seduction money for the merchant's own wife, then at the due date claims that he has already repaid the money to the wife, leaving her to answer for the debt.

Bihoold the murie wordes of the hoost to the shipman and to the lady prioresse

"Wel seyd, by *Corpus Dominus*," quod oure hoost,
"Now longe moote thow saille by the coost
Sire gentil maister, gentil maryneer!
God yeve the monk a thousand last quade yeer!
A ha, felawes! beth ware of swich a jape!   5
The monk putte in the mannes hood an ape
And in his wyves eek by Seint Austyn!
Draweth no monkes moore into youre in.

But now passe over and lat us seke aboute
Who shal now telle first of al this route   10
Another tale," and with that word he sayde
As curteisly as it hadde been a mayde,
"My lady prioresse, by youre leve
So that I wiste I sholde yow nat greve
I wolde demen that ye tellen sholde   15
A tale next if so were that ye wolde:
Now wol ye vouche sauf my lady deere?"
   "Gladly," quod she and seyde as ye shal heere.

94

Domine dominus noster the opening words of Psalm viii. The first stanza of the Prioress's Prologue is a free translation of the first three verses of the psalm.

20　*ysprad* spread.
21　*laude precious* precious praise.
22　*Parfourned* performed, expressed.
23　*bountee* goodness, generosity (to mankind).
24　*soukynge* sucking.
25　*heriynge* praise; cf. Psalm viii, 3 and lines 79-81 and n. below.
26　*kan or may* know how to or have ability to.
27　The white lily is a common symbol of the Blessed Virgin.
28　*Which that the bar* who bore thee.
　　mayde virgin.
29　*do my labour* 'try my hardest'.
32　*soules boote* the remedy (boot) or helper of souls.
33　*moder* mother.
　　free liberal or generous in favours.
34　*unbrent* unconsumed.
　　brennyng burning. The burning bush (cf. Exodus iii, 2-4) was one of the symbols of the virgin motherhood of Mary. This 'wonderful story', says a contemporary preacher, shows 'the moderhed and virginite of oure blessed ladye . . . The busche betokens the moder and maiden enflamed with the speciall grace of the holy gost in conceyvyng and bryngynge forthe oure cheff soveran and lorde god and man' (Owst).
35-9　'. . . who through thy humility drew down from the Deity the spirit which alighted in thee, by whose power, when he had illuminated (or cheered) thine heart, the Father's wisdom (Christ) was conceived, help me to tell it in reverence of thee'.
　　Notice how this sentence, which is complex in construction and cumbersome in translation, nevertheless flows naturally within the verse and brings all the relevant qualities of Mary and the Trinity lucidly together.
42　*science* art, skill.
44　'Thou dost anticipate (goost biforn) us by thy benignity'.
45　*of* by means of.
47　*konnyng* understanding.
　　wayk weak, feeble.
　　blisful blessed.
51　*unnethe* scarcely, hardly; lit. uneasily.
53　*song* poem or story, not necessarily recited or sung with musical accompaniment.
　　seye tell.

Domine dominus noster

"O Lord, oure Lord, thy name how merveillous
Is in this large world ysprad," quod she;   20
"For nat oonly thy laude precious
Parfourned is by men of dignytee
But by the mouth of children thy bountee
Parfourned is, for on the brest soukynge
Som tyme shewen they thyn heriynge;   25

Wherfore in laude, as I best kan or may,
Of thee and of the white lilye flour
Which that the bar, and is a mayde alway,
To telle a storie I wol do my labour;
Nat that I may encressen hir honour,   30
For she hir self is honour and the roote
Of bountee, next hir sone, and soules boote.

O moder mayde! o mayde moder free!
O bussh unbrent brennyng in Moyses sighte
That ravysedest doun fro the deitee   35
Thurgh thyn humblesse the goost that in th'alighte,
Of whos vertu whan he thyn herte lighte
Conceyved was the fadres sapience,
Help me to telle it in thy reverence!

Lady, thy bountee, thy magnificence,   40
Thy vertu and thy grete humylitee
Ther may no tonge expresse in no science;
For som tyme, lady, er men praye to thee
Thow goost biforn of thy benygnytee
And getest us the lyght of thy preyere   45
To gyden us unto thy sone so deere.

My konnyng is so wayk, o blisful queene,
For to declare thy grete worthynesse
That I ne may the weighte nat sustene;
But as a child of twelf month old or lesse   50
That kan unnethe any word expresse
Right so fare I, and ther fore I yow preye
Gydeth my song that I shal of yow seye."

Explicit.

96

54 *Asye* Asia, probably Asia Minor. though the location is deliberately vague.
55 *jewerye* a Jewish quarter c ghetto.
56 *Sustened* maintained.
57 *foule usure* foul usury.
   *lucre of vileynye** evil gain.

Mediaeval social doctrine allowed for merchants and financiers, but was doubtful about the honesty of such callings and indicated their grave danger — the temptation to the sin of avarice. To receive more than was necessary to maintain one's station in life was dishonest and sinful. Both church and popular opinion and sentiment unanimously condemned usury along with any unjust or excessive profits, not from motives of self-interest but on moral and religious grounds. There is, however, abundant evidence that in actual fact doctrine and practice did not always accord. While usury was forbidden by church and state law to Christians, Jews were exempted from such law and were often encouraged as strongly as they were hated for it, to engage in a livelihood closed to Christians.

59 *wende* go on foot.
60 The ghetto was not closed off from the rest of the city, and its main street was a thoroughfare.
63 *an heep* a crowd, a number.
65 'The sort of things it was customary to teach there'.
68 *widwes sone* widow's son.
69 *clergeoun* a diminutive form of 'clerk'; scholar.
70 *wone* custom, habit.
71 *wher as* wherever.
72 *hadde he in usage* he was accustomed, it was his practice.
73 *As hym was taught* as it had been taught him.
74 *Ave Marie* a Latin invocation to the Blessed Virgin Mary, meaning 'Hail Mary'.
78 'For a good child will always learn readily (or quickly)'. For 'sely', see Glossary.
79 'But always when I call this matter to mind, St. Nicholas stands before me continually, for he honoured Christ at so tender an age'. In fact it was said that, except for one meal, he abstained from suckling on Fridays and certain Wednesdays. He was the patron saint of schoolboys and the original Santa Claus.
83 *prymer* the first reading book from which he would learn the alphabet and probably the Lord's Prayer, the Hail Mary, the Creed, and some short prayers.
84 *Alma redemptoris* a Latin anthem sung on feasts of the Blessed Virgin. It begins *O alma redemptoris mater*, O beloved mother of the saviour.   *synge* being sung.
85 *Antiphoner* a book of anthems.
86 *dorste* dared.
   'he drew (himself) nearer and nearer'.
87 *note* melody.
88 'Till he knew the first verse completely by heart'.

Heere bigynneth the Prioresses Tale

Ther was in Asye in a greet citee
Amonges cristene folk a jewerye   55
Sustened by a lord of that contree
For foule usure and lucre of vileynye
Hateful to Crist and to his compaignye,
And thurgh the strete men myghte ryde and wende
For it was free and open at eyther ende.   60

A litel scole of cristen folk ther stood
Doun at the ferther ende, in which ther were
Children an heep ycomen of cristen blood,
That lerned in that scole yeer by yere
Swich manere doctrine as men used there: 65
This is to seyn, to syngen and to rede
As smale children doon in hir childhede.

Among thise children was a wydwes sone,
A litel clergeoun seven yeer of age
That day by day to scole was his wone,   70
And eek also, wher as he say th'ymage
Of Cristes moder, hadde he in usage,
As hym was taught, to knele adoun and seye
His *Ave Marie* as he goth by the weye.

Thus hath this wydwe hir litel sone ytaught   75
Oure blisful lady, Cristes moder deere
To worshipe ay and he forgat it naught:
For sely child wol alwey soone lere.
But ay whan I remembre on this matere
Seint Nicholas stant evere in my presence   80
For he so yong to Crist dide reverence.

This litel child his litel book lernynge
As he sat in the scole at his prymer
He *Alma redemptoris* herde synge
As children lerned hir Antiphoner;   85
And as he dorste he drow hym ner and ner
And herkned ay the wordes and the note
Til he the firste vers koude al by rote.

89 'He had no idea what this Latin was about'.
91 'But one day he begged his friend'.
92 *T'expounden* to explain or translate.
93 *in usage* in use. The child is probably asking what the religious
purpose of the anthem is, or, perhaps, why it is being rehearsed for
a service at this time.
94 *construen* construe, translate, interpret.
95 *knowes* knees.
98 *of* for, (in honour) of.
blisful blessed.
free generous, bountiful.
99 *salue* greet.
100 *socour* succour, comfort.
102 'I learn singing, I know but little (Latin) grammar'.
105 *certes* certainly.
do my diligence try diligently.
106 *konne* know.
107 *for my prymer* for (not having done) my primer.
shent punished.
113 *acordyng with the note* following the notes or melody correctly.
116 *entente* desire, intention.
119 *murily* merrily.
wolde used . . . to.
120 *evere mo* continually.
121-2 i.e. the sweetness of Christ's mother has . . .
123 *stynte of syngyng* cease from singing.
by on.

Noght wiste he what this Latyn was to seye
For he so yong and tendre was of age; 90
But on a day his felawe gan he preye
T'expounden hym this song in his langage
Or telle hym why this song was in usage;
This preyde he hym to construen and declare
Ful ofte tyme upon his knowes bare. 95

His felawe which that elder was than he
Answerde hym thus: "This song, I have herd seye,
Was maked of oure blisful lady free
Hire to salue and eek hire for to preye
To been oure help and socour whan we deye. 100
I kan namoore expounde in this matere:
I lerne song, I kan but smal grammere."

"And is this song maked in reverence
Of Cristes moder?" seyde this innocent.
"Now certes I wol do my diligence 105
To konne it al er Cristemasse be went;
Thogh that I for my prymer shal be shent
And shal be beten thries in an houre
I wol it konne oure lady for to honoure!"

His felawe taughte hym homward pryvely 110
Fro day to day til he koude it by rote,
And thanne he song it wel and boldely
Fro word to word acordyng with the note;
Twyes a day it passed thurgn his throte,
To scoleward and homward whan he wente: 115
On Cristes moder set was his entente.

As I have seyd, thurgh out the jewerye
This litel child as he cam to and fro
Ful murily wolde he synge and crye
O Alma redemptoris evere mo: 120
The swetenesse his herte perced so
Of Cristes moder that to hire to preye
He kan nat stynte of syngyng by the weye.

124 *foo* foe.

126 *Up swal* swelled up; rose up in anger.

127 *honest* honourable.

128 *as hym lest* lit. as it pleases him; i.e. as he pleases.

129 *In youre despit* in spite of you, in scorn of you.

swich sentence* such matter.

130 'As is contrary to the honour or respect (due to) our law'.

132 *chace* drive, hunt.

134 *privee* secret.

135 *gan forby for to pace* was passing by.

136 *hente* seized.

138 *wardrobe* a 14th century euphemism, like the 20th century 'lavatory'.

139 *entraille* bowels.

140 'O cursed race of entirely new Herods'; cf. the Massacre of the Holy Innocents, St. Matthew ii, 16: 'Then Herod, perceiving that he was deluded by the wise men, was exceeding angry; and sending killed all the men children that were in Bethlehem and in all the borders thereof, from two years old and under, according to the time which he had diligently inquired of the wise men'.

142 *Mordre wol out* 'murder will out'; a proverb.

143 'And especially where the honour of God shall increase'.

145 *souded* dedicated, vowed.

virginitee. The word applies to chastity in either sex.

146 *maystow* a contraction of 'mayest thou'.

evere in oon always, for ever.

148-9 See Revelation xiv, 3-5: 'And they sung as it were a new canticle, before the throne . . . and no man could say the canticle, but those hundred forty-four thousand who were purchased from the earth.

These are they who were not defiled with women; for they are virgins. These follow the Lamb whithersoever he goeth. These were purchased from among men, the first-fruits to God and to the Lamb.

And in their mouth there was found no lie; for they are without spot before the throne of God'.

151 *That* (are those) who. Another way of coping with the confused syntax is to omit the second   in line 149.

flesshly carnally, in the nesh.

155 'With face pale from fear and anxious thought'.

157 *she gan so fer espie* she did make out this much.

101

Oure firste foo, the serpent Sathanas
That hath in Jewes herte his waspes nest,   125
Up swal and seyde, "O Hebrayk peple allas!
Is this to yow a thyng that is honest,
That swich a boy shal walken as hym lest
In youre despit and synge of swich sentence
Which is agayns oure lawes reverence?"   130

Fro thennes forth the Jewes han conspired
This innocent out of this world to chace:
An homycide therto han they hired
That in an aleye hadde a privee place,
And as the child gan forby for to pace   135
This cursed Jew hym hente and heeld hym faste
And kitte his throte and in a pit hym caste.

I seye that in a wardrobe they hym threwe
Wheras thise Jewes purgen hir entraille.
O cursed folk of Herodes al newe!   140
What may youre yvel entente yow availle?
Mordre wol out! certeyn, it wol nat faille!
And namely ther as th'onour of God shal sprede,
The blood out crieth on youre cursed dede.

O martir souded to viginitee!   145
Now maystow syngen folwyng evere in oon
The white lamb celestial — quod she —
Of which the grete evaungelist, Seint John
In Pathmos wroot, which seith that they that gon
Biforn this lamb and synge a song al newe   150
That nevere flesshly, wommen they ne knewe.

This poure wydwe awaiteth al that nyght
After hir litel child but he cam noght;
For which as soone as it was dayes lyght
With face pale of drede and bisy thoght   155
She hath at scole and ellis where hym soght
Til finally she gan so fer espie
That he last seyn was in the jewerie.

164 *wroghte* did.
166 *frayneth* enquires.
168 *wente oght forby* (had) passed by at all.
170 *Yaf in hir thought* i.e. put (it) into her mind.
   inwith within.
   space time.
172 'Nearby (the place) where he had been thrown into a pit'.
173 *parfournest* declarest.
174 *lo here thy myght* behold here (in this case) thy might.
175 *emeraude* emerald.
177 *Ther* where.
   ykorven cut.
   lay upright lay on his back, face upwards.
181 *coomen* came (plural).
182 *provost* chief magistrate.
183 *anon* immediately.
184 *herieth* praises.
186 *leet he bynde* he caused to be bound.
190 *nexte* 'nighest', nearest.
192 *Unnethe* scarcely, with difficulty.
193 *This newe Rachel* this second Rachel. St. Matthew's account of
the Massacre of the Innocents, concludes with these words (ii, 17-18):
'Then was fulfilled that which was spoken by the prophet Jeremias,
saying: A voice in Rama was heard, lamentation and great mourning;
Rachel bewailing her children and would not be comforted, because
they are not'. Rachel is thus seen as an archetypal figure of bereaved
motherhood.

With modres pitee in hir brest enclosed
She goth as she were half out of hir mynde   160
To every place wher she hath supposed
By liklyhede hir litel child to fynde;
And evere on Cristes moder meke and kynde
She cryde, and at the laste thus she wroghte:
Among the cursed Jewes she hym soghte.   165

She frayneth and she preyeth pitously
To every Jew that dwelte in thilke place
To telle hire if hir child wente oght forby.
They seyde nay, but Jesu of his grace
Yaf in hir thought inwith a litel space   170
That in that place after hir sone she cryde
Wher he was casten in a pit bisyde.

O grete God that parfournest thy laude
By mouth of innocentz, lo here thy myght!
This gemme of chastitee, this emeraude   175
And eek of martirdom the ruby bright,
Ther he with throte ykorven lay upright
He *Alma redemptoris* gan to synge
So loude that al the place gan to rynge.

The cristen folk that thurgh the strete wente   180
In coomen for to wondre upon this thyng
And hastily they for the provost sente;
He cam anon withouten tariyng
And herieth Crist that is of hevene kyng
And eek his moder, honour of mankynde;   185
And after that the Jewes leet he bynde.

This child with pitous lamentacioun
Up taken was, syngynge his song alway,
And with honour of greet processioun
They carien hym unto the nexte abbay.   190
His moder swownyng by his beere lay:
Unnethe myghte the peple that was there
This newe Rachel bryngen fro his beere.

194 *torment* torture.
194-7 'This provost caused each one of these Jews who knew of this murder to die by torture and by a shameful death, and that immediately: he would not tolerate such wickedness'.
198 'Evil will get what evil deserves'.
199 'Therefore he caused them to be drawn by wild horses'.
200 *heng* hanged.
by in accordance with.
201 *lyth* lieth.
202 *chief auter* the main altar.
203 *covent* company of monks.
204 *Han sped hem* have made haste.
206 *spreynd* sprinkled.
210 *conjure* to beseech, entreat, make a solemn appeal to.
211 *halsen* entreat.
212 *In vertu of* by the power of.
214 *Sith that* since.
to my semynge as it seems to me.
216 *as by wey of kynde* according to the law of nature.
219 *Wol* desires.
221 *loude and clere* loudly and clearly.
223 *after my konnynge* according to my skill.
224 *forlete* give up.
226 *verraily* truly, faithfully.
228 *a greyn.* The word has been variously interpreted as meaning a grain of wheat, a pearl, and even a rosary bead. Robinson prefers the 'pearl' interpretation since the pearl was a symbol of the Virgin. Boyd H. Hill has suggested that Chaucer may be referring to the 'grain' that was thought to reside in the heart, as the home of the spirit, the point of connection between body and soul. Since the child's neck was cut to the bone, this connecting link needed to be re-established, at least between his soul and voice, for the miracle to occur.

With torment and with shameful deth echon
This provost dooth thise Jewes for to sterve   195
That of this mordre wiste, and that anon:
He nolde no swich cursednesse observe.
Yvel shal have that yvel wol deserve:
Ther fore with wilde hors he dide hem drawe
And after that he heng hem by the lawe.   200

Upon this beere ay lyth this innocent
Biforn the chief auter whil the masse laste;
And after that the abbot with his covent
Han sped hem for to buryen hym ful faste
And whan they holy water on hym caste   205
Yet spak this child whan spreynd was holy water
And song *O Alma redemptoris mater!*

This abbot which that was an holy man
As monkes ben, or ellis oghten be,
This yonge child to conjure he bigan   210
And seyde, "O deere child I halsen thee
In vertu of the holy Trinitee
Tel me what is thy cause for to synge
Sith that thy throte is kit to my semynge?"

"My throte is kit unto my nekke boon,"   215
Seyde this child, "and as by wey of kynde
I sholde have dyed, ye longe tyme agoon.
But Jesu Crist as ye in bokes fynde
Wol that his glorie laste and be in mynde,
And for the worship of his moder deere   220
Yet may I synge *O Alma* loude and clere.

"This welle of mercy, Cristes moder swete
I loved alwey as after my konnynge,
And whan that I my lyf sholde forlete
To me she cam and bad me for to synge   225
This antheme verraily in my deiynge
As ye han herd, and whan that I hadde songe
Me thoughte she leyde a greyn upon my tonge.

233 *now* at that moment.
235 *agast* afraid.
237 *out caughte* pulled out.
238 *softely* quietly, peacefully.
241 *gruf* face downwards; cf. Mod. E. 'grovel'.
     plat flat.
244 *herying* praising.
245 'And after that, they rise and hage gone forth'.
247 *cleere* bright.
249 'God grant us to meet where he is now'.
250 *Hugh of Lyncoln.* A 13th century chronicle reports that an eight-year-old child named Hugh was tortured and crucified by Jews in Lincoln in 1255. Saint Hugh, as he was known, was buried in Lincoln cathedral; his tomb became a place of pilgrimage, and miracles were reported to have occurred there.
251 *With* by.
     notable well-known.
252 Just over a century in fact; cf. 250n. above.
253 *unstable* fickle, weak-willed.
254 *merciable* merciful.
255 *multiplie* may multiply (subjunctive).

107

"Wher fore I synge, and synge moot certeyn
In honour of that blisful mayden free   230
Til fro my tonge of taken is the greyn;
And after that thus seyde she to me,
'My litel child now wol I fecche thee
Whan that the greyn is fro thy tonge ytake.
Be nat agast, I wol thee nat forsake'."   235

This holy monk, this abbot hym mene I,
His tonge out caughte and took awey the greyn
And he yaf up the goost ful softely.
And whan this abbot hadde this wonder seyn
Hise salte teerys trikled doun as reyn   240
And gruf he fil al plat upon the grounde
And stille he lay as he hadde been ybounde.

The covent eek lay on the pavement
Wepynge and herying Cristes moder deere;
And after that they ryse and forth been went   245
And toke awey this martir from his beere
And in a toumbe of marbilstones cleere
Enclosen they this litel body swete.
Ther he is now, God leve us for to meete!

O yonge Hugh of Lyncoln slayn also   250
With cursed Jewes, as it is notable
For it is but a litel while ago,
Preye eek for us we synful folk unstable,
That of his mercy God so merciable
On us his grete mercy multiplie   255
For reverence of his moder Marie.
    Amen.

Heere is ended the Prioresses Tale.

108

55 *widwe* widow.

som del stape in age somewhat stepped, or advanced in age.
56 *narwe* narrow, i.e. confined.
61 *hire catel and hire rente* her chattels or property and her income.
62 *housbondrye* economical management.
63 *She foond hir self* she supplied herself; cf. Mod. E. 'all found'.
65 *kyn* kine, i.e. cows.

Malle Moll, a common name for a sheep.
66 *hire bour . . . hire halle* an ironic use of the terms applied to the inner sleeping apartments and great hall of a large house. Such a 'narwe cotage' would probably have consisted of only one room, perhaps with a loft over it.

hERE BIGynneth the nonnes preestes tale of the cok and hen, chauntecleer and pertelote

A poore widwe som del stape in age   55
Was whilom dwellyng in a narwe cotage
Biside a grove, stondyng in a dale.
This widwe of which I telle yow my tale,
Syn thilke day that she was last a wyf,
In pacience ladde a ful symple lyf,   60
For litel was hire catel and hire rente;
By housbondrye of swich as God hire sente
She foond hir self and eek hire doghtren two.
Thre large sowes hadde she, and namo,
Thre kyn and eek a sheep that highte Malle.   65
Ful sooty was hire bour and eek hire halle

67 *sklendre* small, frugal.
68 *never a deel* never a jot. For this line cf. the Franklin's tastes, GP353-4.
70 *acordant to hir cote* in keeping with her cottage.
71 *Repleccioun* repletion, a medical term for eating and drinking to excess.
72 *Attempree* temperate, moderate.
73 *hertes suffisaunce* 'heart's satisfaction, i.e. contentment.
74 *lette hire no thyng* did nothing to prevent her.
75 *shente* harmed, injured. Apoplexy was thought to result from overeating.
77 *bord* table.
78 *in which she foond no lak* probably 'which she found quite sufficient', rather than 'of which she had plenty'; cf. 67 above.
79 *Seynd bacoun* usually translated as 'singed bacon', but perhaps meaning 'broiled'. *ey* egg.
80 *a maner deye* a kind of dairy woman, one whose province was poultry and pigs, as well as milk, butter and cheese.
84 *nas* (there) was not.
85 *orgon* regularly a plural form, in M.E.; consequently the verb 'gon' is in the plural.
86 *massedayes* days when the Mass was sung.
87 *sikerer* surer, more reliable.
logge lodge or resting place. Throughout the tale, everything connected with the house is described with mock-heroic grandeur.
88 *abbey orlogge* the main clock of an abbey. Such clocks were of great importance, since they marked not only the hours of the day but also the canonical hours or periods of monastic devotion. Many of them were magnificently elaborate and indicated the position of the Zodiacal signs and various heavenly bodies as well as the time.
89-90 *By nature* from the instinct natural to him as a cock.
The equinoctial or celestial equator ascended fifteen degrees above the horizon every hour, completing the full revolution around the earth each day. Chauntecleer knew by instinct just where the heavens should be at every hour, viewed from his particular spot on the earth, and crowed on the hour.
92 *that it myghte nat been amended* i.e. in a way that brooked no denial.
93ff. These colours have been variously taken to signify the Golden Spangled Hamburg fowl, the arms of Bolingbroke, and the clergy.
94 *batailled* as in battlements.
95 *byle* bill.
96 *toon* toes.
98 *burned* burnished, brilliant.
99 *in his governaunce* under his control. The irony of this statement will become apparent.
103 *hewed* coloured; cf. 'hue'.
105 *Curteys** courteous. The language from line 99 is the formal language of courtly love and Pertelote here displays all the traditional qualities of the courtly lady. 'Discreet and debonaire' indicates a nicely managed, decorous gaiety of behaviour.
106 *bar* behaved.

111

In which she eet ful many a sklendre meel;
Of poynaunt sauce hir neded never a deel,
No deyntee morsel passed thurgh hir throte;
Hir diete was acordant to hir cote.   70
Repleccioun ne made hire nevere syk,
Attempree diete was al hir phisyk
And exercise and hertes suffisaunce.
The goute lette hire no thyng for to daunce,
N'apoplexie shente nat hir heed: 75
No wyn ne drank she, neither whit ne reed;
Hir bord was served moost with whit and blak,
Milk and broun breed, in which she foond no lak,
Seynd bacoun and som tyme an ey or tweye,
For she was, as it were, a maner deye.   80
   A yeerd she hadde enclosed al aboute
With stikkes and a drye dych withoute,
In whiche she hadde a cok hight Chauntecleer.
In al the land, of crowyng nas his peer:
His voys was murier than the murie orgon   85
On massedayes that in the chirche gon;
Wel sikerer was his crowyng in his logge
Than is a clokke or an abbey orlogge.
By nature he knew ech ascencioun
Of the equinoxial in thilke town,   90
For whan degrees fiftene were ascended,
Thanne crew he, that it myghte nat been amended.
His comb was redder than the fyn coral
And batailled as it were a castel wal;
His byle was blak and as the jeet it shoon;   95
Lyk asure were his legges and his toon;
Hise nayles whitter than the lylye flour,
And lyk the burned gold was his colour.
This gentil cok hadde in his governaunce
Sevene hennes for to doon al his plesaunce,   100
Whiche were hise sustres and his paramours
And wonder lyk to hym as of colours;
Of whiche the faireste hewed on hir throte
Was cleped faire damoysele Pertelote.
Curteys she was, discreet and debonaire   105
And compaignable and bar hir self so faire

107 *seven nyght oold.* The age of seven years was considered the end of infancy; cf. PrT69. In this detail, Pertelote recalls Leece (Gladness), the mistress of Deduiz (Pleasure) in *Le Roman de la Rose.* 832-5: 'Gladness . . . the fine singer who from her seventh year had given him all her love'.

108 *in hoold* in her possession.

109 *loken in every lith* locked in every limb.

113 '*My lief is faren in londe*' probably *My love is far away,* a popular song. Skeat has printed the following stanza from Trin. Coll. Camb. MS. R.3.19:

My lefe ys faren in lond;
Allas! why ys she so?
And I am so sore bound
I may not com her to.
She hath my hert in hold
Where ever she ryde or go,
With trewlove a thousand-fold.

116 *a dawenynge* a dawning, i.e. 'early one morning'.

121 *drecched* vexed, annoyed.

125 *verray* true, i.e. good, sound.

127 *take it nat agrief* take it not in grief, i.e. do not be annoyed by it.

128 *me mette* an impersonal construction, lit. (it) dreamed to me.

meschief mischief, directed against Chauntecleer, i.e. danger.

130 *swevene* dream.

recche aright interpret favourably, i.e. bring to a good issue.

134-5 *hound* dog.

maad areest Upon i.e. seized.

137 *erys* ears.

138 *herys* hairs.

140 *Yet* still.

142 *Avoy!* cf. 'Avaunt!'

hertelees lacking courage; cf. the phrase 'take heart'.

146 *what so* whatever.

113

Syn thilke day that she was seven nyght oold,
That trewely she hath the herte in hoold
Of Chauntecleer, loken in every lith;
He loved hire so that wel was hym ther with.   110
But swich a joye was it to here hem synge,
Whan that the brighte sonne gan to sprynge,
In swete acord, "My lief is faren in londe!"
For thilke tyme, as I have understonde,
Beestes and briddes koude speke and synge.   115
    And so bifel that in a dawenynge,
As Chauntecleer among his wyves alle
Sat on his perche that was in the halle,
And next hym sat this faire Pertelote,
This Chauntecleer gan gronen in his throte   120
As man that in his dreem is drecched soore;
And whan that Pertelote thus herde hym rore,
She was agast and seyde, "Herte deere,
What eyleth yow to grone in this manere?
Ye ben a verray slepere; fy, for shame!"   125
    And he answerde and seyde thus: "Madame,
I pray yow that ye take it nat agrief.
By God, me mette I was in swich meschief
Right now, that yet myn herte is soore afright.
Now God," quod he, "my swevene recche aright   130
And kepe my body out of foul prisoun!
Me mette how that I romed up and doun
Withinne oure yeerd, wher as I say a beest
Was lyk an hound and wolde han maad areest
Upon my body and han had me ded.   135
His colour was bitwixe yelow and red
And tipped was his tayl and bothe his erys
With blak, unlik the remenaunt of his herys;
His snowte smal, with glowyng eyen tweye.
Yet of his look for feere almoost I deye;   140
This caused me my gronyng, doutelees."
    "Avoy!" quod she, "fy on you, hertelees!
Allas!" quod she, "for, by that God above,
Now han ye lost myn herte and al my love:
I kan nat love a coward, by my feith!   145
For certes, what so any womman seith,
We alle desiren, if it myghte be,

114

148 *hardy, wise and free* bold, of good management or judgement and generous. This whole description of the ideal husband is the conventional image of the courtly lover, matching the previous description of Pertelote.

149 *secree* discreet (in the conduct of love).

150 *tool* weapon.

151 *avauntour* boaster (of favours received).

152 *dorste* durst, dared.

154 *a berd* a beard.

156 *vanitee.* The word has rather the meaning of 'unimportant trifles and fancies' than the commoner modern meaning.

157 *engendren of* are engendered by. Mediaeval writing on the subject of dreams was copious. It distinguished between the dream engendered by disorders of the complexion and humours (see Explanatory Notes—Medicine), which was of no prophetic value, and those genuine prophetic dreams vouched for by the Bible and by popular histories like those Chauntecleer subsequently invokes. If Chauntecleer's dreams were of the first type, Pertelote's advice would be sound mediaeval doctrine.

158 *fume* vapour, thought to permeate the brain from excessive or indiscreet eating or drinking.

complexions. As the next line states, a person's complexion was the result of an imbalance in the four humours.

160 *met* dreamed.

164 *arwes* arrows.

lemes flames.

to-nyght this night (just passed).

165 *that they wol hem byte* i.e. the dreamers dread that they will be bitten.

166 *contek* conflict.

whelpes pups or cubs.

lyte little.

169 *beres or boles* bears or bulls.

172 'That causes many a man much distress in sleep'.

174-5 *Catoun* Cato, to whom was attributed a popular collection of moral sayings, one of which is *'somnia ne cures'*, 'pay no heed to dreams'.

178 *Up* on.

181 *for* so that.

tarye tarry, delay.

184 *heele* recovery, health.

prow profit, benefit.

186 *by kynde* by nature.

To han housbondes hardy, wise and free
And secree and no nygard ne no fool,
Ne hym that is agast of every tool,   150
Ne noon avauntour, by that God above!
How dorste ye seyn, for shame, unto youre love
That any thyng myghte make yow aferd?
Have ye no mannes herte, and han a berd?
Allas! and konne ye ben agast of swevenys?   155
No thyng, God woot, but vanitee in sweven is.
Swevenes engendren of replexions
And ofte of fume and of complexions
Whan humours ben to habundant in a wight.
    Certes this dreem which ye han met to-nyght,   160
Comth of the grete superfluitee
Of youre rede colera, pardee,
Which causeth folk to dreden in hir dremes
Of arwes and of fyr with rede lemes,
Of rede beestes, that they wol hem byte,   165
Of contek and of whelpes grete and lyte;
Right as the humour of malencolie
Causeth ful many a man in sleep to crie
For fere of blake beres or boles blake
Or ellis blake develes wol hem take.   170
Of othere humours koude I telle also
That werken many a man in sleep ful wo,
But I wol passe as lightly as I kan.
    Lo Catoun, which that was so wys a man,
Seyde he nat thus, 'Ne do no fors of dremes?'   175
    Now sire," quod she, "whan we fle fro the bemes,
For Goddes love, as taak som laxatyf.
Up peril of my soule and of my lyf,
I conseille yow the beste, I wol nat lye,
That bothe of colere and of malencolye   180
Ye purge yow; and for ye shal nat tarye,
Thogh in this town is noon apothecarye,
I shal my self to herbes techen yow
That shul ben for youre heele and for youre prow;
And in oure yeerd tho herbes shal I fynde   185
The whiche han of hire propretee by kynde
To purge yow bynethe and eek above.
Foryet nat this, for Goddes owene love!

189 See Explanatory Notes—Medicine.
190-1 'Beware that the sun in his ascension does not find you full . . .'
193 *a fevere terciane* tertian fever.
194 *bane* destruction, cause of death.
195 It was good medical doctrine that 'digestyves', medicines to disperse or absorb the excess humour, should precede the purgatives. One authority even discusses earth worms as treatment for tertian fever.
197-200 'Of spurge-laurel, centaury, fumitory,
     Or else of hellebore that groweth there,
     Of caper-spurge or of buck-thorn (once known as goat-tree) berries,
     Of herb-ivy'.
200 *ther merye is* probably 'where it is pleasant', i.e. in the garden.
204 *graunt mercy* cf. grammercy, meaning 'thank you'.
205 *as touchyng* on the matter of.
209 We would say 'of more authority'.
210 *so mote I thee* as I hope to thrive.
211 *of this sentence** i.e. of the saying of Cato.
217 *The verray preeve* the actual proof or demonstration.
218-9 The story is related both by Cicero and Valerius Maximus, though Chaucer probably read it at second hand.
221 *happed so* it so happened.
223 *so streit of herbergage* so restricted as to lodgings.
224 *o* one, a.
225 *ylogged* lodged.
227 *departen* separate, part (company).
229 *as it wolde falle* 'just as it came'.

Ye ben ful coleryk of complexioun;
Ware the sonne in his ascencioun   190
Ne fynde yow nat replet of humours hote.
And if it do, I dar wel leye a grote
That ye shul have a fevere terciane
Or an agu that may be youre bane.
A day or two ye shul have digestyves   195
Of wormes er ye take youre laxatyves
Of lauriol, centaure and fumetere,
Or ellis of ellebor that groweth there,
Of katapuce, or of gaitrys beryis,
Of herbe yve, growyng in oure yerd ther merye is; 200
Pekke hem up right as they growe and ete hem in.
Be myrie, housbonde, for youre fader kyn!
Dredeth no dreem, I kan sey yow namoore."
      "Madame," quod he, "graunt mercy of youre loore.
But natheless, as touchyng daun Catoun,   205
That hath of wysdom swich a greet renoun,
Thogh that he bad no dremes for to drede,
By God, men may in olde bookes rede
Of many a man moore of auctoritee
Than evere Catoun was, so mote I thee,   210
That al the revers seyn of this sentence,
And han wel founden by experience
That dremes ben significaciouns
As wel of joye as of tribulaciouns
That folk enduren in this lyf present.   215
Ther nedeth make of this noon argument;
The verray preeve sheweth it in dede.
      Oon of the gretteste auctour that men rede
Seith thus: that whilom two felawes wente
On pilgrymage, in a ful good entente;   220
And happed so, they coomen in a toun
Wher as ther was swich congregacioun
Of peple, and eek so streit of herbergage,
That they ne founde as muche as o cotage
In which they bothe myghte ylogged be.   225
Wher fore they mosten of necessitee,
As for that nyght, departen compaignye;
And ech of hem gooth to his hostelrye,
And took his loggyng as it wolde falle.

230 *That oon* the one.
231 *Fer in a yeerd* i.e. away at the end of a yard.
233 *aventure* chance.
236 *This man* as opposed to 'that oon' above.
239 *ther* where.
242 *abrayde* started up.
244 *took of this no keep* paid no attention to this.
248 *slawe* slain.
250 *morwe tyde* morning; cf. eventide.
253 *pryvely* secretly.
254 *Do . . . aresten* cause . . . to stop.
260 *in* lodging place, not necessarily an inn.
262 *After* we would say 'for'.
268 *lette* delay.

That oon of hem was logged in a stalle,   230
Fer in a yeerd, with oxen of the plow;
That oother man was logged wel ynow
As was his aventure or his fortune
That us governeth alle as in commune.
    And so bifel that, longe er it were day,   235
This man mette in his bed, ther as he lay,
How that his felawe gan upon hym calle,
And seyde, 'Allas! for in an oxes stalle
This nyght I shal be mordred ther I lye.
Now help me, deere brother, or I dye.   240
In alle haste com to me!' he sayde.
    This man out of his sleep for feere abrayde;
But whan that he was wakned of his sleep,
He turned hym and took of this no keep.
Hym thoughte his dreem nas but a vanitee.   245
Thus twies in his slepyng dremed he;
And atte thridde tyme yet his felawe
Cam, as hym thoughte, and seyde, 'I am now slawe.
Bihoold my blody woundes depe and wyde!
Arys up erly in the morwe tyde,   250
And at the west gate of the town,' quod he,
'A carte ful of donge ther shaltow se,
In which my body is hid ful pryvely;
Do thilke carte aresten boldely.
My gold caused my mordre, sooth to sayn.'   255
And tolde hym every poynt how he was slayn,
With a ful pitous face, pale of hewe.
And truste wel, his dreem he foond ful trewe,
For on the morwe as soone as it was day,
To his felawes in he took the way;   260
And whan that he cam to this oxes stalle,
After his felawe he bigan to calle.
    The hostiler answerde hym anon
And seyde, 'Sire, your felawe is agon.
As soone as day he wente out of the toun.'   265
    This man gan fallen in suspecioun,
Remembrynge on hise dremes that he mette,
And forth he gooth — no lenger wolde he lette —
Unto the west gate of the town, and fond
A dong-carte, went as it were to donge lond,   270

120

271 *arrayed* arranged, appointed; i.e. it looked the same.
wise manner.
272 *devyse* describe.
273 *hardy* bold.
274 *felonye* crime, wickedness.
276 *gapyng upright* on his back with his mouth open.
277 *I crye out on* I call upon.
ministres officers.
283 *al newe* newly.
284 *blisful* blessed.
285 *biwreyest* betrayest, i.e. reveals.
286 *Mordre wol out* a proverb; cf. PrT142.
287 *wlatsom* loathsome.
abhomynable. The word was mistakenly thought to be derived from the Latin *ab homine* 'contrary to man' — hence the meaning here is 'unnatural' as well as 'horrible'.
289 *heled* concealed.
293 *pyned* tortured.
294 *engyned* i.e. subjected to the engines of torture.
297 *to drede* to be feared.
298-9 See 218-9n. above.
300 *I gabbe nat* 'I'm not just talking'.
305 *myrie* pleasantly.
an haven syde i.e. on one side of a secure harbour.
306 *agayn the even tyde* towards evening.
307 *as hem leste* lit. as it liked them, i.e. as they wished.
309 *casten* planned or prepared.
310 *that o man* the one man.
311 *That oon* the one, i.e. the same man as in the previous line.

That was arrayed in the same wise
As ye han herd the dede man devyse.
And with an hardy herte he gan to crye
Vengeaunce and justice of this felonye.
'My felawe mordred is this same nyght,   275
And in this cart heere he lyth gapyng upright.
I crye oute on the ministres,' quod he,
'That sholden kepe and reulen this citee.
Harrow! allas! heere lyth my felawe slayn!'
What sholde I moore unto this tale sayn?   280
The peple out sterte and caste the cart to grounde
And in the myddel of the dong they founde
The dede man, that mordred was al newe.
   O blisful God that art so just and trewe,
Lo, how that thow biwreyest mordre alway!   285
Mordre wol out, that se we day by day.
Mordre is so wlatsom and abhomynable
To God that is so just and resonable,
That he ne wol nat suffre it heled be,
Though it abyde a yeer, or two, or thre.   290
Mordre wol out, this is my conclusioun.
And right anon, ministres of that toun
Han hent the cartere and so soore hym pyned,
And eek the hostiler so soore engyned,
That they biknewe hir wikkednesse anon,   295
And were anhanged by the nekke bon.
Heere may men seen that dremes ben to drede.
   And certes in the same book I rede,
Right in the nexte chapitre after this —
I gabbe nat, so have I joye or blis —   300
Two men that wolde han passed over see
For certeyn cause into a fer contree,
If that the wynd ne hadde ben contrarie
That made hem in a citee for to tarie
That stood ful myrie upon an haven syde;   305
But on a day, agayn the even tyde,
The wynd gan chaunge and blew right as hem leste.
Jolif and glad they wente unto hir reste
And casten hem ful erly for to saille.
   But to that o man fil a greet mervaille: 310
That oon of hem, in slepyng as he lay,

122

312 *agayn the day* towards the daytime.
315 *wende* go.
316 *dreynt* drowned.
318 *to lette* to abandon.
323 *my thynges* my affairs, my business.
325 This line is an echo of the first couplet of *Le Roman de la Rose*
(Chaucer's translation):
> Many men seyn that in sweveninges
> Ther nis but fables and lesinges.

japes jokes.
326 Owls and apes were commonly figures of absurdity.
327 *maze* a delusive fancy.
330 *forslewthen* waste by sloth.

tyde time.
331 *it reweth me* it makes me sorry.
334 'I know not why, nor what mischance harmed it . . .'
335 *casuelly* accidentally.
340 *maystow leere* may you learn.
341 *recchelees* careless, unheeding.
342 *sey* tell.
343 *ful soore is for to drede* is to be dreaded most sorely.
344 Kenelm succeeded to the throne of Mercia in 821 at the age of
seven. He was murdered on the order of his aunt, and was subsequently
made a Saint. A little before his death he dreamed he climbed a tree,
which was then cut down by one of his best friends, whereupon he
flew off to heaven as a bird.
348 *in his avysioun he say* in his vision or dream he saw.
349 *norice* nurse.
350-1 *to kepe hym wel For traysoun* to guard himself well for fear
of treason.
352 *litel tale hath he told* he took little notice. 'Tale' in this sense
means 'reckoning', 'tally'.

Hym mette a wonder dreem agayn the day.
Hym thoughte a man stood by his beddes syde
And hym commanded that he sholde abyde,
And seyde hym thus: 'If thow tomorwe wende,   315
Thow shalt be dreynt; my tale is at an ende.'
     He wook and tolde his felawe what he mette
And preyde hym his viage to lette;
As for that day, he preyed hym to abyde.
     His felawe, that lay by his beddes syde,   320
Gan for to laughe and scorned hym ful faste.
'No dreem,' quod he, 'may so myn herte agaste
That I wol lette for to do my thynges.
I sette nat a straw by thy dremynges,
For swevenes ben but vanytees and japes.   325
Men dreme al day of owles and of apes
And of many a maze therwithal;
Men dreme of thyng that nevere was ne shal.
But sith I see that thow wolt here abyde
And thus forslewthen wilfully thy tyde,   330
God woot it reweth me, and have good day!'
And thus he took his leve and wente his way.
But er that he hadde half his cours yseyled,
Noot I nat why, ne what meschaunce it eyled,
But casuelly the shippes botme rente,   335
And ship and man under the water wente
In sighte of othere shippes it bisyde,
That with hem seyled at the same tyde.
And ther fore, faire Pertelote so deere,
By swiche ensamples olde maystow leere   340
That no man sholde ben to recchelees
Of dremes; for I sey thee, doutelees,
That many a dreem ful soore is for to drede.
     Lo, in the lyf of Seint Kenelm I rede,
That was Kenulphus sone, the noble kyng   345
Of Mercenrike, how Kenelm mette a thyng.
A lite er he was mordred, on a day,
His mordre in his avysioun he say.
His norice hym expowned every del
His swevene and bad hym for to kepe hym wel   350
For traysoun; but he nas but seven yeer old,
And ther fore litel tale hath he told

354 *I hadde levere* I had rather.

357 *Macrobeus*. In about 400 A.D., Macrobius edited, with a commentary, the *Somnium Scipionis* (The Dream of Scipio) by Cicero. In this edition the work was popular throughout the Middle Ages.

359 *Affermeth* speaks in favour of, declares the importance of.

362 Daniel vii. Of his vision of the four kingdoms of the earth and of anti-christ, Daniel wrote: 'I, Daniel, was much troubled with my thoughts and my countenance was changed in me: but I kept the word in my heart'.

364 See Genesis xxxvii, xl, xli, for Joseph's dream of his future eminence as ruler over all Egypt under Pharoah, and for his interpretations of Pharoah's dreams.

365 *Wher* whether.

366 *falle* befall.

370 *actes* records.

remes realms.

372 *Cresus* Croesus, king of Lydia, 560-546 B.C. The last tragedy related in the Monk's Tale is of Croesus who dreamed that he was in a tree being washed by Jupiter and dried on a towel by Phoebus. His daughter interpreted the dream correctly as a prediction of his being hung from a gallows, washed by rain and dried by the sun.

375 This dream of Andromache is not found in the original account of Hector's final defeat at the hands of Achilles; it is an addition to the legends of Troy.

378 *lorn* lost.

388 'I set no store by laxatives'.

389 *venymes* poisonous substances.

390 *deffie* repudiate, reject.

391 *stynte* stop.

392 *so have I blis* as I hope for bliss (i.e. heaven).

393 *o* one.

large grace bountiful favour.

Of any dreem, so holy was his herte.
By God! I hadde levere than my sherte
That ye hadde rad his legende, as have I.   355
Dame Pertelote, I sey yow trewely,
Macrobeus, that writ the avysioun
In Affrike of the worthy Cipioun,
Affermeth dremes, and seith that they been
Warnynge of thynges that men after seen.   360
    And forther moore, I pray yow, looketh wel
In the olde testament, of Danyel,
If he heeld dremes any vanitee.
Rede eek of Joseph and ther shul ye see
Wher dremes be som tyme — I sey nat alle —   365
Warnynge of thynges that shul after falle.
    Looke of Egipte the kyng, daun Pharao,
His bakere and his butiller also,
Wher they ne felte noon effect in dremes.
Whoso wol seke actes of sondry remes   370
May rede of dremes many a wonder thyng.
    Lo Cresus, which that was of Lyde kyng,
Mette he nat that he sat upon a tree,
Which signified he sholde anhanged be?
    Lo heere Andromacha, Ectores wyf,   375
That day that Ector sholde lese his lyf,
She dremed on the same nyght biforn
How that the lyf of Ector sholde be lorn,
If thilke day he wente into bataille.
She warned hym, but it myghte nat availle;   380
He wente for to fighte natheles,
But he was slayn anon of Achilles.
But thilke tale is al to long to telle,
And eek it is ny day, I may nat dwelle.
Shortly I seye, as for conclusioun,   385
That I shal han of this avisioun
Adversitee, and I seye forther moore
That I ne telle of laxatyves no stoor,
For they ben venymes, I woot it wel;
I hem deffie, I love hem never a del!   390
    Now let us speke of myrthe and stynte al this.
Madame Pertelote, so have I blis,
Of o thyng God hath sent me large grace;

126

395 *eyen* eyes.
397-8 *siker* sure. The meaning of this couplet is probably: 'For as surely as *In the beginning* . . . (the opening words of St. John's Gospel), woman is man's ruin'. The latter sentiment was a mediaeval commonplace. The Friar in the General Prologue uses *In principio* somewhat similarly as a word of power and holiness.
399 *sentence** meaning.
406 *fley* flew.
409 *corn* a grain of wheat.
410 *Real* royal, regal.
411 *fethered* i.e. 'mated with'.
412 *pryme* prime; either the canonical hour, 6 a.m. or the period from 6 a.m. to 9 a.m.
419 *in his pasture* at his feeding.
421ff. It was a common mediaeval belief that the world was created at the vernal equinox, the beginning of spring. Skeat has calculated that the date intended for Chauntecleer's adventure was May 3, the phrase 'Syn March bigan' being rather awkwardly parenthetical; thus thirty-two days had passed since March was complete. The necessity for such a reading is that the sun would only be in the given position on May 3. The sun having run 21° in the sign of Taurus fixes the date, and having risen slightly more than 41° up the sky sets the time at 9 a.m. The elaborate date setting reminds us of the opening of the General Prologue, and this is clearly part of the mock-heroic machinery of the Tale.
430 *by kynde* by his natural powers.
431 *stevene* sound, voice.

For whan I se the beautee of youre face,
Ye ben so scarlet reed aboute youre eyen, 395
It maketh al my drede for to dyen;
For al so siker as *In principio,*
Mulier est hominis confusio, —
Madame, the sentence of this Latyn is,
'Womman is mannes joye and al his blis.' 400
For whan I feele a-nyght your softe syde,
Al be it that I may nat on yow ryde,
For that oure perche is maad so narwe, allas!
I am so ful of joye and of solas
That I deffie bothe swevene and dreem." 405
And with that word he fley doun fro the beem,
For it was day, and eke his hennes alle,
And with a chuk he gan hem for to calle,
For he hadde founde a corn, lay in the yerd.
Real he was, he was namoore aferd. 410
He fethered Pertelote twenty tyme,
And trad as ofte, er that it was pryme.
He looketh as it were a grym leoun,
And on hise toos he rometh up and doun;
Hym deyned nat to sette his foot to grounde. 415
He chukketh whan he hath a corn yfounde
And to hym rennen thanne hise wyves alle.
Thus real, as a prince is in his halle,
Leve I this Chauntecleer in his pasture,
And after wol I telle his aventure. 420
    Whan that the monthe in which the world bigan,
That highte March, whan God first maked man,
Was complet, and passed were also,
Syn March bigan, thritty dayes and two,
Bifel that Chauntecleer in al his pryde, 425
His sevene wyves walkynge hym bisyde,
Caste up his eyen to the brighte sonne
That in the signe of Taurus hadde yronne
Twenty degrees and oon, and som what moore,
And knew by kynde and by noon oother loore 430
That it was pryme, and crew with blisful stevene.
"The sonne," he seyde, "is clomben up on hevene
Fourty degrees' and oon, and moore ywis.
Madame Pertelote, my worldes blis,

128

438 *cas* chance, event.
441 *rethor* rhetorician, a man learned in eloquent and effective speaking or writing.
   endite write.
443 'For a chief notable observation (on life)'.
445 *also* as.
446 *Launcelot de Lake* the knight of King Arthur's court.
448 *sentence** theme, story.
449 *colfox* coal-fox, a fox with black tips to ears and tail.
450 *woned* lived.
451 *forncast* forecast. 'High imagination' is the divine foreknowledge of events that has given the dream to Chauntecleer and is soon to be discussed at length.
452 *thurghout* through.
   hegges hedges.
   brast burst.
455 *wortes* herbs.
456 *undren* an indication of time, whose meaning shifted from 9 a.m. to various other hours, such as midday and mid-afternoon. The context here seems to indicate the original 9 a.m.
459 'That lie in wait to murder men'.
461 *Scariot* Judas Iscariot.
   Genylon the traitor in the *Chanson de Roland*.
462 *Synoun* the Greek who remained with the Trojan Horse, to persuade the Trojans of its harmlessness and religious value.
463 *outrely* utterly.
464 *morwe* morning; or 'morrow' in the general sense of 'the morrow brought ill fortune'.
468 'What God foreknows must needs be'. This is the crux of the popular mediaeval disputation about free will or predestination − if God has foreknowledge, events must be predestined: if our actions are known and predestined, how can we have freewill?
469 *clerkis* learned men.
470 *Witnesse on hym* take witness of him.
471 *scole* the schools, i.e. universities.
474 'But I can not sift it to the bran' i.e. distinguish the wheat from the chaff.
475 St. Augustine, the great 'doctor' or learned man of the early church, was the authority called upon by the orthodox theologians in this controversy.

Herkneth thise blisful briddes how they synge,   435
And se the fresshe floures how they sprynge;
Ful is myn herte of revel and solas!"
But sodeynly hym fil a sorweful cas,
For evere the latter ende of joye is wo.
God woot that worldly joye is soone ago;   440
And if a rethor koude faire endite,
He in a cronycle saufly myghte it write
As for a sovereyn notabilitee.
Now every wys man, lat him herkne me;
This storie is also trewe, I undertake,   445
As is the book of Launcelot de Lake,
That wommen holde in ful greet reverence.
Now wol I torne agayn to my sentence.
    A colfox, ful of sly iniquitee,
That in the grove hadde woned yeres three,   450
By heigh ymaginacioun forncast,
The same nyght thurghout the hegges brast
Into the yerd ther Chauntecleer the faire
Was wont, and eek his wyves, to repaire;
And in a bed of wortes stille he lay   455
Til it was passed undren of the day,
Waitynge his tyme on Chauntecleer to falle,
As gladly doon thise homycides alle
That in awayt liggen to mordre men.
O false mordrour, lurkynge in thy den!   460
O newe Scariot, newe Genylon,
False dissimilour, o Greek Synoun,
That broghtest Troye al outrely to sorwe!
O Chauntecleer, acursed be that morwe
That thow into the yerd flaugh fro the bemes!   465
Thow were ful wel ywarned by thy dremes
That thilke day was perilous to thee;
But what that God forwoot moot nedes be,
After the opinioun of certeyn clerkis.
Witnesse on hym that any parfit clerk is,   470
That in scole is greet altercacioun
In this matere, and greet disputisoun,
And hath ben of an hundred thousand men.
But I ne kan nat bulte it to the bren
As kan the holy doctour Augustyn,   475

130

476 *Boece.* Boethius discusses the question in his *Consolation of Philosophy*, Book IV, Prosa 6 and in Book V. Bishop Bradwardyn, died 1349, was Professor of Divinity, Chancellor of Oxford University and Archbishop of Canterbury; he was a notable contributor to the discussion.

477 *forewityng* foreknowing.

478 *Streyneth* constrains.
    nedely necessarily.

479 *clepe* call.
    symple necessitee a necessity unaffected by man's free will, for example, 'man must die'.

484 *necessitee condicionel* a necessity that does not interfere with free will; for example, 'if you know a man is walking, he must, of necessity, be walking'. The examples in this and the previous note are translated from Chaucer's *Boece.*

487ff. Here begins the debate on the sovereignty of women in marriage which is one of the main themes of the Tales, and is argued out chiefly by the Wife of Bath, the Clerk, the Merchant and the Franklin.

489 *met* dreamed.

490 *colde* baneful, fatal. The line is a version of a common proverb.

493 *Ther as* where.

495 'If I should blame women's advice'.

496 *game* playfulness.

500 'I can discover nothing to woman's disadvantage'.

501 *sond* sand.

503 *Agayn* in; lit. against, confronting.
    free magnanimous, expansive, cf. 148n. above.

505 *Phisiologus.* The Latin *Physiologus de Natura XII Animalium* was a bestiary describing various real and fabulous creatures, interpreted as moral symbols. There is a chapter 'On Syrens'. An early English Bestiary gives the following *significatio* for the siren or mermaid: 'Few men understand the signification of the sirens, (half maiden, half fish). Outside they wear lamb's skin, within they are completely wolf; they utter holiness but their deeds are wicked; their deeds are totally foreign to their speech. Duplicity is in their hearts: they swear by the cross, by the sun and by the moon, and straightway they lie. By their speech and by their singing they will betray you too — your possessions by treachery, your soul with lies'. The mere mention of Physiologus would recall 'moralitee' like this to the audience. It is typical of the Nun's Priest's sententious style that he should make so ironically unfitting an allusion. Still, there is an element of foreboding generated by the comparison which the following lines bear out.

509 *war* aware.

510 *No thyng ne liste hym . . . for to* he had not the slightest desire to.

513 *naturelly* by nature.

515 *erst* first, i.e. before.

516 *gan hym espye* spied.

131

Or Boece, or the Bisshop Bradwardyn,
Wheither that Goddes worthy forewityng
Streyneth me nedely for to doon a thyng —
'Nedely' clepe I symple necessitee —
Or ellis, if free choys be graunted me   480
To do that same thyng, or do it noght,
Though God forwoot it er that it was wroght;
Or if his wityng streyneth never a del
But by necessitee condicionel.
I wol nat han to do of swich matere;   485
My tale is of a cok, as ye may heere,
That took his conseil of his wyf, with sorwe,
To walken in the yerd upon that morwe
That he hadde met that dreem that I yow tolde.
Wommens conseils ben ful ofte colde;   490
Wommanes conseil broghte us first to wo,
And made Adam fro Paradys to go,
Ther as he was ful myrie and wel at ese.
But for I noot to whom it myght displese,
If I conseil of wommen wolde blame,   495
Passe over, for I seyde it in my game.
Rede auctours, where they trete of swich matere,
And what they seyn of wommen ye may heere.
Thise ben the cokkes wordes and nat myne;
I kan noon harm of no womman devyne.   500
   Faire in the sond to bathe hire myrily
Lith Pertelote, and alle hir sustres by,
Agayn the sonne, and Chauntecleer so free
Song myrier than the mermayde in the see;
For Phisiologus seith sikerly   505
How that they syngen wel and myrily.
   And so bifel that, as he caste his eye
Among the wortes on a boterflye,
He was war of this fox that lay ful lowe.
No thyng ne liste hym thanne for to crowe,   510
But cryde anon, "Cok! cok!" and up he sterte
As man that was affrayed in his herte,
For naturelly a beest desireth flee
Fro his contrarie, if he may it see,
Though he never erst hadde seyn it with his eye.   515
   This Chauntecleer, whan he gan hym espye,

132

521 *wolde* in the more active sense of 'wished'.
522 *conseil* private affairs.
525 *stevene* voice.
528 *Boece.* Boethius wrote a philosophical treatise *De Musica,* 'Of Music'. The allusion is ironic. Far from claiming to be a performer at all, Boethius places practical musicians in the ranks of slaves, and claims that the only true musicians are the speculative philosophers and critics who contemplate and analyse musical works, but never perform them.
530 *of hire gentillesse** through her courtesy, out of courtesy.
534 *brouke* use, 'retain the use of'.
536 *morwenynge* morning.
537 *Certes* certainly, indeed.
  of herte from the heart.
539 *peyne hym* exert himself, take pains.
540 *wynke.* To 'wink' meant to shut one eye or both eyes, as in the phrase, 'to take forty winks'.
543 *discrecioun* discernment.
545 *passe* surpass.
546 Chaucer refers to a Latin poem of the 12th Century by Nigellus Wireker. The cock takes his revenge by crowing late on the morning the 'preestes sone' was to be ordained, causing him to over-sleep and miss the ceremony.
549 *nyce* foolish.
  he i.e. the 'preestes sone'.
550 *lese* lose.
553 *subtiltee* skill.
554 *seinte* holy.
555 *countrefete* imitate; not 'counterfeit'.
557 *his traysoun* i.e. the treason plotted against him.

He wolde han fled, but that the fox anon
Seyde, "Gentil sire, allas! wher wol ye gon?
Be ye affrayd of me that am youre freend?
Now certes, I were worse than a feend   520
If I to yow wolde harm or vileynye!
I am nat come youre conseil for t'espye,
But trewely, the cause of my comynge
Was oonly for to herkne how that ye synge.
For trewely, ye have as myrie a stevene   525
As any angel hath that is in hevene.
Ther with ye han in musyk moore feelynge
Than hadde Boece or any that kan synge.
My lord youre fader — God his soule blesse! —
And eek your moder, of hire gentillesse,   530
Han in myn hous yben to my greet ese;
And certes, sire, ful fayn wolde I yow plese.
    But, for men speke of syngyng, I wol seye,
So mote I brouke wel myne eyen tweye,
Save yow I herde nevere man so synge   535
As dide youre fader in the morwenynge.
Certes, it was of herte, al that he song.
And for to make his voys the moore strong,
He wolde so peyne hym that with bothe his eyen
He moste wynke, so loude he wolde cryen,   540
And stonden on his tiptoon ther withal
And strecche forth his nekke long and smal.
And eek he was of swich discrecioun
That ther nas no man in no regioun
That hym in song or wisdom myghte passe.   545
I have wel rad in 'Daun Burnel the Asse',
Among his vers, how that ther was a cok,
For that a preestes sone yaf hym a knok
Upon his leg whil he was yong and nyce,
He made hym for to lese his benefice.   550
But certeyn, ther nys no comparisoun
Bitwix the wisdom and discrecioun
Of youre fader and of his subtiltee.
Now syngeth, sire, for seinte charitee;
Lat se, konne ye youre fader countrefete?"   555
    This Chauntecleer his wynges gan to bete,
As man that koude his traysoun nat espie,

134

558 We would say 'So ravished was he by . . .'
559 *ye lordes.* This is a rhetorical address to the great of the land, not to the pilgrims. *flatour* flatterer.
560 *losengeour* flatterer.
562 *soothfastnesse* truth.
563 *Ecclesiaste* Ecclesiasticus xii, 10ff.; xxvii, 26: 'Never trust thy enemy; for as a brass pot his wickedness rusteth. Though he humble himself and go crouching, yet take good heed and beware of him. Set him not by thee, neither let him sit on thy right hand, lest he turn into thy place and seek to take thy seat; and at the last thou acknowledge my words, and be pricked with my sayings . . . an enemy speaketh sweetly with his lips: but in his heart he lieth in wait to throw thee into a pit . . . In the sight of thy eyes he will sweeten his mouth, and will admire thy words: but at the last he will writhe his mouth, and on thy words he will lay a stumbling-block'.
564 *Beth war* be wary, on your guard.
568 *daun Russell.* Russell was a traditional name for the fox, derived from its red colour, as, perhaps, Burnell is derived from *brun*, brown.
569 *gargat* throat. *hente* seized.
571 *sewed* pursued.
572 *eschewed* avoided.
574 *ne roghte nat of* cared nothing for, paid no heed to.
578 *dide al his power* exerted all his energy.
579 The Wife of Bath, another servant of Venus, picks up this argument. She too revels in pleasure (sexual delight) for its own sake rather than seeing it as the Church enjoined, as a treacherous by-product of the reproduction of the species. See further Appendix E.
580 *woldestow* wouldst thou.
581 *Gaufred.* Geoffrey de Vinsauf published a treatise on poetry, *Poetria Nova*, containing a lament for Richard I, who had received his fatal wound on Friday, March 26, 1199. The treatise was extremely popular and held in high esteem, though not apparently without some amusement on the part of Chaucer who has in the previous lines been imitating the over-rhetorical lament for Richard.
583 *shot* arrow. *compleynedest* lamented.
584 *sentence** moral wisdom.
 loore lore, the rules of eloquence.
587 *pleyne* complain, i.e. lament.
588 *peyne* distress, suffering, rather than simply pain.
590 *of* by. *Ylioun* Ilion, Troy.
591 *wonne* taken, captured. *streite swerd* drawn sword.
593 *Eneydos* Virgil's *Aeneid*, ii, 487-90; 552-3. Chaucer telescopes these two passages relating to the assault on the Trojan palace, and the death of Priam at the hand of Pyrrhus:
'But inside, the house is in confusion with shrieks and pitiful uproar, and in the inmost part the lofty halls ring with the womanly wailing. The clamour strikes the golden stars. Then the fearful mothers wander through the vast rooms, clinging to the door-posts and pressing kisses on them . . .
'Now die!' Saying this, Pyrrhus dragged Priam right to the altar-stones, trembling and sliding in the profuse blood of his son, and seized his hair in his left hand, and with his right hand raised the flashing sword and buried it to the hilt in his side'.
594 *clos* enclosure, yard.

So was he ravysshed with his flaterie.
Allas! ye lordes, many a fals flatour
Is in youre court, and many a losengeour   560
That plesen yow wel moore, by my feith,
Than he that soothfastnesse unto yow seith.
Redeth Ecclesiaste of flaterye;
Beth war, ye lordes, of hir trecherye.
This Chauntecleer stood hye upon his toos,   565
Strecchynge his nekke, and heeld hise eyen cloos
And gan to crowe loude for the nones.
And daun Russell the fox stirte up atones
And by the gargat hente Chauntecleer
And on his bak toward the wode hym beer,   570
For yet ne was ther no man that hym sewed.
O destinee, that mayst nat been eschewed!
Allas, that Chauntecleer fleigh fro the bemes!
Allas, his wyf ne roghte nat of dremes!
And on a Friday fil al this meschaunce.   575
O Venus, that art goddesse of plesaunce,
Syn that thy servant was this Chauntecleer,
And in thy servyce dide al his power,
Moore for delit than world to multiplye,
Why woldestow suffre hym on thy day to dye?   580
O Gaufred, deere maister soverayn,
That whan thy worthy kyng Richard was slayn
With shot, compleynedest his deth so soore,
Why ne hadde I now thy sentence and thy loore
The Friday for to chide, as diden ye?   585
For on a Friday, soothly, slayn was he.
Thanne wolde I shewe yow how that I koude pleyne
For Chauntecleres drede and for his peyne.
Certes, swich cry ne lamentacioun,
Was nevere of ladyes maad whan Ylioun   590
Was wonne, and Pirrus with his streite swerd,
Whanne he hadde hent kyng Priam by the berd
And slayn hym, as seith us *Eneydos*,
As maden alle the hennes in the clos
Whan they had seyn of Chauntecleer the sighte.   595

136

596 *shrighte* shrieked.
597 *Hasdrubales wyf.* Hasdrubal, king of Carthage, killed himself when the city was burnt by the Romans in 146 B.C.; his wife threw herself into the flames.
600 *rage* violent passion and grief, rather than anger.
601 *wilfully* of her own volition.
604 *Nero.* The Monk has previously told the 'tragedy' of Nero, including the following lines:
  'He Rome brende for his delicasie;
  The senatours he ,slow upon a day
  To heere how that men wolde wepe and crie'.
607 *Withouten gilt* i.e. without feeling guilt.
609 *sely** simple, good, poor. The scene of the pursuit of the fox which is bearing away the cock (or goose) was a favourite late mediaeval subject for both story and visual representation. The *Roman de Renard*, to which Chaucer's version is closely related, also has a catalogue of dogs by name.
617 *oure.* A colloquial usage sometimes still heard in dialects; cf. the friendly 'How are *we* today?' or the doctor's 'How are *our* spots this morning?' There is no suggestion, therefore, that the Nun's Priest owns the dog.
624 *dokes* ducks.
 quelle kill.
628 *Jakke Straw and his meynee.* Jack Straw and his gang, in the Peasant's Revolt of 1381, massacred a large number of the Flemings who were competing with the English as labourers and artisans, particularly in the cloth trade.
630 *wolden . . . kille* were (engaged in) killing.
632 *bemes* trumpets.
 box boxwood.
633 *horn* Cf. horn-pipes, originally a wind instrument usually made of horn.
 boon probably ivory rather than bone.
634 *howped* whooped.

But sovereynly dame Pertelote shrighte
Ful louder than dide Hasdrubales wyf
Whan that hir housbonde hadde lost his lyf
And that the Romayns hadden brend Cartage.
She was so ful of torment and of rage   600
That wilfully into the fyr she sterte,
And brende hir selven with a stedefast herte.
    O woful hennes, right so cryden ye,
As, whan that Nero brende the citee
Of Rome, cryden senatours wyves   605
For that hir housbondes losten alle hir lyves —
Withouten gilt this Nero hath hem slayn.
Now wol I turne to my tale agayn.
    This sely widwe and eek hir doghtres two
Herden thise hennes crye and maken wo,   610
And out at dores stirten they anon
And seyen the fox toward the grove gon
And bar upon his bak the cok away
And cryden, "Out! harrow! and weilaway!
Ha! ha! the fox!" and after hym they ran,   615
And eek with staves many another man.
Ran Colle oure dogge and Talbot and Gerland
And Malkyn with a distaf in hir hand;
Ran cow and calf and eek the verray hogges,
So fered for berkyng of the dogges   620
And showtyng of the men and wommen eek,
They ronne so hem thoughte hir herte breek.
They yelleden as feendes doon in helle;
The dokes cryden as men wolde hem quelle;
The gees for feere flowen over the trees;   625
Out of the hyve cam the swarm of bees.
So hydous was the noyse, a benedicitee!
Certes, he Jakke Straw and his meynee
Ne made nevere shoutes half so shrille
Whan that they wolden any Flemynge kille,   630
As thilke day was maad upon the fox.
Of bras they broghten bemes, and of box,
Of horn, of boon, in whiche they blewe and powped,
And therwithal they shryked and they howped.
It semed as that hevene sholde falle.   635
    Now goode men, I prey yow herkneth alle:

646 *Maugree youre heed* in spite of anything you can do.
650 *delyverly* agilely.
651 *fley* flew.
654 *trespas* injury, wrong; cf. 'Forgive us our trespasses'.
656 *hente* seized.
660 *shrewe* curse.
664 *Do me to* make me, cf. Fr. *faire,* to make or do.
666 *thee* thrive.
668 *undiscreet of governaunce* i.e. lacking in self-control.
669 *jangleth* chatters, gabs. Many sermons, including that of Chaucer's Parson, attacked unnecessary chatter and gossip as a sin.
670 *recchelees* lacking in care, with some of the sense of self-abandon implied by the modern 'reckless'.
672 *a folye* a foolishness, mere pleasantry.
674 *the moralitee* the moral.
675 St. Paul, Epistle to the Romans, xv, 4: *Quaecumque enim scripta sunt, ad nostram doctrinam scripta sunt,* 'For what things so ever were written, were written for our learning'.
677 This very common piece of literary advise – to separate the moral instruction from the pleasant clothing of fable – was frequently put in terms of wheat and chaff; cf. PPro. 35-6.
fruyt the edible part of any vegetable; cf. 'the fruits of the earth'.
be stille i.e. remain behind.

Lo, how Fortune turneth sodeynly
The hope and pryde eek of hire enemy!
This cok, that lay upon the foxes bak,
In al his drede unto the fox he spak,   640
And seyde, "Sire, if that I were as ye,
Yit sholde I seyn, as wys God helpe me,
'Turneth agayn, ye proude cherles alle!
A verray pestilence upon yow falle!
Now I am come unto the wodes syde,   645
Maugree youre heed, the cok shal here abyde.
I wol hym ete, in feith, and that anon.'"
The fox answerde, "In feith it shal be don!"
And as he spak that word, al sodeynly
This cok brak from his mouth delyverly,   650
And hye upon a tree he fley anon.
And whan the fox say that the cok was gon,
    "Allas!" quod he, "O Chauntecleer, allas!
I have to yow," quod he, "ydon trespas,
In as muche as I maked yow aferd   655
Whan I yow hente and broghte out of the yerd.
But, sire, I dide it in no wikke entente.
Com doun, and I shal telle yow what I mente;
I shal seye sooth to yow, God help me so!"
    "Nay thanne," quod he, "I shrewe us bothe two,   660
And first I shrewe my self, bothe blood and bones,
If thow bigile me any ofter than ones.
Thow shalt namoore, thurgh thy flaterye,
Do me to synge and wynke with myn eye;
For he that wynketh whan he sholde see,   665
Al wilfully, God lat him nevere thee!"
    "Nay," quod the fox, "but God yeve hym meschaunce
That is so undiscreet of governaunce
That jangleth whan he sholde holde his pees."
    Lo, swich it is for to be recchelees   670
And necligent and truste on flaterye.
    But ye that holden this tale a folye,
As of a fox, or of a cok and hen,
Taketh the moralitee, goode men.
For Seint Poul seith that al that writen is,   675
To oure doctrine it is ywrite, ywis;
Taketh the fruyt and lat the chaf be stille.

679 *As seith my lord.* There has been no conclusion as to who or what is meant by this phrase. Possibly the priest refers to Christ, though a note in the Ellesmere manuscript identifies 'my lord' as the Archbishop of Canterbury.

681 As usual, and in comic obliviousness of the moral value of the tale, the Host seizes on a minor aspect to turn into by-play; that is, he gathers the 'chaf' rather than the 'fruyt'.
682 *breche* breeches; buttocks.
    stoon stone; testicle.
684 *seculer* i.e. a layman, not a priest.
685 *tredefoul* tread-fowl; cf. 411-2 above.
    aright indeed: 'a real tread-fowl'.
686 *corage* emotional force, libido.
    myght physical strength.
687 *Thee were nede of* you would need.
    wene think, guess.
689 *whiche* what.
    braunes muscles.
691 *sparhauk* sparrow-hawk.
692 *colour* i.e. complexion.
693 *brasile* red dye produced from brazil-wood.
    greyn of Portyngale the dye, also bright red, produced from the Coccus insect and imported from Portugal.
694 *faire falle yow* i.e. good fortune befall you.
695 *cheere* countenance or behaviour.
696 The fragment breaks off here and it has been suggested that the last two or three lines are not genuine, 'a spurious attempt at patch-work' (Robinson).

141

Now, goode God, if that it be thy wille,
As seith my lord, so make us alle goode men,
And brynge us to his heye blisse! Amen.   680

Heere is ended the Nonnes Preestes Tale.

"Sir Nonnes Preest," oure hoost seyde anoon,
"Yblessed be thy breche and every stoon!
This was a myrie tale of Chauntecleer.
But by my trouthe, if thow were seculer,
Thow woldest have been a tredefoul aright.   685
For if thow have corage as thow hast myght,
Thee were nede of hennes, as I wene,
Ya, mo than seven tymes seventene.
See, whiche braunes hath this gentil preest,
So gret a nekke and swich a large breest!   690
He looketh as a sparhauk with his eyen;
Hym nedeth nat his colour for to dyen
With brasile ne with greyn of Portyngale.
Now, sire, faire falle yow for youre tale!"
    And after that he, with ful myrie cheere,   695
Seide unto another, as ye shullen heere.

explanatory notes
and commentaries

explanatory notes

The text of this edition has been established from the material assembled in J. M. Manly and Edith Rickert: *The Text of the Canterbury Tales*, 8 vols. (Chicago, 1940). We have consulted the work of other editors, especially Skeat, Robinson, Baugh and Donaldson, and have had frequent recourse to the Chaucer Society's Six-Text edition. We follow Manly's reconstruction of the archetype more closely than some recent editors have done, and this in general accounts for the majority of our small divergences from, say, Robinson, and those editors who follow him. On some points either of dispute or of editorial decision which we feel have interest and significance for the student and the general reader, we have provided textual notes. No attempt has been made to 'regularize' the text since Manly has shown that much of the metrical regularity which used to be claimed for Chaucer's verse is suspect, and the result of editorial interference.

No attempt has been made to present a simplified spelling of the text, nor even an entirely internally consistent one. By taking the spelling of the Hengwrt MS as our base and making occasional reference to the Ellesmere MS, we have tried to give spellings which, while they are authentic for the period 1400-1410, are not unduly difficult or confusing for the beginner. In this respect we have had in mind the undergraduate studying Chaucer's language, and have not normalized variant spellings of significance.

In punctuation, the text differs considerably from some previous editions; to some readers it may appear under-punctuated. Yet modern conventions of punctuation too frequently do not fit mediaeval writing; in Chaucer's case they too often force his fluid, colloquial syntax into unnaturally rigid forms. For example

> Ful thredbare was his overeste courtepy
> For he hadde geten hym yet no benefice
> Ne was so worldly for to have office,
> For hym was levere have at his beddes heed
> Twenty bookes clad in blak or reed . . . *GP 292ff.*

Here both the 'For . . .' clauses can be seen as dependent upon the main clause 'Ful thredbare . . .'. But the second 'For . . .' clause is in some degree dependent upon both preceding clauses. Our punctuation allows this flexibility. Skeat's punctuation of these lines (which is that of numerous editors after him) is curiously limiting:

146

Ful thredbar was his overest courtepy;
For he had geten him yet no benefyce,
Ne was so worldly for to have offyce.
For him was lever have at his beddes heed
Twenty bokes, clad in blak or reed,. . . .

The strict punctuation of modern English prose sits very uncomfortably on Chaucer's poetry.

We have tried to limit the use of commas to contexts where ambiguity is likely to occur, or where the reader, particularly the reader unfamiliar with Chaucer, may need help with the syntax. We use colons and semi-colons more liberally than modern usage allows in an attempt to retain the movement of the verse; these signs connect where the full stop divides. In many instances the recognition of a line-end is sufficient for complete intelligibility. As might be expected in a work designed for oral delivery, many apparent difficulties of interpretation resolve themselves when the verse is read aloud with natural expressiveness.

TEXTUAL NOTES

GENERAL PROLOGUE

196 The line, a difficult one in any case, may well have read
He hadde of gold ywroght a ful curious pyn. Of the MSS which have *ywroght,* only two omit *ful.*
217 There seems little justification for adding *eek* to the line which, in fact, gains from its brevity.
220 Robinson omits *his* in this line; MS authority is strongly in favour of its inclusion.
225 As the OED points out the letter *u* in *poure* is ambiguous (being either *u* or *v* in pronunciation) so that contemporary pronunciation of this word is difficult to ascertain. On the basis of the frequent spelling *poore* in both the Hengwrt and Ellesmere MSS, which suggests a vocalic value for *ou* in the form *poure,* we have retained this spelling where it appears, and have not adopted *povre* at all.
253-4 These two lines, included here between square brackets, are generally held to be Chaucer's work, though their appearance in so few MSS (only five or six) is taken to indicate Chaucer's subsequent exclusion of them—probably on the grounds that they fit rather awkwardly at this point; as Manly suggests, they add little to the picture of the Friar.
344 *nowher.* Manly reads *nevere.* He notes that there is considerable

147

variation between the two words throughout the *Tales*, and that this often makes a decision difficult in a given case. While the MSS evidence supports his reading, we have adopted the more usual reading since there is an undeniable *nevere* in the next line.

423   We follow Manly in omitting *they*.

518   Manly admits that the negative is erroneously placed in his reading—*He was noght to synful men despitous*—but is of course bound to it by his method. We adopt the usual emendation.

662   *hym* has some MS authority and is usually adopted to avoid an otherwise ungainly line.

688   On not very strong MS authority some editors add *lay* in this line. It is not rhythmically necessary. *Walet* appears to have been stressed on the second syllable.

743   The parenthesis gains point in this line as it stands, without the questionable addition of *that* after *who so*.

826   One small group of MSS, among them El., reads *all in a flok*.

PARDONER'S TALE

215   *Ther* has the strongest MS support as the first word of the line. *They* has some support. Manly comments that *r* and *i* in some scripts are very much alike, so that the original could very well have been *thei*, which was subsequently mis-copied. *They* does seem preferable.

611   A very large group of MSS reads *tounes* for *myles*. *Myles* has the weight of authority, though Manly suggests it may be an exaggeration of the original *tounes* for humorous effect.

PRIORESS'S TALE

59   The choice between *and* and *or* is an arbitrary one on the part of a scribe.

121   *hath his herte* has little authority but may be correct.

130   The MSS evidence is in support of *oure* rather than *youre*. Some editors, probably feeling that the implied identification of Satan as one of the Jews is too unpalatable, have preferred the less authoritative reading. In addition to its support in the MSS, *oure* seems to us completely in accord with the Prioress's attitude to the Jews throughout the tale.

PRONUNCIATION

While it is impossible to reconstruct exactly the pronunciation used by Chaucer and his contemporaries in fourteenth century London, we can with a fair degree of certainty come close to it. If we fail to

148

observe some of the most characteristically different features of
Chaucer's English from our own, we not only destroy the fine rhythms
of Chaucer's lines, but also lose many of his best auditory effects, not
least among them, his rimes. The following is a schematic account of
the chief features of Chaucerian pronunciation which most readers
with practice ought to be able to master readily. Gramophone records
of some parts of *The Canterbury Tales* are available, made or directed
by specialists in the history of English pronunciation, and these
provide a pleasant aid to the lively and accurate reading of Chaucer.

CONSONANTS

gh   was pronounced in words like *droghte, boghte, night, bright.*
  After a back vowel, as in the first two examples, it was pronounced
  [x] as in Scots *loch;* after front vowels, as in the second pair of
  examples, it was pronounced [ç] as in Ger. *ich.*
gn and kn   were pronounced as spelt in words like *gnof, knight,
  knarre.*
h   was frequently silent in unstressed pronouns — *him, his, hem, hir.*
  It was also silent in words of French origin like *hostelrye, host,
  honour.*
l   In words like *half, folk, palmeres,* — i.e. before f, k and m, — l was
  almost certainly pronounced.
g in the group ng   was probably pronounced medially, as in *singen,*
  and possibly finally in words like *yong, song,* though not in the ending
  -ing.
r   was pronounced wherever written.
w before r   was pronounced; e.g. in *write, wrighte.*

VOWELS

a   closer to the *u* in Mod.E. *hut* than the *a* in Mod.E. *hat: whan,
  hath, and, that, palmeres, Stratford.*
e   as in Mod.E. *let: perced, vertu, every, sette, dette.*
i   as in Mod.E. *hit: with, his.*
o   as in Mod.E. *cot: of, holt, croppes.*
u   as in Mod.E. *put* but not as in *cup.* Note that this sound is
  frequently spelled *o,* especially before the nasal consonants *n* and *m:
  but, ful, sondry, sonne, loved.*
ā   as in Mod.E. *father,* not as in *name: Aprill, bathed, smale, stables,
  table.*

149

ē (open) as in Fr. *père* in words usually now spelled with *ea:* *breeth, heeth, esed, deel.*

e (close) as in Fr. *nè* in words usually now spelled *ee: seeke* (sick), *seke* (seek), *degree, eek, see, be, grief, frere.*
Note that in their subsequent history these two sounds fell together as e (close) before being finally raised to their modern sound.
Chaucer could, at a pinch, actually rime the two as when he rimes *See* (sea) with *be*—an open with a close *e*—though there may be another explanation for this case. He usually keeps them separate.

ī as in Mod.E. *machine,* not as in Mod.E. *hive: I, nyne, ryde, ryse, lif, time.* Note that this sound is very frequently spelt *y: y* has the same value as *i* except, of course, where, as in Mod.E., it represents the consonantal sound it has in *yes, year.*

ō (open) as in Mod.E. *ball: open, goon, holy, old, stoon, foo, also.*

ō (close) as in Fr. *haut,* near the initial position of the Mod.E. diphthong in *hope: soote, roote, doon.*
The open *o* should generally be used with words which today rime with *hope;* the close *o* with words which today rime with *food, good,* or *blood.*

ū is closer to Fr. *tu* than to the Mod.E. *ū* in *fluke: vertu, aventure.* It is spelt *ou* in *devout, oure, trouthe, honour, cours, loude,* i.e. in words which today rime with *house, course,* or *through.*
Notice this pronunciation (and spelling) in the ending of words like *resoun, condicioun,* in rime. Elsewhere the vowel in this ending may already have been weakening.

DIPHTHONGS

ai, ay, ei, ay all represent [æi]:*veyne, day, lay, fair, mayde, sayde, wey.*

au, aw represent the sound in Mod.E. *how: lawe, Caunterbury, felaweshipe, daunce, ytaught, saugh.* The variant spellings in words like *chambres, chaumbres* and in the endings *-aunce* and *-ance, -aunt* and *-ant,* suggest that the simple vowel sound *a* occurred also.

eu, ew There is some difficulty over this sound. In general the pronunciation [eu] or [iu] will serve: *newe, knew, fewe, beautee, snewed, mortreux.*

ou, ow Where it is not the simple vowel *ū* described above − i.e. in words which today rime with *know* or *sought*—it should be pronounced to rime with Mod.E. *know* in all cases: *thought, soules.*

150

In colloquial speech, disyllabic loan words from French must have had either alternative stress patterns (like the modern loan *garage*) i.e. *ver'tu, 'vertu,* or two equal stresses. In verse Chaucer seems to use them with a metrical stress on either syllable according to the demands of the context. Some words treated in this way are *vertu, corage, viage, honour,* all of which in Mod.E. have a fixed first syllable stress.

The *e* of endings like *-ed(e), -es, -eth* is in general to be clearly pronounced as [ə] or [i], though it may at times be syncopated—as sometimes indicated by such spellings as *comth* for *cometh*—if the rhythm seems to require it.

The interpretation of the *-e* at the end of words like *smale, ferne, ende,* is still uncertain. Chaucer's use of *-e* in certain rimes is undoubtedly for humorous effect; he rimes *Rome* and *cinamome* with *to me,* and *blame* with *'com pa me'.* In each case, however, some reference to music or song is involved, and the effect may be one of parodying the distortions which song produces. ɪt is fairly certain that such *-e's* were not pronounced in late fourteenth century London speech, and their occurrence in verse seems to have been dictated not by grammar, as was previously thought, but by rhythmical considerations. In such instances as *smale foweles, straunge strondes, ferne halwes,* it is suggested, the *-e* on the adjective prevents two heavy stresses from falling together. Yet the evidence of the MSS is variable on this point; cf. *half cours, greet strengthe;* and the question of realization in speech remains. In view of this doubt, we suggest that intuition and experience are the best guides: some lines require recognition of the *-e,* if only in the sense of giving full weight to the final consonant of the word concerned. What is to be avoided as far as possible is the rocking sing-song of giving fulsome syllabic weight to the *-e,* particularly at the end of lines: e.g. *sma-le, en-de.*

VERSIFICATION

If we exclude the *Tale of Thopas* in which Chaucer for purposes of parody imitates a balladic stanza form, there are two kinds of verse to be found in *The Canterbury Tales.* The first is a stanza form usually known as rime-royal, which consists of seven decasyllabic lines riming *ababbcc.* The only use of this stanza in the present edition is in The Prioress's Tale. The second kind of verse which Chaucer uses throughout most of *The Canterbury Tales* is the rimed decasyllabic couplet.

To appreciate the metrical structure and the aesthetic effectiveness of verse involves the recognition of two things—the sense of a regularly recurring 'pulse' which sets up an expectation of recurrence like the succession of bars in music, and the rhythmic variety, the 'tune' of the words. In later English verse, metrical patterns like the iambic pentameter regulated the form of the bars or feet of a line fairly strictly, as in Gray's lines:

The curfew tolls the knell of parting day,

The lowing herd winds slowly o'er the lea . . .

where each line consists of five bars, each composed of a lightly-stressed followed by a heavily-stressed syllable. The kind of variety possible in this scheme is illustrated in the second line where *winds* as a verb demands a stronger stress than its position as a metrical off-beat allows. By comparison, while retaining the succession of pulses, Chaucer's much freer verse permitted quite striking verbal tunes by varying the structure of the bars. As the Elizabethan critic George Gascoyne observed:

. . . our father Chaucer hath used the same libertie in feete and measures that the Latinists do use: and who so ever do peruse and well consider his workes, he shall finde that although his lines are not always of one self same number of syllables, yet, beying redde by one that hath understanding, the longest verse and that which hath the most syllables in it, will fall (to the eare) correspondent unto that which hath the fewest syllables in it; and likewise that whiche hath in it fewest syllables shalbe founde yet to consist of words that have suche naturall sounde, as may seeme equall in length to a verse which hath many more sillables of lighter accentes. And surely I can lament that wee are fallen into such a playne and simple manner of wryting, that there is none other foote used but one; wherby our poemes may iustly be call Rithmes, and cannot by any right challenge the name of a Verse. But, since it is so, let us take the forde as we finde it, and lette me set downe unto you suche rules or precepts that even in this playne foot of two syllables you wrest no woorde from his naturall and usuall sounde.

There have been modern readers of Chaucer, not as perceptive as Gascoyne, who have thought that his lines should scan regularly as iambic pentameters. It is frequently the case in *The Canterbury Tales*—for example, in line 10 of the General Prologue—that the metre and the normal word stress exactly coincide to make a 'text-book' iambic pentameter:

152

/ / / / /
That slepen al the nyght with open eye

But, as Gascoyne says, Chaucer did not restrict himself to this kind of line and its perfectly regular feet. And though it is technically possible to analyse most of Chaucer's lines according to the classical terminology of the iambic pentameter and its permitted variants, to do so imposes a certain expectation, a strictness and a kind of regularity which only interferes with our appreciation of his 'natural music'. For instance, to make lines like the following scan in this way, as some recent editors have done, is to produce a pretty sing-song in reading, but to miss the sense and the music of Chaucer's verse:

/ / / / /
Upon the cop right of his nose he hadde
/ / / / /
But soore wepte she if oon of hem were deed

The real effect of these lines lies in the expected five 'bars' not being regularly constructed:

/ / / / /
Upon the cop right of his nose he hadde
/ / / / /
But soore wepte she / if oon of hem were deed

Similarly in lines like

/ / / / /
Cheseth youreself which may be moost plesaunce

although the five expected metrical beats are there they fall not on every second syllable, but where the rhythm or the 'tune' of the line requires. In some lines even to attempt an iambic reading is absurd, yet the pentameter, or five-beat structure is undoubtedly there as expected:

/ / / / /
Pekke hem up right as they growe, and ete hem in

Occasionally one senses that an expected beat falls not on a word or syllable at all but, like a syncopated beat in music, just precedes a word:

/ /   / /   /
Thogh he never erst hadde seyn it with his eye

Such syncopations may occur at the cæsura or sense-pause which
is found in most lines, and which indeed some MSS indicate by a
bar-line /.

Thus in reading the opening lines of the General Prologue, we are
always aware of the pentameter, or five-beat movement, even when
the syllables which receive normal stress in speech are not regularly
arranged in iambic feet, and when an expected metrical beat may fall
upon silence, as in the first line.

/   / /   /   /
Whan that Aprill with his shoures soote
/   /   / /   /
The droghte of March hath perced to the roote
/   /   /   /   /
And bathed every veyne in swich licour
/   /   /   /   /
Of which vertu engendred is the flour,
/   /   /   /   /
Whan Zephirus eek with his sweete breeth
/   /   /   /   /
Inspired hath in every holt and heeth
/   /   /   /   /
The tendre croppes, and the yonge sonne
/   /   /   /   /
Hath in the Ram his half cours yronne,
/   /   /   /   /
And smale foweles maken melodye
/   /   /   /   /
That slepen al the nyght with open eye,
/   /   /   /   /
So priketh hem nature in hir corages,
/   /   /   /   /
Thanne longen folk to goon on pilgrimages
/   /   /   /   /
And palmeres for to seken straunge strondes
/   /   /   /   /
To ferne halwes kouthe in sondry londes . . .

This freedom from the monotonous metrical regularity which
characterises his contemporary Gower, for example, enables Chaucer
to move easily from the controlled utterances of formal rhetoric to the

154

lively tones and rhythms of colloquial speech within the same decasyllabic line.

In reading *The Canterbury Tales* it is essential to remember that Chaucer was writing for oral recitation and that the 'rightness' of his lines is something which must be heard and felt (as Gascoyne says) rather than analysed in terms of iambs and trochees. To read Chaucer as 'one that hath understanding', it is necessary to avoid forcing his verse into a preconceived metrical pattern, and imagining that the quaint result is Chaucer's antique English; one must be among those who 'do peruse and well consider his works' in order to hear Chaucer's real voice, speaking a language which is—perhaps surprisingly—close to our own.

WORDS ASTERISKED IN THE NOTES

Curteys, curteisye

Curteisye is fundamentally the quality of elegance or civility of manner displayed by the noble persons of the court. One who possesses these qualities is *curteys*. In Mod.E. a courteous person is simply well-mannered, polite, helpful; in earlier times a *curteys* person was one who had the appearance, refinement, manners and accomplishments which were proper to all persons at court. In GP.46, 99, 132 and 727, the sense of 'courtly manners, modest refinement, lacking in any trace of overbearing pride', is present. Ironic uses of various kinds are found in NPT.105, GP.250, and in MT.179 and 243.

Daunger, daungerous

The noun is descended from Lat. *dominarium* meaning 'lordship', or 'the power of lordship'. Since the power of a lord could be seen in two ways — simply as power in itself, and as the power to grant or to withhold (money, position, etc.) — the word developed broadly in two senses. These are both illustrated in Chaucer. From the second developed the most frequently found adjectival sense: 'remote, lacking in humility, stand-offish, chary', as in GP.519 and MT.230. This sense is given a narrower application to a person playing 'hard-to-get' in love, as in WBT.157, 520, 1096. Similarly the Wife of Bath uses the noun *daunger* in WBT.527 to mean 'calculated reluctance'.

The other development in the meaning of *daunger*—the sense of 'power over someone'—is shown in GP.665 where the Summoner is said to have the young people *in daunger*—i.e. 'in his power' or even 'at his mercy'. This is perhaps the closest the word comes in Chaucer's usage to the present sense of 'peril'.

Gentil

Etymologically, the adjective means 'of the same *gens* or family' and hence 'of a good family, well born'. It is often used to describe the characteristic qualities of good breeding — nobility, generosity and chivalrousness. The clearest example of this is in GP.72; it is used with satiric effect in NPT.99. As a noun, it is used to describe the pilgrims of best breeding — *the gentils* (see MT.5).

The noun *gentillesse* means 'courtesy, good breeding, nobility', and is used thus in MT.71, 274; WBT.266, 1115ff; it is used ironically in NPT.530.

Two further observations should be made. (1) Not all persons of wealth or rank possessed the moral qualities of *gentillesse* which ought to have attended upon their birth. Hence we find constant allusion to the conflict between rank and the material possessions of high birth on the one hand, and true *gentillesse*—moral virtue, *noblesse*— on the other. The discussion of where true *gentillesse* is to be found is a commonplace of fourteenth century literature; it is as old as Boethius, Dante and Jean de Meun. See WBT.1115ff, and Appendix C — a short ballad in which Chaucer continued the debate. (2) The word *gentil* is extended to mean simply 'excellent', with no suggestion of rank or even of moral worth. It is possible to use the word in this sense with some degree of irony when talking of a rogue or a worthless person: see GP.569, 649, 671; WBT.29.

Sely

The etymological sense of *sely* is 'happy, blessed'; to this sense is joined 'innocent, virtuous, worthy'. This kind of use is best seen in PrT.78. Elsewhere, the word is rarely used without some kind of emotive or ironical slanting. Thus in MT.296, John is not simply 'innocent' or 'worthy' but 'naïve, foolish, gullible'. In WBT.376 the Wife talks about her much maligned self as *sely* — 'innocent, poor, wretched'; and in 138 she refers to her husband's *sely instrument* — 'innocent, blessed, wrongly-accused'. In RPro.42 the sense seems again to be 'poor, wretched'.

Sentence

The Lat. *sententia* meant 'opinion, way of thinking; maxim'. The two main senses of the word in Chaucer are (1) moral wisdom in general,

156

as in GP.308, WBT.1132, NPT.584, PPro.58, or a particular piece of
advice, a moral maxim, as in McT.226; (2) the matter of what is said,
the content as distinct from the style or form of an utterance, as in
GP.800, PrT.129, NPT.399, 448 and PPro.63. From (1) comes the
sense 'an opinion' or 'a view', as in NPT.211, WBT.168; and from (2)
the sense 'whatever one has to say', as in NPT.36, and the sense
'proposal', as in PPro.17. Rarely is there any suggestion of the pompous
affectation which is present in the Mod.E. adjective 'sententious',
though it is easy to see how such overtones developed from the earlier
meanings. The modern 'sentence' (that which ends with a full stop)
is never meant.

Vileyns, vileynye
Etymologically, a *vileyn* is a country man, a farm labourer, a member
of a servile class, just as a *gentil* man is a member of the upper,
courtly class. As *gentil*, the adjective, describes the attributes of fine
breeding, so the adjective *vileyns* or *vileynous* is used of the attributes
of low-birth and servility (as viewed from above) — vileness, baseness,
ugliness; lack of manners, of breeding, of *gentillesse*. Thus in
WBT.1164 and McT.183 we find the word used to mean 'vile' or 'base'.
The noun is *vileynye*. In GP.70 it means 'language befitting a churlish,
low-born person', while in GP.728 it means 'lack of good breeding'.
In NPT.521 it is extended to mean 'base behaviour, injury or violence'.

As in the case of *gentillesse, vileynye* came to be viewed not so
much as an attribute of social rank, but as a quality which any person
might show by his behaviour, irrespective of rank. Thus in WBT.1164
it is *vileyns synful dedes* which make any person a churl. A churl
or a peasant by rank could exhibit, like the Ploughman, true *gentillesse*.

ASTROLOGY

In the opening scene of *The Canterbury Tales*, we read

   . . . the yonge sonne
   Hath in the Ram his half cours yronne.

On first acquaintance, this sentence seems to be just a metaphoric
expression describing the vivifying warmth of spring sunshine in
terms of the movement of the heavens, and rather out of keeping with
the other details of spring growth. In Chaucer's time, however, it

would have been as vividly real and physical an expression of spring as the rest of the passage, for the heavens were not remote and indifferent objects of no interest except as a spectacle (and . way of telling the time); they were full of radiating power, engenoering and controlling all natural processes, influencing every aspect of man's life on earth.

Nor was this influence merely general and undifferentiated. The earth at the centre of the universe was encircled by nine revolving spheres containing the Moon, Mercury, Venus, the Sun, Mars, Jupiter, Saturn, the Fixed Stars and the Primum Mobile. Each of these rained a specific influence on the earth, and over the centuries of man's consciousness of the heavens, a complex lore had grown up as to just what these influences were and how they interacted in producing all the phenomena of the earth below.

For example, the planet Venus engendered copper in the womb of the earth, beauty and lecherousness in mankind and fortunate events in history. Mars engendered iron, the martial character, and war and strife. The details of this process were as multifarious as the natural world, and as the characters and occupations of man. The planets controlled the bone structure, hair colour, complexion, eyes, wrinkles and energy of a man, were assigned particular limbs and particular illnesses for their special care, were patron powers, as it were, of various professions, and influenced the natural non-human world in just as many ways. And to add to the complication, the planets had particular days and times of the day when they were most or least influential (Sunday is the Sun's day, Friday is Venus's day).

The various spheres of the celestial government interacted by encouraging, modifying or inhibiting the specific powers of each individual sphere. The belt of sky across which the sun, moon and planets appear to move was divided into twelve segments or 'houses' related to the Zodiacal constellation of stars, and each of these houses had its own peculiar character. For example, Aries, the Ram, is fiery, Taurus, the Bull, is earthy. These houses were most influential when in the ascendant—just rising above the horizon—and the planet in that sign at that time was also notably influential, though its power was modified in various ways by its starry environment.

For example the sun and the moon each had one of these houses, the five planets each had two houses, in which they were at home and most favourably reinforced. The sign of Taurus (the Bull) was one of the houses of Venus; in this sign, Venus was most dominating and least distorted by evil influences. A child born when the sign of

158

Taurus, with Venus therein, was ascending the horizon, would show a great number of attractive graces, both of body and mind—a fine skin, good manners, soft voice, love of music, strong but virtuous sexual appetite and a generally benevolent disposition. If, however, Mars, an evil and warlike influence, joined Venus in her house, the benevolent powers of that 'constellation' were distorted in various ways—a character like the Wife of Bath would be the result.

'Venus me yaf my lust, my likerousnesse
And Mars yaf me my sturdy hardynesse;
Myn ascendent was Taur and Mars therinne;
. . .

I loved nevere by no discrecioun
But evere folwed myn appetit . . .'

Mars well placed, in his own house of Aries (the Ram), can engender the useful quality of courage as well as contentiousness; but ill-placed, in Taurus, he only distorts the Wife's amorousness into lust and masculine domination of her husbands.

When Chaucer, in the opening passage of the work, invokes the sun in Aries, it is not just a pleasant metaphor. The sun was the most benevolent and powerful of the heavenly bodies and was 'exalted', most influential, in the sign of the Ram, which itself was hot, masculine, luxuriant and fortunate, a source of sexual vitality. The sun is also 'young', with its connotations of fresh vigour, since the yearly life of the sun was thought to start at the vernal equinox when the day and night were equal (in Chaucer's time, March 12). At this time, therefore, the earth is felt to be undergoing the generative power of a most copious and benevolent astral warmth—the spring fertility is visible evidence of this celestial rain of influence.

These examples only involve the larger and simpler features of the system; the astrologers multiplied the web of cross-influences, the inter-relationship of heavenly bodies in their various conjunctions, aspects, houses, faces and terms, until the amateur is confounded. No doubt the common people of Chaucer's time could handle the most obvious questions of planetary influence, as does the Wife of Bath, but the further complexities practised by professional astrologers gave an aura of secret and powerful wisdom to the system, especially when, as often, it was used to predict future events. (Astrologers claimed to have predicted the Black Death of 1345 from the conjunction of Saturn, Mars and Jupiter at the same time as an eclipse of the moon).

159

The cuckolding of the 'sely Carpenter' by the witty student, 'hende Nicholas' in the Miller's Tale, depends on the latter's power to bluff the Carpenter into a most ridiculous course of action by pretending to such occult wisdom. Nicholas suggests that, like Noah, his private knowledge of God's intention allows him to predict a universal flood, and it is the aura of astrological studies, the instruments and the jargon, that overcome his opponent's usual caution and common sense. Though some of the learned scoffed at the practice of astrological prediction, and at the preciseness of the information culled from the stars, there was little doubt that the heavens were a real force in men's lives; among the ignorant, astrology must have seemed a special and powerful study, conferring almost magical powers on its practitioners.

MEDICINE

Mediaeval medicine was founded on the notion of the four humours mentioned so often in Chaucer—melancholy, phlegm, blood and choler, or in strictly medical terms, black bile, phlegm, blood and yellow bile.

In the cosmic picture, all things 'beneath the visiting moon' were composed of the four elements, earth, water, air and fire, and shared the four qualities of hot and cold, moist and dry. When these elements, these qualities were in proper balance, as nearly in equilibrium as is possible in this mutable world, the substance or thing was durable—diamonds are close to such a balance. When the elements were unbalanced, when one or more predominated, the substance or thing decomposed rapidly—apples have too much of the element water, too much of the cold and moist qualities to maintain themselves for long.

When it came to the description of man himself, these elements and qualities were transmuted into the four humours. Melancholy, like earth, was cold and dry; phlegm, like water, cold and wet; blood, like air, hot and moist; and choler, like fire, hot and dry. The mixture of these humours constituted a man's particular complexion or temperament: just as in modern psychology, there was no boundary between a man's physical and mental make up, so that Chaucer's Reeve, a 'colerik man' shows both the thin boniness and the irascibility of the man in whom choler predominated.

Physiologically speaking, a man was born with a particular

complexion, a dominance of one of the humours over the others—only in Adam before the fall, perfect and immortal, were the humours perfectly balanced and stable. Mortal men, however, could prolong their lives by keeping the humours as balanced as was compatible with their peculiar constitution; illness was a sharp imbalance, a superflux of one humour, which must be remedied if the patient was to survive.

The humours were nourished by food, and a sufficient but moderate and balanced diet was necessary to maintain health. The Doctor of Physic is applying his medical knowledge in keeping his diet 'mesurable', allowing no 'superfluitee' which might upset the balance of humours. The Franklin shows a proper concern with health when he changes his diet according to the season—each part of the year tended to foster a particular humour, and a man's diet should be aimed at counterbalancing this possible source of illness. Above all, the 'poore widwe' of the Nun's Priest's Tale shows natural health:

> Repleccioun ne made hire nevere syk,
> Attempree diete was al hir phisyk.

When, however, the balance of humours was upset more than could be controlled by 'attempree diete', more drastic measures were required. Herbs and other substances, such as parts of animals, potable gold, even earthworms, as Pertelote knows, might be prescribed either to work internally, or as purgatives to evacuate the superfluous humour. (Many of the recipes for herbal cures, being based on centuries of practical observation, are quite sound.) In addition, such external physic as compresses and ointments, composed of appropriate herbs, etc., might be applied. The Summoner has tried many of the external cures for his condition, but his continued consumption of the foods and drinks that produce a superfluity of the wrong humour nullifies all such external treatment.

Combined with physical treatment, the doctor would practise various forms of natural magic. As described in the note on Astrology, the heavens strongly influenced man's life. His constitution was largely determined by the arrangement of the stars at his birth, and the particular qualities of the planets continually interacted with this innate complexion throughout his life. In order to diagnose a disease, a well-practised doctor must ascertain the patient's complexion by studying the stars as they were at his birth, and combine this pattern of humours with the pattern of heat and cold, dryness and moisture, radiating from the stars when the disease began. To

161

prescribe for the disease, the doctor must then co-operate with or combat the continuing influence of the stars, as it affected the particular constitution and disease of the patient. He would do this by the physical means mentioned above, and by means of charms.

Just as the existence of the metals was thought to be a result of the engendering power of the various planets, so a charm, cast and engraved when a planet or zodiacal sign was in its most potent position among the heavenly bodies, was thought to be irradiated with that influence. It could then be used to support a particular humour, or to combat a malignant constellation. To reinforce this power, it might be engraved with symbols of the patient, the diseased part and the heavenly constellation concerned.

Though the system was clearly fanciful, it accorded with the deepest beliefs about the nature of God's universe, and the faith engendered by such mysterious wisdom must often have had the beneficial effect the charms themselves lacked.

commentaries

INTRODUCTORY

Chaucer still affects us as one of the most freshly observant of English writers, imitating with memorable accuracy the typical gestures and accents of mankind. To generations of students, he has seemed one of the most familiar and immediately enjoyable of writers; once the barrier of his unfamiliar language is passed, we find ourselves in our own human landscape, made vivid for us by the newness of the social setting and by Chaucer's eye and ear for the revealing detail, the interesting situation and story.

This much is immediately accessible and has made him more popular in the common estimation than many a later and more 'artificial' writer. And even the scholars, who revived general interest in Chaucer towards the end of the last century, tended to concentrate on this side of *The Canterbury Tales*, seeing the work as a piece of realistic reporting on human nature and on fourteenth century society. A judgement which still lingers is that, in this final work, he freed himself from literary convention, raised his eyes from his impressive library of books, and 'sketched the men and women about him.'

As the devotion to realism in literature declines, however, the recent work of scholars has come to show just how completely Chaucer remained dependent on the conventions and ideas of his time. We cannot say that he ever turned away from the literary tradition that nurtured him, but rather that he became more and more aware of the complex interrelationship between convention, in literature or in morality, and the actuality that appears in people's behaviour. It is difficult to find a detail in the description of the pilgrims or in the tales that does not gain part of its effect from our recognition of conventional meaning: Chaucer lays no claim to the originality that became so dear to later writers, rather he boasts of his sources and depends on our recognizing earlier uses of his material.

As our understanding of Chaucer's literary and social and religious background grows, and as we thence become aware of the meaning behind every detail, the immediately accessible interest takes on richness and depth. The *General Prologue* doesn't merely show a collection of 'characters' whose whole interest for us lies in our empathetic feeling for them as people (an idea that has found expression in the common phrase, 'a gallery of portraits'). Rather, the pilgrims come to be seen as the focal points for a large number of various but related ideas, judgements and typical patterns of behaviour. The brilliance of Chaucer's art—and indeed his actual originality—lies in his power of translating abstract conceptions about mankind, not just into allegorical personifications but into characters who arouse those empathetic reactions which we feel towards our actual fellow beings. It is right that we should first of all meet him at a realistic level, as a fine observer and teller of stories; but the continuing interest and the reward of study lies in the slow unfolding of the universe of thought that is brought to fine focus in the little world of the pilgrimage.

The influence of a writer's own environment on his work is always incalculable but Chaucer's career at least shows interesting parallels with his literary attitude. He was court poet under the chivalric Edward III and the cultured Richard II, he underwent the courtly training of a squire and he clearly catered in his literary career for a courtly audience; it seems likely that he was supported by the King (with an annuity) at least partly for his activity as poet.

However, this side of his environment should be set against his background and his practical career: his father and grandfather were vintners in London and he himself displayed the practical abilities of a member of the middle class. He was early a minor diplomat in the King's service to France, Italy and perhaps Spain. From 1374-1386, he was Controller of the wool custom, the wool subsidy and the petty custom at the wool quay in the Port of London—these were forms of export duty, the first two on wool, skins and leather, the third on other merchandise. The appointment was no sinecure designed to support a court poet—the controller was expected to act in his own person (though Chaucer obtained deputies when he was overseas or especially pressed by business); his task was to check, on the king's behalf, the actual collectors of the custom, keeping a parallel account of all shipments and charges. It seems likely that Chaucer had no staff of any kind, apart from the deputies, to help him in this work. (For fuller details and examples of Chaucer's work as controller, see *Chaucer Life Records*, edited by Martin M. Crow and Clair C. Olson, Oxford 1966, pp. 148-270.)

Chaucer was also a Justice of the Peace for Kent from 1385-1389, he was returned as Knight of the Shire for Kent to the stormy 1386 session of parliament; from 1389-1391, he was appointed clerk of the works, especially concerned with repairing the royal chapel at Windsor; subsequently he was probably some sort of keeper of forests for at least some part of his remaining nine years of life.

Chaucer was, then, a thoroughly practical and busy man, involved in the world of men and money at the same time as being an entertaining writer for the court and a man of wide and imaginative learning. It is fair to see in this double career an image of his literary style, in which the conventionality of court modes and the abstract truths of the learned tradition are taken up into a mind rich with the observation of men's actual passions and practices, a style in which his understanding of what men realistically are in this practical world, is enlarged by the imaginative work of all who had built up the mediaeval vision of mankind.

It is in his last and most exploratory writing, in *The Canterbury Tales*, which he probably began to assemble in 1387 when he was 47, that this fusion of convention and observation is most fully explored. For here we seem to look as with a television camera but find a world of values and ideas. In producing this effect, Chaucer could rely securely on the allegoric temper of the mediaeval imagination, on the habit of mind that presumed every least detail would have abstract significance. His audience would be accustomed to looking through the literary fiction at various levels of ideas. Chaucer builds his pilgrims and the characters in the Tales, from allegoric images—the Pardoner's eyes are staring, like those of a hare: the physiognomists had declared that staring eyes signified shamelessness, and the hare was traditionally a creature of shameless lust. The Miller's bagpipes, carried by so grossly physical a figure, would suggest the coarsest 'music' of sensuality—the Miller could easily be one of the grotesques found lurking in the borders of some late mediaeval manuscripts. The Squire's flowery tunic would evoke the traditional spring floweriness of courtly love and probably, precisely, the God of Love in *Le Roman de la Rose*.

Similarly, Chaucer expects us to recognize the great anti-feminist controversy that stands behind and gives form to the Wife of Bath's every utterance: the Nun's Priest's Tale is an absolute pot-pourri of references to traditional controversies, codes of behaviour and moral ideas about mankind. From moment to moment, however entrancing the character of the story, our minds are directed outwards from the fiction to the abstract world of ideas, rather than inwards to the workings of the human heart. To find our way into Chaucer's real quality, we have to learn the allegoric vision, that sees the Pardoner's draught of corny ale, the Reeve's habit of always riding hindmost, as a focussing in symbolic action of abstract conclusions about human kind. Far from merely sketching the visible scene, he is bringing to fruition a remarkably wide and imaginative absorption in the intellectual tradition of his time.

There are two main literary traditions on which Chaucer draws—the Christian moral system in all its extreme and detailed elaboration on the one hand, and on the other the system of what, in various forms, has come to be called Courtly Love. There are also some subsidiary stock attitudes—the primitive justice and 'realism' of the fabliau in the Miller's Tale, for example, and the blank practicality of the Manciple's Tale with its remnants of pre-Christian tags on 'how to get on in the world.' But the Christian morality of the mediaeval church is a solid background to every attitude and style, and not just in the framing device of the pilgrimage which sets the ideal Christian life of ordinary people before the pilgrims. We are continually reminded of Christian moral judgement in the texture of meaning of even the most secular Tales.

Almost equally wide-spread are references to the ideas and literature of Courtly Love. This was the literature most familiar and acceptable to his audience at court and was indeed the main secular literary tradition open to Chaucer. A highly formulated system or theory of the relation between the sexes, it was remote from mediaeval moral notions on the one hand and from the 'natural' behaviour of men and women on the other.

It reversed most of the church doctrines on the proper submission of woman and on the role of reason and spirit in controlling the desires of the flesh. It was not concerned with the propagation of the species but with pleasure and the over-cultivation of desire, and it was incompatible with the church's sacrament of marriage. Love wounded the Courtly Lover in the heart to the utter overthrow of his reason, and he became but the submissive servant of his lady (see Appendix E). But, though all his powers were abject and humbled in his lady's presence and his main pleasure the long drawn out pain of frustrated wooing, such love was held to ennoble him in his behaviour to others and to foster all the chivalric virtues and social graces. The sequence of emotional events, the kind of behaviour, the language, the style of beauty, all became formalized and conventional; though built on the fundamental role of sexual

166

passion, so artificial a code could be nothing but comic to so downright a sexual enthusiast as the Miller, for example.

Though this love system was elaborately codified, its status in Chaucer's time was as ambiguous as its sources were confused. The impulses behind it were both immoral and heretical—the writers were often deliberately blasphemous in converting religious language and concepts to sensual purposes—but the basic attitude had been elevated by Dante into an exalted mysticism and the code of behaviour in its social aspect was accepted as the authentic manner of the courtly life. It gathered together, not only the cult of sensuality in a highly unnatural form and the refinement of behaviour to a point of fantasy, but also those profoundly important changes in the sensibility of the western world which, as we can now see, took root and transformed society.

Various writers approached courtly love from varying points of view and Chaucer acknowledges most of these views except for the entirely serious one. *Troilus and Criseyde* is the most touching portrayal of the real emotional validity that could inform a courtly love relationship but ends with Troilus's condemnation of his blind lust from the higher viewpoint of the eighth heavenly sphere. The Squire, that 'lovere' and 'lusty bacheler', has his absurdity, but it is clear that Chaucer appreciated all the tender intensity of feeling and the delightful cultivation of courtly manner that stemmed from love literature. By Chaucer's time, courtly love had been explored in all its variations, and also filtered down, in its notions and manners, into the texture of social behaviour at every level. In *The Canterbury Tales,* practically everybody is touched by the code in one way or another, from the Prioress with her affected sensibility to the Miller with his rude laughter.

Chaucer's genius does not lie, however, in the merely artful compiling of traditional moral figures or in the rehearsing of courtly commonplaces. Though he works through a continual reference to conventional literary or moral material, his real interest lies in the way such material may inform the actual world and may be the means of understanding the ways of men. However much we become aware of the traditional and derivative, we never feel that this element triumphs over Chaucer's characteristic grip on human actuality. Like all the greatest writers, he is master of the tradition, not servant. He never drifts off into ideal or remote systems of ideas (and what could be more idealistic and remote than courtly love or ascetic mediaeval Christianity) but uses them as the tools for investigating the human

167

race as it is. Such systems are only interesting to Chaucer in their application to the unsystematized stuff of our world.

There are two ways that Chaucer takes to bring about the fruitful union of literary tradition and the open world. The pilgrims in the *General Prologue* and in the links and preambles, take on an irresistible human presence, so that whatever general considerations may be embodied in the character are understood by us in their proper human context: the abstractions are tested and qualified by so fully human an embodiment. For example, the Monk is a compact summary of all the vices of mediaeval monasticism, the Pardoner may be analysed as the complete Blasphemer but we are persuaded to accept these characters into the imagination as people, with a consequent qualitative change of our judgements. It is the Parson who sets up, in his sermon, the purely theoretic Christian standard and this is clearly a much narrower, more inflexible and less humane approach to the pilgrims than Chaucer's own. Though in the context of heaven the Parson has the last word—and Chaucer's Retraction at the end is a gesture that affirms the transcendent validity of the Parson's Tale— yet in this 'thoroughfare of woe' on earth, it is not only more understanding but even in a sense more just to take people as people rather than as sin-polluted souls. (Indeed, the Parson of the *General Prologue* clearly applies charity in practice, however rigorous may be his preaching.)

Chaucer's means of making us accept the pilgrims with this kind of 'realistic' judgement are complex but one of the most interesting is the device of making himself, as narrator, a part of the group being described. It is probable that at least parts of the work would have been read by him to the court and perhaps to friends and he seems to have this semi-dramatic situation in mind: he gives himself a dramatic *persona* as teller and traveller and our sense of the kind of judgement that might be afforded the pilgrims in reality is embodied in this rather naive, middle-class and uncritical pilgrim Chaucer. Through this figure, with his awe for the beautiful Prioress and the prosperous Monk, his distaste for the Pardoner, his liking for the Shipman, we are given a quite different sort of vision of the pilgrims, the sort of human reaction that is characteristic of our relation with actual people.

Of course, we are meant to view the pilgrim Chaucer's judgements with considerable irony: the *persona* that Chaucer gives himself is obviously at odds with the sophisticated and learned poet his audience would know well, and the humble pilgrim's reactions to his fellows often seems purely comic. But he is not merely a comic device: he

168

does embody a kind of judgement of his fellows that must be taken seriously. And he helps to give that dimension of reality that so qualifies the abstract levels of meaning.

Chaucer also makes us feel the limited validity of each pilgrim's peculiar point of view by bringing them all together in the one unified work. The charitable Parson and Ploughman ride in company with the Miller and the Wife of Bath, the Knight's Tale is followed by the Miller's reply to that vision of Courtly Love, the Monk's dreary tragedies are 'answered' by the Nun's Priest's comic catastrophe. In each case we are presented with a characteristic point of view that has engaged and satisfied one individual's imagination; but the understanding that Chaucer the poet seeks, and offers, does not lie in submitting to any particular point of view—the Knight's or the Miller's or the Pardoner's—but in recognizing the variety of often mutually incompatible views that make up the imaginative fabric of human society.

The Canterbury Tales is a gathering of the widest possible range of such views, and to understand it as a whole, therefore, we set every part against every other part. We read the Miller's Tale, for example, conscious of the kind of mind that could produce such an attitude to human life, conscious of the preceding Knight's Tale, which exalts sexual refinement, of the following Reeve's Tale, which debases sexual gaiety, and of the Christian standard of sexual behaviour embodied in both the Parson's sermon and in the ostensible purpose of the Miller's journey to Canterbury. The Pardoner's Tale, by itself a rousing mediaeval horror sermon, is to be set against the other works of religious imagination, the sentiment of the Prioress and the rigorous charity of the Parson's Tale; and it is qualified strongly by our knowledge of the Pardoner, derived from the General Prologue and from his preamble.

Again, the proper relationship of man and woman in marriage, a subject touched on by the Nun's Priest, is examined from various angles by the Wife of Bath, the Clerk, the Merchant and the Franklin, and is glimpsed in passing flashes in such other tales as those of the Knight, the Miller, and the Manciple; it, too, is given its Christian meaning by the Parson.

The principle of unity in *The Canterbury Tales* is not only in the external form of pilgrimage but also in the internal nerve structure of cross-references. We are aware, not only of the way in which each figure and fiction draws on the beliefs of the mediaeval world, but also of the whole of the rest of the work bearing on each part of it:

169

it is the sense of a mesh of ideas and attitudes, rather than a mere sequence of unrelated stories that gives so strong an internal consistency. The more we read, the more interesting does each tale and the whole work become.

Such a form is an expression of the peculiar Chaucerian irony, which allows him to immerse himself with enthusiasm in so many characteristic human viewpoints or ideas while maintaining an assured and amused objectivity. His famous 'detachment' is not indifference, it does not produce any lack of sympathetic life in his work—the pathos of the Prioress's Tale, the desperate blackness of the Pardoner's story are genuinely powerful. Chaucer has practised almost every literary and moral style available to him with an understanding and skill unsurpassed by even the most straight-faced follower of each tradition. But always, in his mature work, Chaucer adds an ironic perception that every human attitude of mind is not only opposed to but also grates against many other such attitudes. It is as though he delights in 'trying on' the various styles, and the attitudes they embody, and in feeling the imaginative life that has been expressed in the tales, but always remaining aware that they are merely parts in the various human comedy. It is appropriate that Chaucer's most vividly realistic writing should be found at the meeting points of the Tales, in the link passages, for it is the clashing of conventional attitudes of mind that throws us back onto the actual world so refreshingly.

Nowhere in *The Canterbury Tales* does Chaucer 'speak his mind', setting his own beliefs against the pilgrim world. If we feel he is a man of remarkably clear-sighted common-sense, it is not because he peels away the attitudes of men to 'show what life is really like.' Like the proverbial onion, if you peel away the layers, you are left with nothing; but the onion exists, like human life, a reality composed of those layers. In *The Canterbury Tales*, Chaucer has found the perfect literary form to show the interlocking layers of human ideas, each with its own 'truth' and its own limitations, all together making up the real composite onion.

As we get to know the work, irony comes to be felt as the basic underlying attitude, the medium in which the characters and tales exist. It is not the irony that destroys, either from disgust, or in order to preach yet another message: rather, it is a way of delighting in a world whose evils and absurdities are all too plainly clear. A moralist without this quality could do nothing but condemn the Canterbury pilgrims—the Parson is such a man. Chaucer, on the other hand, though perfectly clear in his moral judgement, presents the pilgrimage (which is also the pilgrimage of life) as a thing of teeming abundance and fascination. The ironic stance of his imagination is what allows him to maintain his balance amid this demanding variety, without clinging to a rigid system for support and without shunning any human vice or folly in self-defence. Among English writers, he is unequalled in this central sanity of mind.

The Nun's Priest comes, perhaps, closest to the Chaucerian ironic view—he mocks and enjoys everything in this worldly thoroughfare, leaving us with the sense of a thoroughly unillusioned wisdom about the ways of man. In the Nun's Priest's Tale, however, we are aware of a sure faith in the saving mercy of God: does Chaucer too finally rest his ironic exploration of the World on a non-ironic Faith?

This is a question of some difficulty. Christian orthodoxy clearly has a special status in *The Canterbury Tales:* the Parson and Ploughman are described with no ironic qualification in the General Prologue and, as has been said, the Parson's sermon and Chaucer's Retraction also seem to be presented with a complete suspension of irony. Moreover, the Christian judgement finally made explicit by the Parson has been the standard of judgement by which the pilgrims have been measured throughout: both the fact of pilgrimage and the web of references to Christian ideas have kept this ideal before us continually. However, the Christian ideal is offset by other and more humane reactions when we are actually confronted with the pilgrims. The Parson's summary of their vices and their need for repentance seems an oddly narrow attitude after the humane humour of the rest of the work—and Chaucer's Retraction of all his writings that 'are conducive to sin' is itself attached to a work in which these writings occur: he did not actually eliminate those parts of *The Canterbury Tales.* We are left suspended, unresolved, between an orthodox submission to Christian truth and the common sympathies and interests of this worldly life: each makes its absolute demands, irreconcilable with the other. It is perhaps a measure of Chaucer's maturity that he shows no impatient reaching after an easy resolution one way or the other: certainly his most insistent concern is to study the dilemma and the comedy of mankind caught between two worlds, and the various compromises or choices that individuals make. Though at the end of the pilgrimage of life, faced by the heavenly Jerusalem, there is only one choice to be made—the choice Chaucer makes in his Retraction—nevertheless the problem, for all but ideal figures, is more complex while we have the world still to manage and enjoy.

THE GENERAL PROLOGUE

'In the spring, a young man's fancy lightly turns to thoughts of love'. Chaucer's opening spring-song, complete with young sun, Zephyrs and birds, the shooting of sap and the longings of the human heart, leads the reader to expect some tale of human passion and romantic love. The sequence of spring events seems to lead by inevitable progression to such amorousness as is shown later by the Squire:

> So hoote he lovede that by nyghtertale
> He slepte namoore than dooth a nyghtyngale.

Moreover, this song of 'Spring, the sweet spring', of the re-birth of nature in April and in May, is one of the oldest and most stereotyped of poetic conventions. It was widely employed in the fourteenth century to introduce poems of courtly love, and indeed, it appears to this purpose in several of Chaucer's works, including *Troilus and Criseyde* and his translation of *Le Roman de la Rose:*

> Hard is the heart that loveth nought
> In May whan al this mirth is wrought,
> Whan he may on these braunches here
> The smale briddes syngen clere.

In *The Canterbury Tales,* however, spring prompts a longing, not for love but for pilgrimage. With comic unexpectedness we find, instead of a tale of secular joys, a stirring abroad of pilgrims across the face of the earth, visiting sacred shrines in foreign places, issuing from every shire in England. And the effect of this comic shock is to throw us out of the small, enclosed world of Love into the greater world of common human feelings and pursuits, where the effervescent promptings of the season send people, not into the flowery woods to sigh for their lady's grace, but out on pilgrimages, migrating like birds in the joy of sociable travel and the release of fine weather. This is spring as Chaucer would have seen it around him, a stirring in the blood of ordinary various humanity to be out and about after the constricting cold of winter.

It is of course deeply ironic that pilgrimages which are, in theory at least, penitential disciplines to subdue the wilfulness of the flesh, should be prompted by so purely secular a spirit. The description of the pilgrims, their subsequent behaviour and the tales they tell, make it clear just how little real spiritual purpose was to be found on the

172

trip to Canterbury. Chaucer is echoing a very common criticism of actual pilgrimages, that they were too much like mere holiday junketting. It is perhaps too severe to claim that there was no spiritual aim for the majority of the pilgrims—they no doubt often worshipped devoutly at the shrine they chose, and certainly made very substantial offerings. But in general, the pilgrims were prompted to travel by those prickings of nature that kept the birds waking, rather than by the difficult call to perfection embodied in the saint they were going to visit. It is typical that Chaucer's pilgrimage should be played out of town by the bagpipes of the bawdy Miller and that the earthily sensual Wife of Bath should be the greatest pilgrim of them all.

Under the comedy and the satire on human motives, however, Chaucer is setting up the standard of judgement that persists throughout the work. To the saints, to those who treat human life as a pilgrimage towards the heavenly Jerusalem, to the Parson and the Ploughman, the rebirth of nature may genuinely be a time of spiritual rejuvenation. Lent and its culmination in the Easter festival coincided with the spring season, the rebirth of the natural world being seen as symbolic of Christ's resurrection and his triumph over the powers of darkness. For all the pilgrims, the journey should have been a penitential discipline leading to a joyful rejuvenation of the spirit. As they proceed, immersed in all the folly and vitality of man, we are constantly reminded of the Christian meaning of both spring and of pilgrimage, the ideal against which they must be judged.

THE KNIGHT

Nearly half the description of the KNYGHT is given over to the list of his battles, a fighting career as impressive and 'perfect' as the man himself. Over a period of some forty years, it had covered the whole frontier of beleaguered Christendom—the south of Spain, the north of Africa, Turkey, Prussia, Lithuania and Russia. In a time when chivalry had much decayed before the commercial and political forces of a changing world, such soldiering already makes the Knight something of an ideal.

His personal qualities, too, are a catalogue of what the perfect knight should be, unfalteringly chivalric, Christian and successful; such a figure might be found in many a romance and text book of chivalry.

The Knight may be linked with the Parson and the Ploughman, ideal representatives of the three divisions of the mediaeval Christian social order, Knights, Priests and Labourers. Or, in the pattern of the work as a whole, he may confront the everyday world of the pilgrims as a secular ideal, just as the Parson confronts it with the religious ideal: it is he who opens the telling of tales and the Parson who closes it.

Does Chaucer, however, view the Knight with the same unsmiling idealism that he gives the Parson and his brother? There is at least room for doubt. What gives much of the interest to this portrait is the incongruity between the ideal figure and the context in which he appears. He is placed not in some remote idyllic landscape where perfection is possible, but in the contemporary political situation, fighting battles well known to the audience; and in London, among realistically observed people gathering in an inn of some fame. Although, as an ideal, he may be a reproach to all those who fail in their duty, the vivid reality of the world in which he is placed makes him something of a melancholy anachronism, even perhaps slightly comic. He is a figure from an attractively simple imaginary world who just does not fit the complex, awkward world we know.

THE SQUIRE

The SQUYER is not the knight's son by blood alone; he also embodies in pure form the fantasy and gaiety of the code of courtly love, which bore to the chivalric code very much the relationship of an adolescent offspring to a sober parent. The high-spirited variety and even frivolousness of the Squire contrasts sharply with the drab figure of the Knight, but both belong to the same rather remote world of idealized motives and emotion.

The Squire is a typical 'lusty' bachelor in training for the Knighthood; he is fully equipped by Chaucer with all the accomplishments of military and amorous prowess so lavishly handed out by the poets of courtly love. No young squire was ever lanky or squat, ever lacked agility or strength or failed to bear himself well in battle for his lady's sake. No Lover was ever less than marvellously, unrealistically accomplished at a wide variety of elegant activities, from jousting to drawing and writing the lyrics of love; nor was love ever born in the heart in any season but that of flowers and nightingales.

Indeed, so purely does the Squire represent the young Lover that Chaucer connects him directly with the God of Love himself as depicted in *Le Roman de la Rose*, embroidered like a meadow with the flowers of spring: '. . . nought yclad in silk was he, But all in floures and in flourettes'.

174

Chaucer clearly delights in this figure of young love, and in the tradition he represents. But he is fully awake to his absurdities. In an allegoric dream world like that of *Le Roman de la Rose,* or in the purified world of the Lays of Courtly Love, the Squire would not raise a smile. But on the realistic pilgrimage, setting off from the Tabard, he becomes attractively comic, a fantasy taking form in the real world. Of course, young 'bachelers' did carry on in this way; Chaucer had himself been a squire and was expert in what he later called 'many a song and many a leccherous lay', fulfilling the courtly ideal at least in this particular. His amused mockery is largely directed at those, including perhaps his youthful self, who have chosen to act out the fantastical role of the courtly lover in the common down-to-earth world of London and of the French campaigns.

Absurd as he may be, however, the spirited Squire is greatly to be preferred to many of the more 'realistic' pilgrims. He seems to share much of the innocent vitality of the spring, a joyfulness of heart and mind almost as scarce on this pilgrimage as any spiritual care; Chaucer's mockery of the Squire never takes on the harshness of satire.

THE YEOMAN

Like the Squire, the YEMAN is a colourful figure: the green of his garb and the brown of his complexion are the colours of the forest which is his life's concern. The gay peacock arrows and the bright silver of his St. Christopher stand out sharply in a portrait which is largely vivid visual description. Beneath this brightness we are aware of an alert and efficient man, thoroughly at home in his natural environment. His skill in all the crafts of the forest, and his scrupulous care and preparation of his gear are highlighted in the sharpness of his 'takel'—the sharp arrows and sword, the spear-sharp dagger. Having meticulously sketched the perfect image of a forester, Chaucer is content simply to comment dryly: 'In fact I'd say he was a forester'!

The Yeoman's simple colours and natural vigour are seen to contrast nicely with the Squire's extravagance of appearance and manner—the solid oak against the flowery meadow—and his mastery of woodcraft seems efficiently practical beside the Squire's animated enjoyment of his sophisticated accomplishments. As the Knight's only servant on the pilgrimage, he strikes us as the obvious choice on account of his solid reliability, and his readiness for action should the occasion arise for it.

Chaucer's presentation of the Knight, the Squire and the Yeoman as a group, serves to make the individuality of each emerge more clearly. We recall that the virtuous Knight had good horses but was not himself gay: the gayness of his servant and his son is specifically emphasised. The faithful devotion to duty of both master and servant places the Squire's high spirits and his knightly potential in sharper focus. The Yeoman's involvement with the natural world gives solid backing to the chivalric and courtly life of his masters.

THE PRIORESS

In the description of the PRIORESSE Chaucer seems to reach a peak of enthusiasm—there are some twenty-four superlative expressions in forty-five lines. However, while she is being treated with dazzled admiration by the pilgrim, each enthusiastic phrase comes to be seen in the poet's view as yet another point of satire.

This satirical double view does not depend, as perhaps it does in the case of the Knight, on the meeting of an ideal standard of behaviour with the hard facts of actual life. Rather it depends on the compromise the Prioress has achieved between two parallel but incongruous ideals. Despite her apparent affable calm, we soon come to see her as caught uneasily between, on the one hand, the rules governing the behaviour, dress and attitudes proper to a high-ranking religious woman, and on the other, the perfect behaviour, attitudes and dress laid down so copiously for the ideal lady by the writers in the courtly love tradition. It is thus appropriate that this Prioress is placed in the General Prologue immediately after the courtly group of characters—the Knight, the Squire and their yeoman—but before the genuinely renegade religious—the Monk and the Friar.

The two ideals—religious and courtly—were close enough in manner and even vocabulary for the naive pilgrim not to notice the discrepancy: the carefulness of behaviour, the neatness and restraint of appearance, even the words 'conscience', 'charitable' and 'pitous' belong ambivalently to both traditions. But Chaucer is masterful in indicating that, for this Prioress, all these characteristics have slipped down the moral scale from the discipline and noble christianity of the one ideal to the dainty sensuality and over-refined sensibility of the other.

For example, the founders of religious houses considered the nun's habit as a means of concealing and disciplining the enticements of the flesh, whereas Le Roman de la Rose, Chaucer's chief text-book of

176

courtly behaviour, lays it down as a woman's duty to reveal, display and enhance what points of beauty she possesses. The forehead was one of the important beauties and Chaucer's Prioress has typically modified the rules of her order to display a very fine specimen. The phrase describing her modest and quiet smiling, so suitable to a Prioress, has, in fact, all the wrong connotations, being a conventional description of the courtly heroine. The description of her excellent table manners is a close reworking of a passage from *Le Roman de la Rose* (see Appendix A). Similarly, her extreme tenderness of heart is of the same tradition, and her features are all the standard of courtly beauty.

There is no reason to suppose that the Prioress is intended to be conscious of her devotion to the ideals of courtliness. Her being on pilgrimage, her keeping of pets, her swearing, even by St. Loy, and her adaptation of her clothing and 'accessories'—were all faults slight enough and common enough at the time to evade the notice of her somewhat woolly 'conscience'. *She* thinks, no doubt, that *Amor* means divine love, that she owes it to her position as Prioress to be careful in manner and deportment—even that it is true charity that she feels towards mice and dogs. *We* are aware that the courtliness of manner vitiates her religious life.

Moreover, this courtliness of manner is not an accurate copy; it is 'cheere of court' as imagined in the circumscribed and insulated life of a nunnery. Nowhere does Chaucer make this clearer than in his precise reference to her French. The contrast he makes is between Parisian French—the dominant form of the language in the fourteenth century both in its courtly refinement and in its literary culture—and the provincial Anglo-French dialect—as, for instance, it was spoken and probably taught by the nuns at Stratford atte Bowe. Fourteenth century Anglo-French—which has been described as 'an exotic and artificial dialect needing hot-house culture'—was often ridiculed by speakers of Parisian French, among them of course members of the English court of Richard II. Where Anglo-French *was* still spoken, as it certainly was in some nunneries, it was probably on account of its erstwhile association with the upper classes. It was 'genteel' but anachronistic.

This sheltered convent life which kept the Prioress ignorant of the real language of court, has similarly never enabled her to develop the true compassion and charity shown by the Parson towards his parishioners (especially the sinners) and towards the pilgrims. The kind of sensibility she has developed, while it is exemplified in her attitude to animals, is most fully displayed in her Tale of the little 'clergeoun'.

Every detail in the description of the MONK condemns him at the strict bar of Christian morality. Well-fed, richly clothed, given over to expensive pleasures and profane pursuits, he is a catalogue of the vices of a self-indulgent monasticism so often condemned in late mediaeval satire. Behind this figure of the 'fair prelat' stands the great tradition of Christian asceticism, the pursuit of the knowledge of God by the rejection of the world and retirement from worldly possessions and activities, by humility and the discipline of all the appetites of the flesh that interfere with spiritual grace. Line by line, detail by detail, the Monk betrays this calling.

Yet, paradoxically, there is an engaging vigour about the man—he is associated with images of horses and hunting, of food, of bodily health and physical luxury, images which engage our own enjoyment of life. He is even, in a worldly sense, a 'fair prelat', 'to been an abbot able'; the sense of an imposing presence derives largely from the pilgrim Chaucer's obvious admiration, an admiration so complete that his opinions and even his tone of voice come to echo those of the Monk.

However, we admire him only by setting aside our moral judgment —as Chaucer the pilgrim clearly does in agreeing with his opinions, and as we so often do in real life with such 'good fellows'. To correct such admiration, the poet keeps the moral standard in our minds through a number of pointed metaphors and careful reminders. The bridle bells, so attractive as an image, are compared with the chapel bells he is neglecting; the not implausible argument, that the world may be better served outside the monastery than by driving yourself mad over books and physical labour, is merely used to justify a taste for hard riding and hunting—and what has a *monk* to do with the *world* anyway? The cheerful abuse directed at the venerable St. Augustine and the monastic rule returns against the Monk himself and against all those whose materialistic ignorance of the soul's health looks merely for outward prosperity and good fellowship as the criteria of a man's success in life.

Like the Monk, the FRERE is condemned by the ideals which he represents but fails to uphold, the glad poverty, the humble service to the sick and the poor shown by St. Francis of Assisi. But the Friar lacks even the worldly attractiveness, the honest dishonesty of the Monk; he is close to the traditional figure of Hypocrisy, every detail of whose appearance, thought and speech is part of a devious 'false seeming', put on like a cloak for his own evil ends. (See Appendix D.)

Wherever Chaucer is clearly echoing the Friar's arguments, we find a perversion of religious doctrine, an expert deceitfulness for which the four orders had become notorious. For example, the friars had wider powers of absolution than the village priests, covering more serious sins; this friar manages to suggest his powers are somehow more effective than those of a mere 'curat'. Again, almsgiving may be a sign of the noblest Christian virtue, charity; the Friar suggests that it may be a sufficient substitute for repentance, a perverted doctrine no doubt very pleasing to the rich from whom he made his greatest profits.

Cloaking this inner corruption is the friar's 'charming' manner, not natural but assumed for profit; if we have any doubts they are settled in the last paragraph. Like his lisp, everything sweet or jolly is but profitable mannerism; like his eyes, this jollity, we feel, has nothing of genuine warmth, but is as cold as the frosty night which sets the stars twinkling so 'attractively'. He only takes on the humble service of his order 'ther as profit sholde arise' and even then it is the inappropriate courteous serviceability of the courtly manner, remote from the inner charity of the true friar.

THE MERCHANT

The 'worthy' MARCHANT may be seen as a secular version of the Friar; like that 'ful solempne man', he conceals beneath a somewhat ceremonial manner and an outward prosperity of appearance a single base passion—profit. He has, however, none of the complexity of the Friar; his conversation is confined to the business of making money, and the narrowness even of this interest, is neatly exposed in the lines

> He wolde the see were kept for any thing
> Betwixe Middelburgh and Orewelle.

He is not even concerned about the general security of trade overseas; he is anxious only about the safety of his own trade route to the staple port.

This boring single-mindedness makes his prosperity seem of doubtful value, and we soon find he is not even secure in this prosperity. He is in debt and attempting to recover his position by various illegal expedients; in the process he is concealing his shakiness beneath a stately manner. It is typical of the man that he should use a saddle that gives a false impression of his stature.

Chaucer is perhaps commenting on the darker side of the growing middle-class prosperity, the spiritual and human barrenness that money breeds in its devotees. Like the anonymous Guildsmen, he seems to be so drained of personality that Chaucer does not even learn his name.

THE CLERK

The gaunt abstracted figure of the CLERK, too completely absorbed in learning to trouble himself with worldly prosperity, is in sharp contrast with the Merchant and the Sergeant of Law, with whom he is placed. Their care for outward appearance and their barren devotion to material gain throws him into attractive relief. By comparison with the selfish triviality of so many of the pilgrims, his moral earnestness and high seriousness, his appetite for learning and teaching and his forgetfulness of himself make him thoroughly admirable.

Nevertheless, Chaucer does not take him completely seriously. The Clerk belongs to the ancient tradition of the unworldly scholar, like the famous Thales who was reputed to have gazed on the stars so earnestly that he fell into a marl-pit (an anecdote later referred to by the Miller in his satire on clerks). Though Chaucer was himself greatly devoted to books, he was also a busy man of affairs; and his reading always interacted with a close observation of the world around him. We must take it as ironic, therefore, when he praises that scholarship which renders a man unwilling to concern himself with common human affairs. Indeed, the Clerk is too immersed in his moral philosophy to advance to the practical morality of a benefice, let alone to the worldly usefulness of secular office.

When Chaucer makes the ironic comment that though he was a philosopher yet he had little gold in his chest, he is referring to alchemical philosophers, endlessly and vainly trying to find the process that could turn all things to gold. But there is also a wry comment on the uselessness of all philosophy and on the comicality of the scholar who effects nothing in the practical world. Though the clerk would disown the world for his love of learning, there is still something amusingly ineffectual about a devoted pursuit that leads to such striking unprosperity. There is a certain naivety, a lack of urbanity even in the admirable earnestness of the man, a singlemindedness of approach in striking contrast to the complex variety of outlook of Chaucer himself. Even his speech, in form and substance, has come to sound like the books he reads.

The thin figure on an emaciated horse, with his mind on higher things amid the bustle and vitality of the pilgrimage, is inevitably comic.

The SERGAUNT OF THE LAWE ranks highest among the pilgrims after the Knight, having much of the social standing of the Franklin and a great deal more professional pomp and circumstance.

A Sergeant of Law—'one who serves [the King] in matters of law'— was chosen by king's writ from among the most eminent lawyers of the time, and had to be of at least sixteen years standing in the study and practice of his profession; there were probably no more than twenty Sergeants in Chaucer's time. His duties involved pleading in the Court of Common Pleas, the court where civil, as opposed to criminal, cases were heard; such cases frequently concerned disputes over titles and claims to land. Sergeants were also frequently appointed by temporary patents and commissions as judges of the assize courts, travelling the country to sit at the periodic county sessions. From their number were chosen the permanent judges of the king's courts.

The position was one of ceremonial and privilege: they were, for example, permitted to retain their peculiar head-gear in the presence of the king. Chaucer's Sergeant fills the role with great dignity and competence, to all appearance an admirable representative of Justice, and able to reduce to clear cut certainty the almost inextricable tangles of the law.

But as with the Doctor of Physic, 'all is not sweet, all is not sound' beneath this professional competence. The interest of this description lies in the deft ironies which qualify the admirable figure. Where the manner and matter of the Clerk's conversation, which has just been described, reveals transparently the spirit of the man, the great dignity of the Sergeant seems to be *merely* a matter of wise words, covering up a lack of real virtue. The line 'And yet he semed bisier than he was' also implies a professional facade and we begin to look more closely at the spirit that directs all his professional activities.

Chaucer sets the learning and fame that have raised him to be 'Justice in assise', against a comment, not on any good he may have

181

done, but on the amount of fees and robes it has earned him—and which have allowed him to be 'so greet a purchasour'. Again, his power of simplifying the law serves his own end—acquiring titles to land that no one can challenge; his remarkable knowledge of cases and precedents serves to draw up documents safe from attack, whether actually just or not. Nowhere is there a suggestion that justice is his aim; under the lawyer's facade of dignified activity, the motivating interest is acquisition.

THE FRANKLIN

With no apparent awareness of incongruity, the morally innocent pilgrim-narrator calls the FRANKELEYN 'Epicurus owene sone' and 'Seint Julian' within five lines. Epicurus 'was he who believed that carnal delight was the highest good, and for that, forsook completely the good of the soul and gave himself to the flesh' (Gower, *Miroir de l'Omme*). The Franklin would certainly have seemed to the Parson a figure of gluttony, as one who ate often, of rare and 'deyntee' foods on which excessive care had been expended. In the light of strict Christian teaching he stands condemned.

But Chaucer, the son of a prosperous wine-merchant, living in the court and among solid citizens, must have found such a view over-simple, out of touch with the world he knew. The pilgrim narrator in fact speaks for common judgement in finding no real clash between the Franklin's Epicurean tastes and his Saint Julian-like hospitality: worldly delight may, in life if not in sermons, combine with and indeed foster many amiable and generous virtues.

The traditional figure of gluttony is gross, nauseating and diseased. The Franklin, attuning his diet to the natural cycle of the seasons, is most attractively healthy; Chaucer even compares him with his favourite flower, the daisy. The care expended on food and drink is not mere appetite but an interest as natural as snow and as free to all comers. His 'delyt' overflows into universal generosity, a permanent table always laden with food and drink for all. He comes to seem an almost mythical figure, not of Appetite but of Abundance.

Moreover, he accepts the social responsibility entailed by his wealth. He represents perhaps the best of the growing middle-class, bent on comfort and pleasure, but generous and with a sense of responsibility. It is ironic that, of all the pilgrims, only the ideal Parson and Ploughman and the Epicurean Franklin show active charity.

182

In contrast with the Franklin, whose wealth flows outward in munificence, the FIVE GUILDSMEN present those perennial comic figures, the new rich, whose wealth merely promotes vanity and the pursuit of petty dignities. In this deft piece of mockery, Chaucer seems to build them up to a point of some pomp and circumstance, with the wisdom of Aldermen, the dignity of Merchants and Burgesses; he then deflates them by showing the real basis of their pomp. The proof of their aldermanic wisdom is merely that they are rich enough to qualify for the office; the motive for their 'dignity' is merely the vanity of their wives. And in retrospect we notice that Chaucer's praise never really penetrates beyond the too-new bits and pieces of their accoutrements, the fancy dress of their livery. It is part of Chaucer's comic treatment of their solemn pretension that they remain merely a group, indistinguishable from one another—and they are never mentioned again. Under the brash facade was nothing worth remembering.

THE COOK

To further their dignity, the Guildsmen have their own cook—even the Franklin does not feel the need for such a distinguishing expense! But the COOK merely reveals their real distance from the dignity at which they aim, as do their other social pretensions. In an extended verbal joke, the sumptuous, mouth-watering foods turn to ashes when the disgusting 'mormal', associated with dirt and diseased women, is thrown among them. And the Cook's subsequent behaviour on the pilgrimage shows that his knowledge of London ale concerns quantity, not, as we might suppose, quality. With stinking breath and white face, he is too drunk even to tell his tale.

THE SHIPMAN

The ambiguous phrase 'a good felawe', neatly defines the SHIPMAN. Clearly anything but good in any moral sense, he is nevertheless extremely good at his job and of that cheerful immorality which always qualifies a man to be thought a good fellow. As Chaucer frequently makes clear, it is not the quality of a man's moral life that governs our liking or approval of him. Good humour, confidence, ability to manage his world are the qualities that attract, especially in the more obviously male worlds, like business or the army. Too much troubling of the conscience is mere weakness of mind.

In Chaucer's time, sea-faring was one of the roughest of

occupations. The Merchant is concerned about the amount of piracy in the channel and it seems likely that Chaucer was referring to notorious places and cases in mentioning Dartmouth and the barge 'Maudelayne'. In this lawless country of the sea, the Shipman is cheerfully, healthily competent, the best of 'good felawes'.

On land, however, riding on the pilgrimage, he is but an awkward figure, clearly out of his element. In the comparatively lawful context of London, and in the moral context of Canterbury, his immorality is less acceptable. 'Good felawe' though he may seem, he still has to reckon with the law of man and God.

Nevertheless we are left with the image of the confident seaman, rather than of the awkward pilgrim; the details of the Shipman's craft give a strong impression of his intricate mastery of sea-faring. His natural element is that of storm and sun, open sea and difficult coastlines, and of privateering and the cheating of mere landlubberly merchants. It seems only part of the environment in which he thrives that he should disdain finicky conscience and show the cheerful callousness of sending his prisoners home by water.

THE DOCTOR OF PHYSIC

The DOCTOUR OF PHISIK seems at first to be Chaucer's image of the ideal medical practitioner: the initial description of his method of treating patients is an admirably concise summary of the principles and process of diagnosis and treatment. But by the end of the passage, a narrow outlook and an acquisitive self-centredness has seeped up through the details of his craft, making him an interesting and distasteful character. Like the Shipman before him, he is a man expert at his calling but lacking any knowledge of the Christian conscience that should direct it: in the case of a physician, the lack is striking.

This disparity between his professional ability and his human worth is defined by neat juxtaposition of detail. The efficient organization that makes sure the required drugs and medicines are on tap at an instant's notice was important in a time when the prescribed medicines might be changed hourly to follow the changing influence of the heavens. But the personal motive is then revealed—the profits to be won by both doctor and apothecary; the admirable organization is but another instance of an age-old racket.

This rather unsavoury detail, separating the opening description of the doctor's genuine expertise from the roll-call of authorities, makes us doubt whether that list is evidence of real learning or merely an

184

echo of his impressive bed-side manner. Moreover, this resounding list is followed by an account, not of his self-less devotion to the science of healing, but merely of his care for his own body, as though implying that all this learning is in the end devoted to self-interest of one kind or another.

Again, the luxurious clothes imply no munificence; he wears them in spite of a general 'carefulness' in spending, perhaps as part of the pomp and circumstance that fosters the image of the learned and dignified doctor. Not only is there no generosity in his wealth, but also it derives largely from the national calamity of plague; the conjunction of luxury and distress leaves a bitter taste in the mouth. After all the indications of his motivating money-hunger, the final comment that he loved gold for its medicinal qualities is cuttingly ironic and serves to make clear the gap between the real usefulness of medical knowledge and the constricted spirit of the man who has it to sell.

The character of the Doctor is perhaps shown most subtly in the paragraph comparing his carefulness over diet with his carelessness of the Bible; the riming of 'digestible' and 'Bible' sharply points up the comparison. Doctors were commonly attacked as being atheists, partly because so many of their authorities were pagan, but partly, as Chaucer suggests, because their care was purely for the body of man, not for his soul. The Doctor applies all his science to the preservation of his health, disciplining his appetite according to medical theory, reading widely in medical text books, and totally neglecting the text book necessary for his soul's health. His mental boundaries are limited by the particular science he practises, a narrowness of outlook not uncommon in scientists even in more recent times.

'In al this world ne was ther noon hym lik', at least in the matter of medical knowledge. As a man there are all too many like him.

THE WIFE OF BATH

One of the most lurid threads of mediaeval Christianity was the tradition of anti-feminism which saw woman as the carnal temptress, tearing man from his spiritual good by the strings of sensuality. The WYF OF BATHE is an incarnation of such a figure; her solid, sensual vitality and its effects on those around her are both a confirmation of the traditional Christian distrust of woman, and a criticism of its often arid unworldliness.

Both in the General Prologue and subsequently in her own Prologue and Tale, Chaucer silhouettes the Wife against the clear light of the Christian ideal. Her worldly care for social standing is presented in terms of precedence at the offertory; the feminine extravagance of her clothing is focussed in the hat she wears to church on Sunday; her frequent marriages have brought her time and again to the church door; her moral 'wandering by the way' finds expression in a love of pilgrimage to holy shrines.

We are thus continually reminded of the Christian teaching concerning women and wives, and at every point the Wife violates that teaching. In her almost masculine vigour, sitting astride her horse, with a hat like a soldier's shield and with sharp spurs, she is unlikely to assume the properly submissive role of woman: it is she who has run through a series of husbands. Luxurious, promiscuous, a loud gossiper and immodest, she is a case-history for the preacher's hand-book—the scarlet temptress, eternal Eve.

But Chaucer does not allow any easy condemnation. She is a figure as full of distinctively human energy as one could hope or fear to meet. Colourful, confident, accomplished, there is a value in her gross vitality which finds no place in the narrow Christian orthodoxy of the time. In her there flows the coarse power of the world and the flesh, the deep undercurrent of the unreasonable animal in man, which has puzzled and overcome the moralists and theorisers since the beginning of history. Our final impression from both this description and her more prolonged self-revelation is of one whose real and impatient vitality has burst the seams of the Christian world that seeks to control her.

THE PARSON

The PERSOUN and his brother the Ploughman are the only pilgrims on whom there falls no shadow of criticism or ridicule: they function purely as representatives of the admirable and engaging ideal by which all the other pilgrims are judged, the ideal of Christian charity operative in the world in priest and layman respectively.

The Parson not only sets the standard by his practice of Christianity, as described in the General Prologue, but also by the sermon that forms his Tale. He gives there a detailed analysis of the Seven Deadly Sins, accurately pin-pointing the various sins practised and preached by the other pilgrims. Against these sins he sets the Christian ideal, and forces home the need for repentance and absolution.

To describe such a type figure, Chaucer draws heavily on phrases that echo the Bible, the Church Fathers and the literature of Christian exhortation. The common biblical metaphor of the shepherd and his sheep extends over eighteen lines of the portrait; the image of walking

186

with a staff to the farthest limits of his parish echoes the traditional image of the pilgrim and perhaps the instruction of Christ to the apostles in St. Mark: 'And he commanded them that they should take nothing for the way but a staff only.' The comparison of priests to gold and the laity to iron, and the image of the sinful priest as rusted gold, are taken from the Church Fathers. Such phrases as 'first he wroghte and afterwards he taughte', 'in adversitee ful pacient', 'he koude in litel thyng have suffisaunce' are steeped in the moral atmosphere of church homily, as is the antithesis with which the description begins, between worldly poverty and the riches of holy thought and work.

Though such an ideal figure lacks the vivid presence of many of the other pilgrims (and there is virtually no personal description), the Parson does not seem unreal or unworldly. We see him in close relation with the common world of his time, the world of money-grubbing priest and widespread poverty, of riches and misfortune, of social distinctions and common humanity. Moreover the images which surround him are rich with natural connotations—sheep and wolves, gold and iron, storm, rain and winter mire. The ideal figure is set firmly in the natural world, among the vicissitudes of human emotion and action, having an effect on sinners and sufferers and therefore sharing much of their energy and life.

THE PLOUGHMAN

The Parson is the perfect priest: the PLOWMAN, his brother by both blood and the spirit, is the perfect lay Christian. And these two, who embody the Christian ideal, are the poorest of all the travellers. One of the recurring themes of *The Canterbury Tales* is that avarice produces success in the world's eyes—the Pardoner, Merchant, Sergeant of Law and the Doctor—but is morally destructive of its devotees. By contrast, the poverty which the Parson and Ploughman exhibit may be seen as a necessary part of their virtue. A venerable tradition enjoins destitution as a necessary condition for Christian perfection, a tradition memorably expounded by St. Francis of Assisi and spread throughout Christendom by the mendicant friars. 'It is easier for a camel to pass through the eye of a needle than for a rich man to enter into the kingdom of heaven.'

Chaucer, therefore, found it natural to take his image of the perfect lay Christian from among the poor. And it was natural too to choose a ploughman, one who laboured in the fields in the most basic of all human occupations, growing food. Such a figure may easily be

187

symbolic of the human condition as a whole, and has been from time immemorial. When Adam was cast out of Eden, his lot was to cultivate the soil—'in the sweat of thy face shalt thou eat bread'—and metaphorically it is the task of all men since Adam to be true workers in the fields, cultivating the earth in obedience to God. To be a 'trewe swynkere' is therefore to be a true Christian and Chaucer's Ploughman symbolizes the perfection of lay Christian life of whatever social level. Living according to the commandments—loving God and his neighbour—he shows charity to the poor for the love of Christ, supports the church willingly with his tithes and labours ungrudgingly for the nourishment of men. He is the perfection of Charity, the primary Christian virtue.

Of course, actual labourers were unlike this theoretical ideal; in real life poverty seldom breeds virtue and there were continual diatribes against the avarice, unwillingness and restlessness of the peasants, especially since the Peasants' Revolt of 1381. Chaucer's description gains moral impact from the discrepancy between the ideal and the actuality known to his audience.

THE MILLER

Flanking the Parson and Ploughman are two figures of the roughest secular grossness, the Wife of Bath and the MILLERE, both having a dominating physical presence that contrasts with the spiritual force of the brothers in charity. These two are the representatives of the music of earthly appetites, the Wife knowing well the old dance of sexuality, the Miller being expert in the bagpipe music of all the lower appetites. Gross and all-subduing physicality, with its blind energy and moral ignorance weigh down his description: the sounds that issue from him are the notes of the bagpipe and a bawdy jangling as from the mouth of hell.

A wart on the nose, a thick, short-shouldered physique, red hairyness, flaring nostrils, and a big mouth all combine, according to the physiognomists, to indicate violence and sensuality, with their related qualities of shamelessness and stupidity. In fact, the only way the Miller uses his head, apart from the habitual dishonesty of millers, is in the violent display of breaking down doors!

Yet Chaucer's judgement is never that of the mere moralist—there is something positive in this ignorant energy. The Miller is not vicious but ignorant of higher values; the contrast with the Pardoner makes this clear. He seems partly protected from our distaste by the innocence of his amorality. Like the gargoyles on the mediaeval

188

cathedral, he seems a necessary adjunct to any complete picture of the human race.

THE MANCIPLE

The MAUNCIPLE, like the Parson, is given no physical description at all; he is purely a type and not a character, at least as far as the General Prologue is concerned. At first reading, he seems to be described appreciatively as a figure of unlearned shrewdness, astute in his trading and by God-given natural ability able to outshine all the learning of those he serves. But when we consider the meaning of the phrase 'sette hir aller cappe', we realize the irony that pervades the praise and recognize the type he really represents.

The only way the Manciple can 'make fools of them all' is of course by cheating in his use of the funds entrusted to him for provisioning; it is in his private capacity, not just as agent of one of the Inns of Court, that he is always ahead in his accounting! His masters, moreover, are genuinely praiseworthy, contemporary 'good stewards', of real wisdom and responsibility (if a little unworldly in letting themselves be fooled). In contrast with such beneficial stewardship, in which is represented the ideal relationship between a servant and his lord, the Manciple must seem a figure of mere worldly cunning, a type of the bad servant. It is heavily ironic that his 'wit' is attributed to God's grace, a grace which may give the unlearned innocent a wisdom surpassing that of the learned man, but which certainly gives nothing to a man of 'lewed' cunning.

The comic effect of this portrait lies in the sting in the tail; it is not until the last line, which clinches the contrast between the virtue of the Masters and the immorality of the Manciple, that we see the irony in the former praise, and realize the aptness of setting the man in the midst of a group of ignorant deceivers.

THE REEVE

Our first image of the REVE is of a mean, shorn, grotesquely skeletal figure, with all the unsociable attributes of the 'colerik' man. Chaucer then places this figure in its agricultural environment, the small productive world of the manor, with its dependence on weather and season, its crops and storage barns and its variety of livestock. His dwelling is set handsomely apart among the beauties of nature on the heathland (where Zephirus inspires the 'tendre croppes').

In this vigorous natural world the Reeve exists like a skeleton at a feast, sharing nothing of its healthy life; his only relation with it is suggested in the two lines 'Ther was noon auditour koude on him wynne' and 'Ther koude no man brynge hym in arrerage'. Avarice is his passion: his crooked cunning turns all his undoubted abilities to private profit. He is a country version of that figure of 'lewed wit', the Manciple.

His relationship with the other workers on the manor is equally arid. Though united with them in social rank and, apparently, in dishonesty, there is no fellow feeling. The suspicious vindictiveness of his temperament suppresses any 'good fellowship'. Knowing all their tricks, perhaps because he came up through the ranks himself, he sacrifices his fellows in pursuing his own ends—the prosperity of the estates on which his own profiteering depends. The only person with whom he is on amicable terms is his lord, and in this case too, merely for dishonest profit. His alienation from the manorial community is typified by his house on the heathland; it is not the natural beauty of its surroundings that he seeks but its privacy where he can nurse his choler and his private stores: he seeks the shadows not for solace but for secrecy.

On the pilgrimage, the Reeve presents the same character. The excellent horse, the luxurious 'surcote' (perhaps a perk from his lord) only emphasize the withered body they support and clothe; and as in Norfolk, he separates himself from the sociable crowd, riding suspiciously behind them all.

In the Prologue to his Tale, he is seen as the epitome of Old Age, all his disagreeable characteristics contributing to such a figure; in the General Prologue, however, the description is more of the choleric man, his spirit rusted by the flames of choler rather than by the destructive process of time. Though apparently excellent at his job, either as reeve or as carpenter, he is tarnished in spirit, withered in body by his grasping and grudging character; he is neatly symbolized by the rusty sword he bears.

It seems likely that the reference to 'Baldeswelle' is a reference to a famous or notorious character or estate of Chaucer's time, which may have given some additional local colour to the satire.

THE SUMMONER

The SOMNOUR is diseased, but his condition does not call for pity; not only is it the result of his own gluttonous desires for food and women, but also it is ultimately the physical result, the outward evidence, of a complete moral breakdown.

The disease has been identified by Professor Curry as 'a species of morphia known as *gutta rosacea* (sauce fleem) which has already been allowed to develop into that kind of leprosy called *alopicia*'. It is caused by a corruption of the blood. The first stage covers the skin with 'livid red pustules', the second produces a falling of the hair from the eyebrows and elsewhere and a swelling of the face, with further development of 'matter-infected pustules'.

The Summoner has tried all the acknowledged remedies but before we feel sympathy for his vain efforts to cure himself, Chaucer reveals that he persists in indulging just those appetites which foster the downward course of the disease. The medical treatises quoted by Curry specifically warn against heating the blood by consuming onions, garlic, leeks and red wine in particular. Moreover the disease was thought to be contracted by association with infected women.

The Summoner's continued appetite for the foods and women that are destroying him is a graphic image of the progress of deadly sin. The disease, caused by his gluttony and lechery, can only be relieved by more indulgence in gluttony and lechery, in a descending spiral that has made his body an image of hell. He has reached the point of frenzy, in his drunkenness shouting as though mad, dressing himself as a living parody of an ale-stake, bribable with a mere quart of wine. He has subjected himself to all the five species of drunkenness later described by the Parson: he has lost his reason, his spirit is disturbed, he preserves no decency in his eating, his body is distempered and he has sunk into forgetfulness of everything that concerns salvation.

The real irony of this description is that such a man should be a Summoner, the overseer of the moral discipline of his diocese. His drunken repetition of a few meaningless Latin phrases is a bitter parody of his official function. Similarly, for the benefit of such good fellows as himself, he turns against the whole institution of church discipline which he is supposed to represent, not only corrupting it by encouraging lechery, but also teaching his friends the ins and outs of bribery, and casting scorn on the moral power of excommunication.

Chaucer's interpolation at this point is double edged. On the one hand, the slightly shocked pilgrim is exclaiming that excommunication and absolution *are* powerful moral weapons—and in the context of the pilgrimage he is right. But the afterthought—one must also beware of getting involved in the courts—deflates the force of this claim; for most people it *is* the danger of imprisonment or fines that they fear, rather than the danger to their souls. And this is the fear that gives the Summoner his power (especially over the young and lusty)

191

Chaucer is looking with some irony at the power of the church to inflict temporal punishment for moral offences, and sees the inevitable degradation such church justice undergoes in the popular estimation. It is significant that his Parson is loath to invoke the temporal power of the church.

THE PARDONER

The Summoner seems like a man in a self-perpetuating hell, but the PARDONER is yet more deeply steeped in corruption. On the descending ladder of sinfulness that leads to irrevocable damnation, the last step is for free-will to join with a known evil, making no effort to resist the temptation. The Pardoner seems beyond pardon since, professionally knowledgeable as he is in the necessary condition for God's mercy and having that knowledge constantly in his mouth, he nevertheless gaily and willingly subjects himself to what he knows to be the worst of sins, blasphemy. The abject and ignorant frenzy of the Summoner seems quite human by comparison.

Though he proclaims himself a figure of Avarice, the Pardoner's main aim really seems to be verbal and practical blasphemy, the desecration of religion and of the sacrament of penance for which he claims to be the agent. The tone of voice and the choice of phrase he uses to describe his pardons and relics are clearly contemptuous, as is the choice of the most inappropriate material possible from which to fabricate these relics. He talks of pardons hot from Rome, he uses pigs' bones for saints' relics, a pillow case for the Virgin's veil. And his subsequent Prologue further develops this delight in mocking the faith and the faithful.

The Pardoners were not, despite their popular name, concerned with 'pardon', or forgiveness of sins, directly, but with the distribution of papal indulgences. The purchaser of such a document did not thereby obtain pardon for particular sins: such pardon was obtained only by the sacrament of penance, by true contrition and absolution. The indulgence, in return for the money offered for the good work of the church, remitted the temporal punishment which still remained due to sin after such a pardon had been obtained. The pardoners also commonly displayed relics of the saints for the devout to touch, and often preached as well. The main reason for the notoriety of the profession was that they used their legitimate role, their 'pardons' and relics and preaching, to suggest to the faithful that they actually had the keys of heaven, that they could dispense forgiveness of sins at the drop of a coin.

192

One of the Pardoner's pieces of equipment is the 'vernycle' which he wears on his cap to proclaim that he and his pardons *are* hot from Rome (though we have reason to doubt it). But the 'vernycle' is also an imprint of Christ's face; with it Chaucer produces the striking visual image of Christ—the source of all real forgiveness of sins—presiding over the brimful 'treasury' of pardon.

> A vernycle hadde he sowed upon his cappe,
> His walet biforn hym in his lappe
> Bretful of pardoun comen from Rome al hoot.

In this image we see both the ideal of Christian mercy and the Pardoner's proper role of bringing Christ's mercy to the repentant. We are aware from the tone of these lines that the Pardoner is merely using this pious role to make the priests and the people his apes, but the ideal, so vividly visualised in this way, sets a seal of condemnation on him and his tricks.

Chaucer surrounds this ideal image, moreover, with details of the Pardoner's actual grotesque appearance and behaviour, details which point to a perversion of his nature in striking contrast with the perfected human nature of Christ. He is compared with the hare and the goat, animals noted for their lechery. But it is made clear that his is no ordinary lechery (even the Wife of Bath, for all her fleshly appetite, can be contemptuous of the Pardoner). The effeminate vanity implied by nine lines devoted to his care of his ratty and waxy hair, the lack of any sign of a beard, the thin goat's voice with which he sings the treble part to the Summoner's ground bass, the glaring eyes signifying shamelessness, all lead up to the contemptuous summary 'I trowe he were a geldyng or a mare'. The horse was another image of lust but the homosexual Pardoner is compared with the castrated or female horse, and the object of his perverted lust is apparently the Summoner, his 'freend and his comper'. The peculiar moral corruption which delights in desecrating whatever is of the spirit, is paralleled by a physical and emotional corruption, a desecration of his human nature as well. And to add a last touch of horror to the worst of the pilgrims, there is a high-spirited enthusiasm in all his behaviour which makes him on the one hand a curiously unpleasant version of the Squire and on the other an excellent performer in church.

THE HOST

The HOOST is the first character in *The Canterbury Tales* (apart from the pilgrim narrator) to be revealed through his speech as well as by direct description, and he continues to display himself in this way throughout the work, introducing the pilgrims before they tell their tales and very often showing strong and characteristic reaction to what they tell. He is thus one of the most important links that hold the work together in spite of its various content.

It was a happy invention of Chaucer's to choose the host of an inn, a professional purveyor of 'confort and mirthe' as Master of Ceremonies for the pilgrimage. He is one of the few people one can think of used to handling a group of such variety of type and social station, and it seems realistic that he should attempt to gather such a group into a single party for mutual entertainment. It comes naturally to him to find just the right combination of deference, ribaldry and command for the various pilgrims.

He is obsequious to the Prioress when he asks her to tell a tale, he is a rough-tongued echo of the Knight when the latter interrupts the tedious sequence of the Monk's 'tragedyes', he is condescendingly merry at the expense of the Nun's Priest and cruelly devastating at the expense of the Pardoner.

Already in the General Prologue we find the Host, with blandishments and comic threats, coaxing the pilgrims into a jolly entertainment. Gathering them all into a flock, he makes up the rules for the game and sets them on, rather like an entertainer getting a children's party going. The initial cautious flatness of mood of the pilgrims is deftly caught by Chaucer in their indifference to the Host's jollity and plans, and their lack of discussion among themselves; they are still eyeing each other somewhat warily. 'Us thoughte it was noght worth to make it wys. And graunted hym withouten moore avys'. But the Host quickly breaks the ice, and arouses their amusement with his plan for tale-telling—'This thyng was graunted and oure othes swore With ful glad herte, . . . and thus by oon assent, We been acorded to his juggement. And therupon the wyn was fet anon.'

Much of the amusement of Chaucer's description comes from the blend of heartiness and professional shrewdness in the Host. Though protesting that he is going on the pilgrimage at his own cost for the general entertainment, he is clearly not going to lose money. He turns on the charm only when all the reckonings have been paid— apparently in advance. And the game he devises involves everyone returning to his inn for a supper which may be free to the winner, but which will certainly be paid for in full to the Host.

His physical appearance and his manner are in keeping with his role; he is a 'semely' man to be a 'marchal' of such entertainment.

194

His solidity of body and his energy ally him with the Monk (a manly man with 'eyen stepe') and with the Wife of Bath and the Miller. Like them, he displays a rather crude good fellowship, with an equally crude moral sense—after all, the keeper of an inn cannot afford to be 'nice' about the company he provides for! It is the Host who organizes the secular gaiety of this supposedly devout occasion, asserting that there is no 'confort ne mirthe' in riding silently as stones, and in the subsequent conversation it is he who disperses seriousness and fosters a most unreligious merriment. With his mirth, his resounding blasphemies and his ignorance of spiritual values, he represents most vociferously in this work the outlook of secular man. At the end of every tale, he brings the company back, with a bump, to the common world.

THE PARDONER'S PROLOGUE AND TALE

The Pardoner's Tale itself is an exercise, both by Chaucer and by the Pardoner, in one of the most emotional of preaching styles. Like the Prioress's Tale, its aim is to arouse strong feelings without any appeal to reason, though here disgust and fear of sin replace the lachrymose devotion of the Prioress.

The style and action of the Tale are full of preacher's tricks, rhetorical devices for engendering moral horror in the listeners. For example, we are made to think in emotionally charged slogans— the 'compaignye of yonge folk' don't just eat and drink too much in the tavern, they

'. . . doon the devel sacrifise
Withinne that develes temple in cursed wise
By superfluytee abhomynable.'

They don't just swear; rather, 'Oure blissed lordes body they to-tere', using such oaths as 'Goddes digne bones' and 'Goddes armes'. And the events also are grotesquely heightened; the 'riotoures' don't merely drink, they are set in the tavern 'Longe erst er prime rong of any belle'; the friend whose corpse prompts their search for death did not just die but 'was yslayn to-nyght Fordronke as he sat on his bench upright'. The world we know is reduced to a mere playground for the devil.

This intensification of moral blackness (there is very little moral whiteness in the tale at all) is also effected by exclamatory calls for

195

attention and horror—'O glotonye ful of cursednesse!', 'O traytours homicide, O wikkednesse!'—and by the rhetoric of physical disgust—

'O wombe! O bely! O stynkyng cod
Fulfilled of dong and of corrupcioun!'

But Chaucer is not producing a simple parody of a style, a straightforward mockery of a certain common kind of religious imagination: the tale is genuinely powerful. The rhetorical devices work on us as well as on the Pardoner's victims and in a different voice, could be the utterance of worthy piety: they are quite close to certain passages in the Parson's Tale. However much we may be aware of the deliberate exaggeration of effect, the tale does effectively carry us into a dark and doomed world, where the most potent realities are vice and folly, where the brotherhood of men is an impulse of drunkards soon dissolved in murder, and where mankind is, ignorantly or intentionally, in pursuit of death. It has all the grimness of the mediaeval Christian view of the world as a 'thoroughfare of woe', without the redeeming faith in Christ which so lights up the Parson's and the Nun's Priest's Tales.

In this world of fear and death, the only wisdom is either to be prepared to leave it while young—the 'boy' at the tavern says of Death:

'Beth redy for to meete hym evere moore'—

or to long to leave it when old—the old man says:

'Allas! when shal my bones been at reste?'

Those who love this world, the three young men who set out to kill 'this false traytour Deeth', only deliver themselves into death's clutches. The point is emphasized by the irony that it is their love of this world in the shape of gold that makes their quest for death successful, just at the moment they forget the quest and have the most to live for; they do not find Death but are found by him. The old man is an inhabitant of the same fallen world, but one who knows its worthlessness and treachery: he knows that gold is death to its devotees and he only longs to re-enter the restful oblivion of his mother earth. However, even he is ignorant of anything but the woe of life (such a desire is spiritual defeat): in this death-haunted world, even the wisest has no knowledge of the 'new life' for which the

196

whole creation 'groaneth and travaileth in pain', waiting for redemption. Although the old man is mocking the 'riotoures thre' when he explains that he is only old because he can't find anyone who will 'chaunge his youthe for myn age', he reveals by this very comment his ignorance of the crucifixion by which Christ sacrificed his spiritual youth to redeem the 'old Adam' of fallen human nature. For the Pardoner's audience, Christ has once and for all responded to man's plea to 'chaunge his youthe for myn age'. But in the old man's world, the only mention of Christ is, ironically, in the blasphemy of the young men. As they set off to kill death they crucify Christ in the oaths—'hem thoughte that Jewes rente hym noght ynough'— ignorant that it is only through Christ's crucifixion that man may overcome death.

> And Cristes blessed body they to-rente;
> Deeth shal be deed, if that they may hym hente.

It is of course suitable that one wanting to sell the promise of eternal life should terrify his listeners with such a vision of hopeless mortality. Our attitude to this vision is controlled by our knowledge of the character to whom Chaucer has given it.

The Pardoner is a professional deceiver and, in his chosen field, perhaps the most polished professional on the pilgrimage. But his is not the efficient indifference of the mere professional: we cannot see him just as someone practising falsehood for a living. From a literary point of view, he is descended from the allegorical *Faus Semblant* of *Le Roman de la Rose,* an embodiment of religious and social hypocrisies; and, however much Chaucer may have translated allegory into human character, the Pardoner still shows the same complete absorption in the practice of 'false appearances'. Apart from his deceptions, he does not exist: his whole life and imagination are devoted to practical hypocrisy, his satisfactions arise from the complexity and effrontery of these deceptions and from the consciousness of always making the people his 'apes'.

Of course, the 'confession' of his practices to the pilgrim audience is not deceitful, at least in matters of fact: like the self-revelations of wickedness poured out by such allegorical characters as *Faus Semblant* or the Sins in morality plays, this apparently frank exposure might seem an implausible literary convention. But even this confession, like that of the Wife of Bath, becomes plausible in Chaucer's handling. The pilgrimage is a special occasion and provides a special audience—the Pardoner carefully distinguishes between the 'lewed peple' from whom he makes his money, and the 'lordynges', the 'gentils', to whom he now speaks, and who, he feels, will enjoy the spectacle of his deception as much as he. Though the pilgrim audience sinks out of mind for most of his Prologue, this setting is sufficient to make his uncharacteristic truthfulness both believable and expressive of his character. For it is part of his character to be inordinately self-pleased, and in a way that demands public recognition. We have seen his love of display in the General Prologue; his own Prologue and Tale are an invitation to this (for him) unusual audience to join him in the admiration of his talent and wit. There is nothing 'sincere' in his confession; it is yet another display designed to practise on his listeners and to draw from them reactions gratifying to his self-esteem.

The Pardoner's means of 'making the people his apes' are the sermon which agitates them into fear and guilt, and the relics and pardons which promise rescue from these feelings: the people will pay in proportion to the depth of fear and guilt aroused by the sermon. He is a master of his craft; the sermon is powerfully agitating and he knows all the related tricks most likely to bring people to the offering. He tells (in lines 30-71) now, under the guise of holiness, he appeals to their cupidity and lechery with his miraculous relics and to their fear of slander from him or gossip from their neighbour. He tells of the 'bisynesse' in the pulpit that makes him such a 'noble ecclesiaste', and of the 'olde stories' the 'lewed peple' love to hear. 'Of his craft, fro Berwyk into Ware Ne was ther swich another pardoner.'

The ostensible aim of his performance is Avarice

'I preche no thyng but for coveitise.'

At one level the work is a satire, like many another in the fourteenth century, on the pious fraud perpetrated by the Pardoners, whose intention

'is nat but for to wynne
And no thyng for correccioun of synne.'

The details are not far-fetched—they are to be found in church documents attempting to control these notorious abuses.

But for this pardoner, avarice is only of secondary importance. As he describes it, the core of his performance is to move the congregation to repentance so that they will pay for his pardons and thus satisfy his avarice. But a sermon on any sin would serve such a

198

purpose: why does he choose to attack the very sin that motivates the sermon? When he says:

'Thus kan I preche agayn that same vice
Which that I use, and that is avarice',

he is clearly most interested in the witty immorality of preaching against his own practice rather than in the particular vice itself—avarice is merely the vice handiest to him as a Pardoner. Such a procedure gives him the delighted consciousness of secretly mocking the morality he is preaching; and to see his listeners *moved* against the very sin which he is hugging to himself must seem the most satisfyingly outrageous way possible of making them his 'apes'. This covert joy in the multiplication of witty hypocrisies is what remains in our minds.

For the same reason, he has rhetorical outbursts against the blasphemy which is his basic attitude to religion, and the drunkenness and gluttony which he brings to the pilgrims' (and our) attention by insisting on stopping at the ale-stake for a 'draughte of corny ale' and a cake. And the three young men who die so horribly and so justly, die for the very sins the Pardoner practises. What deeper or more satisfying deception could there be than so to play on people's imaginations that he inspires respect for himself as the 'noble ecclesiaste', on the one hand and on the other, a fearful sense of guilt for the very sins he is revelling in, underneath the false appearance. That he can genuinely make 'oother folk to twynne From avarice and soore to repente', only improves the joke.

To the pilgrims and to us, who know the spirit of the man, there is a peculiar fascination in the sermon. When we read such passages as

'O glotonye ful of cursednesse!
O cause first of oure confusioun!
O original of oure dampnacioun
Til Crist hadde boght us with his blood agayn!'

and

'Thise cokes, how they stampe and streyne and grynde
And turnen substaunce into accident
To fulfillen al thy likerous talent!
Out of the harde bones knokke they
The mary, for they caste noght awey
That may go thurgh the golet softe and soote;

199

Of spicerie of leef and bark and roote
Shal been his sauce ymaked by delit
To make hym yet a newer appetit.
But certes, he that haunteth swiche delices
Is deed whil that he lyveth in tho vices.'

the highly wrought eloquence takes on a new depth when we keep in mind that the Pardoner is revelling, in imagination, in the very sin he is describing—beneath the disgust is a lip-licking relish. Such a style of preaching, conjuring up the vividest images of the sinfulness of man, may easily express a wallowing of the spirit in the forbidden joys—Chaucer's Pardoner embodies in full clarity the potentiality for inner dishonesty latent in such a style.

We are left with the vision of a man for whom the truths and symbols of religion are merely stock-in-trade of deception, vices part of a good joke against the faith and the faithful. But of course, they are much more than that both to the pilgrim audience and to us: part of the fascination of the performance is that, since what he preaches is genuine morality, the total opposition between his preaching and his practice actually condemns *him*. Though he thinks he is using religion and morality as a means of deception, it is he who is ultimately deceived; the truths he mocks are stronger than he, and mock him.

The final inglorious debacle, reducing to silence the man whose tongue is his fortune, makes clear how much the Pardoner is the fool of his own cleverness. Having demonstrated his preaching style—'Lo sires, thus I preche'—he then appeals to the pilgrims to add their applause to his self-congratulation by joining him in the joke against religion and against the poor 'apes' on whom he preys. Every tale ends with a blessing—the Pardoner, with mock sincerity, declares that Christ's pardon is best, 'I wol yow nat deceyve'—as though he were now going to stop the joking and at last admit the Truth. It is a declaration so utterly out of key with everything the Pardoner says and does that he cannot mean it or expect the pilgrims to believe he means it. Rather he is giving them a sample of the mock morality he uses against the people, in this case mockery of the very source of all real pardon, Christ himself. And he immediately proceeds to apply to the undeceived pilgrims a comic version of the same deceiving patter that he has used against the 'lewed peple'. He clearly expects his audience, caught up in the glorious joke, to join in a scene of mock pardoning; imitation is the applause he seeks, and he turns to the

200

Host, who so often speaks for the pilgrims, to be the first to pay him the compliment.

But, however entertaining the Pardoner's self-revelation may have been, it is certainly not of the kind to make the pilgrims join him in the perversion of religion. As the Host justly says in reply to the invitation to kiss, in mockery, the phony relics, 'Nay, nay! thanne have I Cristes curs!' As with the sermon, so with the blessing and the sacrament of absolution—though the Pardoner in his joyful perversity thinks to stand religion on its head, the sermon arouses a real sense of the need of absolution in this 'thorough fare of wo', and the blessing reminds us where that absolution is really to be found. The pilgrims laugh when the Host, with equally heavy-handed joking, reduces the Pardoner to impotent silence.

To do so, he turns to the physical perversion shown in the General Prologue. Moral perversion is just a joke to the Pardoner—no attack on that side could have any effect. But the man seems to think he has concealed what even Chaucer the pilgrim notices—that he is 'a gelding or a mare': he dresses as a young man about town 'al of the newe jet' and claims to have 'a joly wenche in every toun'. On this question he is vulnerable, and, with the Host's coarseness, the great act is over.

THE PRIORESS'S TALE

No other of *The Canterbury Tales* is so exactly suited to its teller as is the legend of the martyred child to the Prioress. As an expression of sentimental piety and insulated charity it is a perfect emanation of the Prioress's 'conscience' as Chaucer defines it in the General Prologue. Though superior in artistry, it is nevertheless fairly typical of homiletic 'miracles' in its uncritical acceptance of dubious legend and in its emotionalism. The story with its references to the 8th Psalm, to Rachel and to King Herod's slaughter of the children, is eminently fitted to be a homily for use on the Feast of the Holy Innocents, the liturgy of which day it so often echoes. It is the kind of pious story the Prioress would frequently hear and love to hear. Yet there are touches in the telling which make it unmistakably the Prioress's own: for instance, her concern for the 'litel child' learning his 'litel book' reminds us inevitably of her concern for small dogs and mice.

There can be no denying that the tale has pathos and emotional power of a kind. And it is clearly intended not to instruct in any literal

201

or factual way but to inspire in the hearer that unreasoning and lachrymose devotion so perfectly displayed by the abbot and his company in the very presence of the miracle. The story itself has no involvement with the real world of men and affairs; characters and action have been removed into a kind of hot-house where they are embellished by the rhetoric of affective sentiment. The Virgin Mary is 'Oure blisful lady, Cristes moder deere'; the devil is 'Oure firste foo, the serpent Sathanas'; the martyred child is 'This gemme of chastitee, this emeraude/ And eek of martyrdom the ruby bright', and he is thrown, not simply into a pit, but into 'a wardrobe . . . wheras thise Jewes purgen hir entraille'. In setting too, the story is made remote and timeless: 'Ther was in Asye in a greet citee'. The stanza form with its pattern of rimes beautifully contains the elaborate and largely uncolloquial syntax to produce an almost liturgical movement. This is best seen in the Prologue to the tale, and in the stanzas in which the Prioress adds pious declamation to her narrative.

This clothing of affective sentiment not only insulates the tale from the world of real things and events, it demonstrates the uncritical and sentimentalized nature of the teller. The last stanza contains the Prioress's sibilant plea for God's mercy, although her earlier identity of the Jews with Satan and his race has allowed her to endorse the torture and shameful death meted out to them by the Provost. Her sheltered life—which allows her charity no further scope than weeping over trapped mice and stories about small boys being murdered—enables her to disregard the existence of Jews as people, and to see them as mere symbols of evil. The tale supplements the portrait of the Prioress in the General Prologue in showing her, as R. E. Kaske has so neatly put it, "as the sentimental product of a sheltered existence weeping excessively over such small violences as she knows, and speaking with naive aplomb of stylized horrors whose reality lies beyond her ken".

This is not, of course, to dismiss the Prioress's Tale any more than it is to denounce the Prioress as a fake, nor is it to conclude that Chaucer is doing so. As an example of pious legend it has an economy of narration and perfection of style that makes it one of Chaucer's significant achievements. Each step in the narrative is moulded exactly to the stanza form, there is never any sense of delay or of padding. Yet Chaucer is not by any means endorsing the attitude of mind expressed in the tale. We can never forget that it is Chaucer's Prioress who is telling this tale—Chaucer specifically reminds us at one point by a carefully placed 'quod she'.

202

In exploring a style of narrative Chaucer is defining an area of experience which, in the setting of *The Canterbury Tales*, is seen for what it is. We, like Chaucer, are able to stand back from the emotion of the tale and see it as the pious substitute for the religion of charity. In sharp contrast to the religion of Parson and Ploughman, which is a serving of the world in Christ-like charity, the Prioress shows us a religiosity which uses people and things as objects for contemplation to induce emotional attitudes of devotion. Only a mind which was closed to the realities of everyday life could credit the unbelievable sanctity of the little child and the grotesque identification of the Jews as the race of Satan. Yet such is the power of the Prioress's Tale that the pilgrims are reduced to silence for some time. Chaucer does not say whether it is a silence of devotion or embarrassment: he does say that it was wonderful to see! Contrary to his custom, the Host offers no comment upon the tale, but laughs and jokes and changes the subject. His earthy good humour, perhaps, makes a significant comment upon the irrelevance of the Prioress's virginal piety.

THE NUN'S PRIEST'S TALE

It was an error of judgement to expect a merry tale from the Monk: as though to requite the Host for various insulting comments on his appearance of vigorous virility, he launched solemnly into an apparently endless series of tragedies—until the Knight calls a halt. In turning to the Nun's Priest, the Host makes a more fortunate choice: in spite of the miserable appearance of his horse, the Prioress's attendant tells the most high-spiritedly comic of all the tales. Moreover, he directly 'requites' the Monk by making his tale a mock tragedy, with open parody in lines 438-447. Chaucer expresses our reaction to the tale by referring to its teller as 'this sweete preest, this goodly man Sir John'. This judgement does, however, emphasize that the teller is a priest. Though our first reaction is one of delight at the range of wit and mockery, we would be doing less than justice to the tale if we saw it as *merely* entertaining. For, in the end, although every facet of human nature and every aspiration or belief becomes mere folly of the fowlyard, we are still aware both of a central faith in the care and power of a good God and of the charity that each foolish man should feel towards his fellows.

Just what is the Nun's Priest mocking? Already, in Chaucer's

probable source, the French version in *Le Roman de Renart,* the cock
is an amusing characterization of hen-witted vainglory, refusing out
of a kind of arrogant cowardice the advice of both his hen-wife and
his dream. The animal fable is used to bring into full clarity the
particular human qualities traditionally associated with the cock, the
hen and the fox, and also to prevent the close identification that
could take them seriously. Human behaviour can only be the object
of amused contemplation when it appears in the lives of hens,
however serious it may be in our own world. In Chaucer's re-working,
this satire on human nature deepens and proliferates. The vainglory
of the cock comes to be seen as one aspect of the central folly of man,
the folly that caused his Fall, and around this drama there gathers a
wide spectrum of related human follies.

Chauntecleer is the bright singer. Like the organ and the abbey
clock, he calls men to the praise and worship of God, awakening them
in the morning and marking the canonical hours. As in Eden garden,
his only task, for which he is naturally equipped, is the song of praise.
But, like Man, he falls to the wiles of the devil-fox; he is first blinded
to the warning of God by subjecting his reason to sensuality and he
then symbolically closes his eyes to the fox's evil flattery of his
God-given talent.

The dream is clearly a genuine warning by God. Chantecleer's own
learned argument proves, in admirable mediaeval fashion, the validity
of such dreams as

Warnynge of thynges that men after seen:

his conclusion is impeccable

'I shal han of this avisioun
Adversitee,'

(and the event proves him right). But Pertelote has said she 'kan nat
love a coward'; in defiance of all that reason has taught him, and in
spite of quoting the dictum 'Woman is man's confusion', he discards
the warning of God for the uxorious pleasure of her 'softe syde'.
As Milton says of Adam, he is

Against his better knowledge, not deceav'd
But fondly overcome with female charm.

204

With both eyes open he discards reason for sensual pleasure; soon the ravishing flattery of the fox playing on his over-confidence and vanity, makes him shut his eyes to the fulfilment of the warning and he falls.

Chaucer is not, of course, just retelling the story of the Fall in animal guise—rather, by numerous references, he is drawing on that archetypal drama to make the story of the cock and the fox more than just a 'folye'. It becomes the Christian vision of every man's state, warned and watched over by God but falling through sensuality and pride into the jaws of the universal Fox. The happy ending signifies, perhaps, the power of man to release himself from sin when once his eyes are opened by experience:

> For he that wynketh whan he sholde see
> Al wilfully, God lat him nevere thee.

Every episode of the rambling, multifarious tale relates this central analysis of folly to further aspects of human society and thought. Courtly love is a systematized subjection of man to the sovereignty of woman and sensuality: the image of the courtly lover as always courageous and obedient is what makes Chantecleer reject the proper fear of God and the warning of the dream.

The peculiar value of woman, represented by the housewifely practical advice of Pertelote on the medical treatment of dreams, needs, according to orthodox mediaeval ideas, to be completed and placed in perspective by the wider wisdom of man.

Theologically speaking, revelation from God should be supported by human reason and learning: here, we see the dream and the ponderous scholarship of Chantecleer's dream lore being overcome by the demands of sensuality.

The discussion of pre-destination, free-will and destiny raise the sense of God's continual care for man; and the confusion of that discussion casts doubt only on man's understanding, not on God's omniscience. The truth remains that if Chantecleer had heeded revelation and reason, in obedience to God, he would have avoided catastrophe, the Destiny that (according to mediaeval belief) 'may nat been eschewed' by one subjected to the pleasures of the senses, by one of Venus's servants.

The heroic style, the tragic outcries serve to gather the classical world into the central Christian drama of the moral fall of man. And so on, in every detail of the apparently rambling tale.

But clearly, all this moral reference is absorbed into comedy. It is wrong to consider the animal fable just a pleasant clothing for a fundamentally serious message; rather it is a device to set the human issues at a comic distance. The problem of man's relationship with God and the world, so solemn a subject for so many religious men, is seen as a folly of the fowlyard by the Nun's Priest. We are kept teetering in comic suspense between the human order in all its brilliance and variety and the actual scene in the grimy 'halle' and drab 'yarde' of the widow; Chaucer is masterly in finding the exact common phrase or image that will make the double vision most absurdly obvious. The beauty of his paramour's face, which makes all Chauntecleer's 'drede for to dyen' is focussed specifically on the scarlet red about her eyes. In the midst of his scholarly discourse on dreams, Chauntecleer exclaims:

'By God, I hadde levere than *my sherte*
That ye hadde rad his legende, as have I.'

Chaucer exaggerates this effect still further by applying to the plain fowlyard events all the rhetorical devices of heroic poetry:

Whan that the monthe in which the world bigan
That highte March, whan God firste maked man . . .

O false mordrour, lurkynge in thy den,
O newe Scariot, newe Genylon . . .

The hens embody throughout, not plain human nature (that is the widow's role), but man's highest aspirations after brilliance and dignity and profundity, his courtliness and learning, his heroic and tragic visions of himself—none of which can but seem absurd in such a setting.

Moreover the various attitudes and styles mock themselves even without the comic effect of the animal setting. The courtliness is absurd in a 'paramour' who so quickly launches into thoroughly plain and detailed medical lore on laxatives and indigestion; and in a courtly lover who is rapidly transformed into a long-winded, complacent mediaeval clerk. The heroic apostrophes are parodies of Geoffrey de Vinsauf; the learned discussion of predestination only reveals the total confusion of man's efforts to understand God. Indeed the whole tale is a parody, the Nun's Priest is himself a caricature of that incurably moralizing and digressive mediaeval mind for whom a story is merely an opportunity for related speculation and parallel instances. His discursiveness becomes at times uncontrollable: the burst of anti-feminism is hardly tactful in the Prioress's attendant; the diversions onto Phisiologus and the source of natural fear in lines 511-515 are delightful irrelevancies.

We are left with a hilarious version of the most serious possible human drama. What does this 'sweete preest' intend? The final vision is of the complete absurdity of man in every aspect of his earthly existence—the completeness of this vision even extends to the Nun's Priest's behaviour. But it is only man's earthly drama that is so comic— the Nun's Priest's amusement at man's activities leaves untouched his faith in the love of the unsearchable God. His is a Christian view of man that sees him not as vile but as absurd, not as suffering God's frown but rather his appreciative laughter. Man's antics are ridiculous and even delightfully so. We come to feel that it is the Nun's Priest's sense of man's absurdity that allows a forgiveness of behaviour which, in stricter and more solemn eyes, would be merely evil. Where all of man's behaviour, including one's own, is seen as folly, how can one look on man except with sympathetic amusement; in a world of universal absurdity, what can the man of faith do but wait on God and watch the world go by? And where vices are seen as folly, the observer can enjoy rather than condemn the brilliance and fantasy of a spectacle so inextricably entangled with human weakness. The tale is popular not merely as entertainment, but also because it shows a most attractively humane and mature understanding of man,

The glory, jest and riddle of the world.

appendixes

APPENDIX A

Le Roman de la Rose by Guillaume de Lorris (c.1212-1237) and Jean de Meun (c.1237-1305).

These extracts are from the lengthy advice of *La Vielle* to *Bel Aceuil*, 13408ff,. where she is explaining how women set about gaining men's love:

|At meals|, she should take good care that she does not wet her fingers up to the joints in sauce or gravy, nor soil her lips with soup, garlic or fatty meat; she should not heap up too much food, nor put too much in her mouth. With the tips of her fingers she should handle the morsel that she dips in the sauce, be it green or white or yellow: then she should carefully lift the mouthful so that no bit of soup, sauce or pepper falls on her breast. And so gracefully should she drink from her cup that she does not spill a drop on herself; for anyone who sees this happen might well consider her far too rude or gluttonous. She should take care that she does not drink from the common cup while there is still a morsel in her mouth. She should also wipe her mouth so well that she leaves no grease adhering to it, at least to her upper lip; for when grease remains thereon, specks of it might be seen in the wine: this is neither becoming nor neat.

La Vielle continues:

When she's moved to laughter she smiles so well and so beautifully that she reveals two dimples, one on either side of her little lips . . . She should be careful not to seclude herself, for when she stays indoors the less is she seen by people, and her beauty is less sought after; fewer covet and solicit her. She should often go to church and make visitations, go to weddings, processions, games, festivities, carolings, for in those places the god and goddess of Love hold school and celebrate mass for their pupils.

But she should always first look in her mirror to make sure that she is well dressed. When she feels that all is perfection, she will walk through the streets in her most alluring manner — not too languidly nor yet too stiffly, neither too high nor two low, but pleasantly through the crowds. Her shoulders and her hips move with such grace that no-one could imagine a more beautiful movement. She walks gracefully in her small, fine shoes, which fit her feet so well that there is never a wrinkle.

And if her dress has a train, or hangs close to the pavement, she raises it at the side or in front as if to feel a breath of wind, or to enable her to cross the threshold, or as if she desires to draw it back that she may step more freely. But she takes good care that the beautiful form of her foot is revealed to the view of passers by. If she happens to be wearing a mantle, it should hang in such a way that it doesn't hide from view the fair form it protects.

This idealized description of the *Lady Ydelnesse* appears in the early part of *Le Roman de la Rose* (by Guillaume de Lorris) 527ff:

> Hir heer was as yelowe of hewe
> As ony basyn scoured newe;
> Hir flesh as tendre as is a chike,
> With bente browis smothe and slyke,
> And by mesure large were
> The opening of hir yen clere;
> Hir nose of good proporcioun,
> Hir yen grey as is a faucoun,
> With swete breth and wel savoured;
> Hir face whit and wel coloured,
> With litel mouth and round to see,
> A clove chin eke hadde she . . .

> — from the English *Romaunt of the Rose*
> probably translated by Chaucer.

APPENDIX B

The following extract 'Concerning Pardoners' is from a fourteenth century English manual for the guidance of clergy, the *Regimen Animarum* — The Rule of Souls. It provides an illuminating summary of papal legislation which strove, too often in vain, to control the activities of pardoners.

What is the law concerning pardoners who travel about through the churches with letters of pardon and who preach abuses? I say that those pardoners who idle away their time with eating and drinking ought not to be admitted unless they show appropriate letters, or the letters of the diocesan bishop; and they are not permitted to preach to the people anything in addition to what is contained in those letters — of which the form is common:

Quoniam ut ait Apostolus . . . etc.

Note that they (the pardoners) ought to be modest and discreet; they ought not to lodge in taverns or any other unsuitable place, nor indulge in unfitting or extravagant expenditure, nor falsely wear the habit of a religious . . .

Furthermore, Pope Clement IV in that decree which begins *Sedis Apostolice,* published *in curia,* decrees that bishops, rectors and all parish curates are not bound to receive them in hospitality nor provide them with necessities; also, whoever are of religion or in orders are not bound to call a congregation of the people for their sermons or exhortations; also, although such gatherings are mentioned in their letters, the Pope revokes them; and if because of this any sentence of excommunication or interdict is pronounced (by the pardoners), it is null and void. And Pope Clement V says of this that pardoners seeking alms ought not to be admitted to any place unless they exhibit letters from the diocesan bishop, nor may they preach to the people, nor expound anything but that which is contained in the aforesaid letters. And diocesan bishops should carefully examine apostolic letters — through which, previously, pardoners have been admitted (to a diocese or parish) — lest they give authority to the initiation of a fraud, because some large number of pardoners grant indulgences to the people on their own authority, to the deception of souls; without any right they grant pardons upon the offering of money; they absolve penitents from perjuries, murders and other sins; they remit sins forgiven and uncertain in exchange for gifts of money; they relax a third or a quarter of the statutory penance; they claim deceitfully that they release from purgatory and conduct to the joys of paradise the souls of the parents or friends of those who give alms to them. Pardoners are found with the liberal alms-givers of any place whatever; they illegally grant plenary remission of sins, and they absolve them all *a pena* and *a culpa.*

The Lord Pope, wishing to abolish these kinds of abuses, by which the jurisdiction of the church is rendered vile and the authority of the keys of the church is brought into contempt, expressly revokes all and singular privileges whether they are previously issued or conceded to any of them in any places, orders or persons of pardoners of whatever kind at all, lest this material previously granted by such apostolic authority be made any longer favourable as a pretext for these men.

— 'De Questoribus' from *Regimen Animarum* (1343)
The Latin text, from which this translation is done, is edited from MS Harley 2272 by Professor A. L. Kellogg and Professor L. Haselmayer in PMLA 61, 1951, pp. 256-7.

APPENDIX C

Gentilesse

Moral Balade of Chaucier

The firste stok, fader of gentilesse —
What man that claymeth gentil for to be,
Must folowe his trace, and alle his wittes dresse[1]
Vertu to sewe, and vyces for to flee:
For unto vertu longeth dignitee
And noght the revers, saufly dar I deme,
Al were he mytre, croune or diademe.

This firste stok was ful of rihtwisnesse,
Trew of his word, sobre, pitous and free,
Clene of his goste, and loved besinesse
Ageinst the vyce of slouthe, in honestee;
And, but his heir love vertu as dide he
He is noght gentil thogh he riche seme,
Al were he mytre, croune or diademe.

Vyce may wel be heir to old richesse
But ther may no man, as men may wel see,
Bequethe his heir his vertuous noblesse:
That is appropred unto no degree
But to the firste fader in magestee
That maketh hem his heires that him queme,[2]
Al were he mytre, croune or diademe.

[1] In this line the first *his* refers to the father of *gentilesse*, the second *his* to the man who claims to be *gentil*.
[2] queme — please.

APPENDIX D

In *Le Roman de la Rose*, the God of Love assists the Lover in his quest for the Rose by enlisting, among others, the services of *Faus Semblant* (False

Seeming) who, in the dress of a friar, gives an account of his deceits and reveals his hypocritical nature:

I dwell with the proud, the cunning, the artful, those who covet worldly respect and exploit the great need of others; who pursue the highest salaries, and buy the acquaintance of powerful men, and follow them; those who make out they are poor and yet live on delicious food and drink expensive wine; those who'll preach you poverty at the same time that they are fishing for immense wealth . . .

By means of my dispensations I make the world fall into my hands; I can hear confession and give absolution, that no prelate can invalidate, to all men wherever I find them. I know of no prelate who can do so excepting only the Pope, who granted this privilege to our order. There is no prelate or priest who will dare criticise or grouse against my men. I have seen to it that their mouths are shut. But they are up to my tricks and I am not so well received as I might desire, because I've put it over them too often. But I don't care how it goes — I've got the cash and the collection. So much have I done, so much have I preached, so much have I appropriated, so much they've given me—everyone in their folly—that I lead the gay life because of the single-minded credulity (*simplece*) of the clergy, who are thoroughly scared of my traps.

I am a hypocrite, |I| preach abstinence . . . but I fill my paunch with the very best food and wine as befits a divine . . . Wealth has power, and no matter how poor I feign to be, I make jolly certain I'm *not* poor! By Our Lady, I'd prefer the acquaintance of the King of France a hundred thousand times to that of a pauper even if he had as good a soul! When I see these naked vagabonds trembling on stinking dunghills, crying out and moaning from cold and hunger, I don't get myself involved in their affairs. If they are carried to an Ostel Deu (hospital) they won't be comforted by me, for those who aren't worth an oyster won't fill my mouth with any alms at all. What can he give who even licks his knife (after a meal)? It's much more sensible to pay a visit to a rich usurer who is ill; I'll go and comfort him so that I may have a chance of getting his cash; and if wicked death should end him, I'll be only too glad to convey him to the grave. And if anyone should reprove me because I keep away from the poor, do you know how I pass it off? I make it quite clear by the quality of my cloak that the rich are more tainted with sin than the, poor . . .

212

I meddle in matters of court, make reconciliations and arrange marriages; sometimes I act as attorney or executor or go as an envoy; I take messages and hold inquests, none of which things fall within my province at all.

Another Friar makes quite certain that False Seeming never hears the confession of one sweet little nun; he gives her frequent shrivings himself:

They made their confession with so great devotion, that it seemed to me that there were two heads together in one hood.

APPENDIX E

Reason instructs the Lover in the nature of Love in *Le Roman de la Rose*, 4376ff. The basic distinction he makes is between sexual pleasure as an end in itself, and sexual pleasure as an encouragement to the propagation of the human race. In the first case he distinguishes further between courtly love and honest lust, and he finds the former the more culpable.

Love, if I have been well instructed, is an illness of thought which is spread freely between two persons of opposite sex; it comes as a desire, born of disordered sight, to embrace and kiss, and to have mutual fleshly pleasure. Lovers don't desire any other thing but these ardent pleasures. They care not to have offspring; they are bent on sensual pleasure. There are some kinds of people who discount this love, but feign being fine lovers, not deigning to love for love itself, but rather mocking ladies, promising them their bodies and souls, and swearing lies and fables to those they find deceivable, until they have had their pleasure. But they are the less deceived: for it is much better, my fine friend, to deceive than to be deceived, especially in this battle, when they know that there's no middle course. Although I'm no theologian, I'm telling you that every man who goes to bed with a woman ought to desire, as far as he's able, to continue the divine being, and perpetuate his likeness, since all are subject to corruption, so that by succession, the race may not fail. For when father and mother die, Nature demands that they leave children to continue afresh this work in such a way that the one fills the place left by other[s]. Nature has made this a pleasurable job so that the workers may not dislike or shrink the task; for many of them would never lift a finger if the pleasure didn't entice them.

Thus Nature employs subtlety. No one is in the right if he hasn't the right intention — who instead covets sensual delight. Do you know what they are doing — those who desire only pleasure? They are putting themselves in the power of the prince of all vices, as Cicero set it down in his book *Of Old Age* (the which state he praises and esteems more than Youth). Youth leads lads and girls to put their bodies and their souls in jeopardy; and it is a difficult thing for them to come through without danger to life and limb, or without doing shame or ill to themselves or to their progeny.

BIBLIOGRaPhy

Works referred to by author in the notes and commentary:

BAUGH, A. C., *Chaucer's Major Poetry*, Routledge and Kegan Paul, 1964.
CARUS-WILSON, E., in *The Cambridge Economic History of Europe*, Vol. 2.
CURRY, W. C., *Chaucer and the Medieval Sciences*, George Allen and Unwin, 2nd. ed., 1960.
MANLY, J. M., *Some New Light on Chaucer*, Henry Holt, 1926 (reprint Peter Smith, 1959).
OWST, G. R., *Literature and Pulpit in Medieval England*, Oxford, Blackwell, 1961.
POWER, E., *Medieval English Nunneries*, Cambridge, 1922.
ROBINSON, F. N., *The Complete Works of Geoffrey Chaucer*, Oxford, 2nd. ed., 1957.
SKEAT, W. W., *The Works of Geoffrey Chaucer*, Oxford, 1894-7.
TYRWHITT, T., *The Canterbury Tales*, Routledge, repr. 1830.

Translations from the following are our own:

GUILLAUME DE LORRIS and JEAN DE MEUN, *Le Roman de la Rose*, SATF, repr. 1965.
OVID, *Ars Amatoria* and *Metamorphoses*.
HORACE, *Epistolae*.
VERGIL, *Æneid*.
DANTE, *Purgatorio*.

References to the Bible are to the Latin Vulgate. We give either our own translations or quote from the Douay-Rheims version (CTS, London, 1956).

Suggested Further Reading:

(i) Background Works

HUSSEY, M., SPEARING, A. C. and WINNEY, J., *An Introduction to Chaucer*, Cambridge, 1965.
BOWDEN, M., *A Commentary on the General Prologue*, McMillan, 1948.
RICKERT, E., *Chaucer's World*, Columbia, 1948.

Loomis, R. S., *A Mirror of Chaucer's World*, Princeton, 1965.
French, R. D., *A Chaucer Handbook*, Appleton Century Crofts, 1947.
Coulton, G., *Chaucer and his England*, Methuen, 1908.
Jusserand, J. J., *English Wayfaring Life in the Middle Ages*, Barnes and Noble, 1950.
Brewer, D. S., *Chaucer*, Longmans, 1953.
    Chaucer in his Time, Nelson, 1963.
Robertson, D. W., *A Preface to Chaucer*, Princeton, 1962.
Lowes, J. L., *Geoffrey Chaucer*, Oxford, 1929.
Lewis, C. S., *The Allegory of Love*, Oxford, 1959.
McKisack, M., *Fourteenth Century England*, Oxford, 1959.
Crow, M. M. and Olson, C. C., *Chaucer Life Records*, Oxford, 1966.
Bryan, W. F. and Dempster, G. eds, *Sources and Analogues of Chaucer's Canterbury Tales*, Routledge and Kegan Paul, 1941.

Langland, W., *Piers the Ploughman*, trans. J. F. Goodridge, Penguin, 1959.
Gower, J., *Confessio Amantis*, trans. T. Tiller, Penguin, 1963.
The Romance of the Rose, trans. H. W. Robbins, Dutton, 1962.
Middle English Romances, ed. A. C. Gibbs, Arnold, 1966.
Lays of Courtly Love, trans. P. Terry, Doubleday, 1963.

(ii) Critical Works:

Bronson, B. H., *In Search of Chaucer*, Toronto, 1960.
Coghill, N., *The Poet Chaucer*, Oxford, 1949.
Craik, T. W., *The Comic Tales of Chaucer*, Methuen, 1963.
Ford, B., ed., *The Age of Chaucer*, Penguin, 1954.
Lawrence, W. W., *Chaucer and the Canterbury Tales*, Columbia, 1950.
Muscatine, C., *Chaucer and the French Tradition*, California, 1957.
Preston, R., *Chaucer*, Sheed and Ward, 1952.
Shoeck, R. J. and Taylor, J., eds., *Chaucer Criticism*, Vol. 1, Notre Dame, 1960.
Speirs, J., *Chaucer the Maker*, Faber, 1960.
Wagenknecht, E., ed., *Chaucer: Modern Essays in Criticism*, Galaxy, 1959.

a Basic Word List

algate always, in any case.
anon at once, immediately.
atones at once.
benedicitee Lat. imperative *benedicite*, 'bless ye'. Used as an exclamation like 'Bless me!', often pronounced 'ben-chit-ay'.
cleped, ycleped called, named.
certes for certain, certainly.
de(e)l bit, piece; *every deel* every bit; *never a deel* not one bit.
eek, eke also, too, moreover.
er, er that before.
gan began; often simply auxiliary 'did'.
hem them.
highte called, named.
ilk, thilke same, the same, that same.
kan can, know (how to . . .), knows.
koude pa.t. of *kan;* knew, could.
mo more.
moot, mote must, ought to, may.
moste pa.t. of *moot.*
nas was not: *ne + was.*
nat know not: *ne + wat.*
nere were not: *ne + were.*
niste knew not: *ne + wiste.*
nolde would not: *ne + wolde.*
noot know not: *ne + woot.*
o, oon one.
pardee Fr. *par dé* by God! Generally weaker in emphasis than in Mod. E.
quod quoth, said.
sikerly surely, certainly.
sith since.
soothe truth.
swich such.
syn since.
thee thrive, prosper. Usually in *so theech, so moot I thee,* as I hope to thrive.
thilke the same, that same.
trowe believe, think, trust.
unnethe scarcely, hardly, with difficulty.
verray true. Never an adverb; cf. Mod.E. 'He's the very man'.

217

whilom once (upon a time).
wight man, person, chap, creature.
wiste knew.
wot, wolde will, would.
woot know.
yeve, yive give. *yaf* gave.
ywis certainly, truly.

ABBREVIATIONS

GP	General Prologue
McT	Manciple's Tale
MT	Miller's Tale
NPT	Nun's Priest's Tale
PaT	Pardoner's Tale
PPro	Parson's Prologue
PrT	Prioress's Tale
RPro	Reeve's Prologue
WBT	Wife of Bath's Tale

fig.	figuratively
Fr.	French
Lat.	Latin
lit.	literally
M.E.	Middle English
Mod.E.	Modern English
O.E.	Old English
O.E.D.	Oxford English Dictionary
O.Fr.	Old French